Apologia Politica

Apologia Politica

States & Their Apologies
by Proxy

Girma Negash

LEXINGTON BOOKS

A division of
ROWMAN & LITTLEFIELD PUBLISHERS, INC.
Lanham • Boulder • New York • Toronto • Oxford

LEXINGTON BOOKS

A division of Rowman & Littlefield Publishers, Inc.
A wholly owned subsidary of The Rowman & Littlefield Publishing Group, Inc.
4501 Forbes Boulevard, Suite 200
Lanham, MD 20706

PO Box 317
Oxford
OX2 9RU, UK

British Library Cataloguing in Publication Information Available

Library of Congress Cataloging-in-Publication Data

Negash, Girma.
  Apologia politica : states & their apologies by proxy / Girma Negash.
    p. cm.
  Includes bibliographical references and index.
  ISBN-13: 978-0-7391-1094-2 (cloth : alk. paper)
  ISBN-10: 0-7391-1094-2 (cloth : alk. paper)
  1. Apologizing—Political aspects. I. Title.
BF575.A75N44 2006
172'.4—dc22   2006003209

Printed in the United States of America

♾™ The paper used in this publication meets the minimum requirements of American
National Standard for Information Sciences—Permanence of Paper for Printed Library
Materials, ANSI/NISO Z39.48–1992.

In memory of my father, Negash Wolde Selassie, and my mother, Mamite Tekle

Contents

Preface

My interest in questions of forgiveness, apology, and reconciliation has been in gestation since the 1970s when I was a graduate student assistant to sociologist Elise Boulding and political scientist Francis A. Beer, and several other prominent scholars who developed the Conflict and Peace Studies Program at the University of Colorado (Boulder). More recently, I was simply intrigued by the idea of political apology. Political apologies, often in the headlines, have drawn all kinds of reactions ranging from the positive responses to public atonement for crimes against humanity to the deserving derision, especially in the last decade or two, in the ever expanding apologia for sins committed in the past. The Vatican probably leads in the apology count but nations are producing confessionals just as fast. Curiosity about the apology phenomenon is generating new scholarship to dispel misperceptions, clarify meaning, and better understand the dynamics of different kind of apologies. My contribution here is to add to this exploration. I particularly address questions about whether states can successfully apologize to begin with, the extent of political constraints on their apologies as well as their moral limits.

I propose in this work an ethic of apology based on a blend of political and moral theories that informs a critical and systematic examination of state apologies. Accordingly I construct an interdisciplinary theoretical framework and a standard of effective apology against which I measure the validity of historical political attempts to apologize and move towards reconciliation. Following a theoretical introductory chapter, I treat the cases of Germany and Israel, Japan and its neighbors, Rwanda and the international community, and the recent U.S. China standoff over the Belgrade and spy plane incidents. In each of these cases I assess the actions of leaders on both sides against a standard for an effective apology to illustrate the successes, failures, and yet-to-be-completed apologies by states.

My intellectual debts are too many to enumerate but they are acknowledged in my citations. However, since I began this project I have been exceptionally fortunate in having a number of people who gave their time and energy to my project. Their generosity and my association with them in the last few years have been the best part of this scholarly journey.

I owe special debt to two colleagues and mentors, Nicholas Tavuchis and Donald Shriver Jr. who encouraged and assisted me from the very first time I presented a paper on the subject in 2000. Both of these scholars were most generous with reading and discussing parts of the manuscript and imparting their conceptual and editorial advice. I am grateful to the critical insights of David Rudrum and Michael Barnett. I owe thanks to Thomas Butler who read two chapters and contributed subtle and critical suggestions. I am indebted to Michael Shapiro, Lili Cole, Robert Weyeneth, Yanrong Chang and Mark Whitaker who all shared their thoughts and gave me advice on my project. My appreciation also goes to Serena Leigh Krombach, Kathryn Funk, Christopher Case, Rowena Lund and Tom Brent of Lexington Books for initiating me into the inner workings of a press and assisting me through the editorial and publication process. I have also benefited from the dedicated service by USC Aiken librarians Brigitte Smith and Paul Lewis. At USC Aiken, I wish to acknowledge with gratitude the support of my department head, Valdis Lumans, who stood out in his understanding of the burden of this project in addition to my other univeristy duties. A special thanks go to Michael Fowler for artfully designing the image on the book cover, preceded by my daughter Tobya and my friend Xinmin who also worked on the design. In the last minutes of the preparation of the manuscript my son, Ezana, put his computer wizardry to work. In spite of all the care and assistance from people I have mentioned so far, this project would not have materialized without the support and assistance of my life partner Sara Gueret-Negash. I benefited a great deal from her probing questions, the many discussions we have had during the writing of the manuscript, and her editorial skills.

G.N.
Aiken, S.C.
January 2005

Chapter 1

The Problematic of Political Apology

Holy Roman Emperor Henry IV, German Chancellor Willy Brandt, American President Bill Clinton, and Japanese Prime Minister Tomiichi Murayama share in common the ritualistic act of public contrition. But the similarities end there. The image of the emperor, in 1077, pleading for the reversal of his excommunication by the Roman Catholic Church, waiting for three days barefoot in the snow outside the castle of Pope Gregory VII in Canossa, Italy, is the archetype of such apologies.[1] Public remorse has lost much of its power since, with few exceptions. A lasting image of public contrition in modern times is that of Willy Brandt, the German Chancellor, kneeling before the memorial for Nazi victims in Warsaw in 1971. Brandt's act was bold and unprecedented at the time in conveying sincerity of remorse in its apologetic gesture. More than 30 years later, at the end of the last genocide of the 20th century, American president Bill Clinton, delivered a cursory apology at Kigali Airport in Rwanda while in transit. It was another reminder of the huge gap between a super power, whose action or inaction is of grave consequence, and a people in a continent at the periphery.[2] When, on the 50th anniversary of the Asia-Pacific War, Japanese Prime Minister Omiichi Murayama apologized for Japanese war crimes from his residence, while his cabinet members paid homage to Japanese dead (including war criminals) at the Yasukuni Shrine, the actions drew both protest and praise worldwide. In all these cases the actors were individuals performing in the public domain in their capacity as state agents.

State Apology

Do collectivities, groups and corporate entities act and respond differently from individuals in their approach and disposition to conflict resolution? At first

1

glance there seems to be no distinction between individuals and corporate groups when it comes to apology toward reconciliation, for instance. Yet as we move from individual to group, to corporate entities and finally the nation-state, reconciliatory acts such as apology are differentiated in representation.

By way of representation, the requisites of apology apply to groups as they do to individuals except that group to group apology needs to be delegated by leaders or appointed delegates. Such groups are less formal. In July 1999 some 400 European and North American Christians, members of an amorphous Reconciliation Walk group prayed in Jerusalem's Old City and offered to local religious leaders framed copies of their apology for the slaughter of mainly Jew and Muslim inhabitants of Jerusalem by Crusaders in 1099. It took a little more than three years for the Reconciliation Walk group, numbering 2,500 at different stages, to trek the path of the Crusaders from Europe to the Holy City.[3] Such a disparate group is different from a more organized corporate entity. For example, the Irish Republican Army made a splash in the news when it publicly apologized to the relatives of hundreds of innocent civilians killed in its 30-year violent campaign.[4] The IRA is a corporate group with legal if not moral personality that can be held accountable for any apologizable transgression. Even the Roman Catholic Church can be held responsible for its deeds as its pontiff made the most extravagant apology in the millennial year on behalf of Catholics for the Church's 2,000 years of sins that included persecutions, errors and violence.[5] In spite of the moral authority it commands, the Church remains a quasi-sovereign entity that does not hold the power and legal authority of nation-states and the responsibilities we expect of them.

Political apology is apology that directly involves nation-states or that in which states have taken interest to apologize on behalf of many or are on the receiving end on behalf of victims of grievous transgressions. Under the rubric of political apology come - state apology that is rendered between states, apology that is delivered by a state to groups or individuals, and finally, an apology that involves the international community or an international organization with legal personality. The present inquiry is limited to political apology with international dimensions dealing primarily with state-to-state apologies but also with apologies where states and the international community are parties to transnational and transhistorical grievances about past crimes.[6]

There is something distinctive about state apology, apology between states in this instance, which differentiates it from those between groups and among individuals. Specifically, apologies between individuals are direct and unmediated compared to apologies between collectivities, requiring the acceptance or rejection by the recipient free from external considerations. As soon as apologies are given in front of witnesses, the expectations of others and established norms transform them into public acts. Even individual apologies have their sacramental roots in the way they invoke the language of penance as God is their witness. But when the apology is socially sanctioned and linked to more universal moral standards it becomes exclusively public in nature. Thus when governments are either compelled or voluntarily giving apologies to individuals, groups or other governments the authority of state is a mediating factor. When the state is the perpetrator, government leaders claim to have the legitimacy to speak for that state and its people. The public admission by President Jacques Chirac in 1995 that the state bore responsibility for the roundup of 13,000 Paris Jews for deportation to Nazi concentration camps during Vichy regime recalls the moral debt of contemporary Frenchmen to the deportees.[7] In this political apology, the state mediates between perpetrators and victims. We are looking then at three levels of public discourse and exchange. First are exchanges between individuals. Second, apologies between corporate groups, normally rendered through their representatives. For example, Christian groups have apologized to indigenous peoples for exploitations of the past. Our immediate interest is in a third group - apologies by nation-states represented by their state agents - that has recently invited intellectual queries and debates about their peculiar nature and consequences.

In dealing with historical injustice, social constructionists tell us that perpetrators and victims come to redefine their identities, as the respective histories of Germans after World War I, Jews after the Holocaust, and Palestinians after 1948 attest. The complex politics that involve identity, memory, and relative power makes this last level of public discourse on apology extremely contentious. It also makes it imperative that we reconsider the meaning of apology as a speech act employed in the public arena. We should finally reach a better understanding of the meaning of apology with regard to its evolution in its capacity to signal reconciliation, to facilitate conflict resolution and to promote remedies for deep societal afflictions and trauma. A potentially fruitful approach to addressing these questions is to get to the roots of the concept of apology - to its genealogy. This effort will shed light on the convergence between the associated notions residing in restorative justice such as apology, forgiveness and reparations, and the pressing demands made by individuals, groups, and states for apology and restitution.

A Genealogy of Apologies

Let us begin by considering the etymology of apology as proposed by Nicholas Tavuchis.[8] Tavuchis directs our attention to the Greek root of *apologos*, which means "a story," and by extension *apologia*, which then evolved to mean "an oral or written defense." This simply means that if you injure someone, you justify your act without any expression of remorse for it. The original meaning of "defense" or "account" gradually changed "whereby the expression of regret itself serves as reparation without requiring additional actions on the part of the transgressor."[9] A*pologia* – taken as a speech in defense – has shifted to the modern understanding of apology in which acknowledgement of wrongdoing and expression of regret are expected even if additional actions are not taken.

A second area that informs the language and forms of apology is religion, as examinations of Judeo-Christian roots and traditions confirm with respect to confession. Peter Brooks' *Troubling Confessions* is instructive on this score. It traces the evolution of confession in the Roman Catholic Church "from an emphasis on public penance, as a manifestation of one's sin and need for restoration to the Christian community, to an emphasis on the verbal act and fact of confession itself, and the corresponding speech act of absolution."[10] By the Middle Ages private confession had taken precedence over public penance. Individual self-examination gradually assumed prominence and by the time of the Renaissance a modern sense of guilt and individual responsibility had emerged.[11] The move from public penance to individual confession, especially in the Catholic tradition, is accompanied by the parallel ascendance of the modern subject. The powerful symbols and metaphors of Christianity, especially those of sin and redemption are foundational, as are the associated rituals of confession and atonement. Consider Marina Warner's reappraisal of modern apology in light of those traditions exemplified by St. Augustine's *Confessions* and the Jewish prayer on the Day of Atonement. Warner claims that the language of repentance and atonement has been usurped lately by modern government leaders who are performing priestly acts in their apologetic acts. These official apologies unite two different forms of speech, according to Warner; one is the "theological and sacramental, the language of repentance and atonement;" and the other is "psychoanalytic: the practice of talking cure."[12] This part of her observation thus seeks to throw light upon the probable motives for the symbolic uses of sacramental language by secular leaders as well as the contingent factors that has made them current.

The third source of our use and misuse of apology is in the psychology of moral behavior. The need for and the appropriate use of apology in psychoanalytic terms can be linked to at least three sets of inter-related concepts regarding the apology process. The first includes such morally relevant emotions as guilt, shame, and empathy that we often associate with the affective responses to wrongdoing by perpetrators and bystanders. Furthermore, our inquiry benefits by the changing views of the role of emotions in morality on the part of philosophers, political theorists, and psychologists.[13] The renewed recognition that much of human action is emotionally driven will benefit our attempt to explore the underside of the politics of remorse. The second set involves those ideas related to societal trauma and the resulting negative responses. Scholars like Dominick LaCapra adapt "psychoanalytic concepts such as melancholia and mourning, acting out and working through" to historical analysis and sociocultural and political critique in order to elucidate trauma and its aftereffects on society.[14] Such an inquiry is often aimed at victims' amnesia and perpetrators' denials. Post-traumatic stress disorder manifested at individual, family and societal levels involves loss and melancholia and demands coming to terms with the painful past.[15] The final set subsumes the different aspects of healing from working through trauma to healing in therapeutic terms. The conventional reference to "healing" from societal trauma is often metaphorical, although the medical implications are evident. Theories and methods of psychotherapy for victims of mass violence have advanced since the Holocaust, from the days of Bruno Bethelheim and Frantz Fanon to modern psychotherapists who have worked with victims in such places as Bosnia, Chile, and Rwanda.

The fourth origin of the idea and practice of apology, at least in the case of apology between collectivities, can be traced to the philosophically liberal traditions that ushered in the democratic and socialist revolutions, and promoted the first and second generations of human rights. It is in the wake of major human crises and catastrophes that advances were made in humanitarian law, and institutions were established to safeguard international human rights. What I have in mind here are events that led to the establishment of structures of authority and habits of cooperation that allowed the creation of the United Nations and the adoption of the Universal Declaration of Human Rights.[16] Human rights have firmly been asserted since the Holocaust and World War II increasingly challenging the norms of the Leviathan that is the state. As John Torpey has pointed out, "The human rights instruments promulgated by the United Nations after World War II were drafted to ensure that human beings would not, in the future, exercise their barbarous impulses on others without the latter having a juridical leg to stand on – especially when the perpetrator was the victim's own government."[17] More recently it is the continuation of this evolution in human rights that ushered in the rise of a culture of apology. In the assessment of one observer, "the modern apology stands traditional notions of prestige and power on their heads by giving priority to the concepts of justice and mercy so that in the end what becomes most crucial is reconciliation."[18]

The New Apologies and Intellectual Traditions

The increased frequency of public apologies, especially between national states, raises other questions as to why there are so many and why they are taking place now. One answer comes from Michel-Rolph Trouillot who contends that collective apologies in our late modern age are the result of the transference of the attributes of the liberal self to states, and changing historical perceptions played out globally. As Trouillot argues, "We may not have reached the universal history dreamed of by Enlightenment thinkers, but collective apologies are increasing in part because offers, demands, denials or rejections are all projected on to a global stage which is now the ultimate horizon of a new historicity."[19] Trouillot's explanation of the new wave of apologies is rejected by Jeffrey Olick and Brenda Coughlin who argue that Trouillot "has the order of logic reversed; the confessional individual mimics the regretful state, not the other way around – or at the least they are codetermined phenomena." For Olick and Coughlin "the rise of regret in all its forms is a sign of the failure of the state to generate adequate psychological defense mechanisms, not of the state's success in doing so."[20] It is possible to conclude that the cross-influences between the confessional individual and the state might be codetermined because either Olick and Coughlin or Trouillot are correct in their seductively parsimonious but sweeping conclusions to explain the new wave of apology. It is true that the modern liberal state has imitated the liberal individual, when we take into consideration, for example, that government has assumed the role of providing for society from the economy to welfare. By the same token, individuals and groups have taken the initiative in transnational actions in those cases where the liberal state has miserably failed or proven unsuited to solve certain global problems. In any event, there is a convergence of three philosophical traditions specifically informing the burgeoning apology practice.

The first tradition comes from the accumulated wisdom of liberalism and those ideas and practices that we now understand to have promoted peace and cooperation among states in the past. Among the two strands of that tradition, the first is faith in rationality with its instrumental value of preference for cooperation over conflict and its commitment to building institutions to promote them. The second tendency of liberalism established itself through faith in universal rational moral duty to achieve peace. International law to a great extent is state-centric considering how the Nuremberg trials set a precedent for judging a crime against humanity. This is also the case of reparations to Israel, which were administered outside the jurisdiction of international law since the recipient state did not exist at the time the crimes were committed. In other words, the new morality based on the Kantian faith in democratic peace had not yet fully evolved. In a way, modern criteria for successful apologies impose the universal values of today on the actions and discourse of another period.

Converging with the liberal tradition of accumulated wisdom is the movement of states and their agents to become active movers of peace processes in ways other than traditional conflict resolution procedures would dictate. What makes this new approach a departure from the past is that statesmen, out of their own volition or under public pressure, are found apologizing for past and recent injustices, accepting accountability, taking responsibility, and displaying their remorse publicly. In such cases states and their agents are trying to lead their peoples towards reconciliation. Where successful, intransigent enemies may eventually be reconciled as a result of the actions taken by visionary leaders. On the other hand, the initiatives of individuals may be taken up by states to promote rapprochement. For example, Frenchmen Robert Schuman and Jean Monet developed the idea of a united Europe that would prevent wars by creating crosscutting economic linkages. That integration theory, dubbed as functionalism, is in a way similar to the pragmatic policies of Germany towards Israel. Neofunctionalists think along the same line, arguing that states can be the driving forces of integration by committing to taking more bold and binding actions instead of waiting for a grass roots and evolutionary approach. Such approaches to reconciliation and integration remind one of arranged marriages in traditional societies where the wise say: "the couple will grow to love each other." The advocates of state initiatives in the apology process point to the advantages of beginning with the commitments and restraints of more or less binding agreements, frameworks or institutions before bringing people into the mix. The assumed advantage here is that if the institutions of cooperation exist, people will eventually make a habit of interacting with others, even their former enemies.

There can also be a delayed appreciation of such institutional approaches by those who suffered injustices when the healing process has already begun. The changes of attitude and behavior toward their former enemies can simply begin with a rationalizing acceptance of a degree of justice rendered, with symbolic satisfaction, and the appreciation of peace and stability. This approach to reconciliation is more political in nature than social, we might say. One could point out that beginning the apology process with political reconciliation suited the needs of societies like South Africa, Guatemala and El Salvador.

The third area of inquiry with several tributaries is moral theory as it relates, more narrowly, to explanatory accounts of how various ways of moral communities come into being. The social construction of identity and its relevance to an apology process comes from various intellectual traditions. Sociologists link apology and forgiveness to social norms and compliance as the offer of apology involves some kind of fall from social grace and community and thus it is aimed at social restoration. Erving Goffman saw apology as a remedial social interchange.[21] Tavuchis reinforces Goffman's notion of identity by considering an apology as "a form of self-punishment that cuts deeply because we are obliged to retell, relive, and seek forgiveness for sorrowful events that have rendered our claims to membership in a moral community suspect or defeasible."[22] Going through an apology is a painful experience but necessary in so far as it effects a transformation of the participants' relations and the world around them. The social constructionist approach to identity has also been the mainstay of postmodernist schools who pay attention to the power of discursive practices in the imagining of new communities.

Among such critical theories is Habermas's discourse ethics that presupposes an ideal speech situation wherein "the practice of reaching understanding is public, is universally accessible, is free of external and internal violence, and permits only the rationally motivating force of the better argument."[23] Discourse ethics also entails the universal exchange of roles in which "by entering into a process of moral argumentation, the participants continue their communicative action in a flexible attitude with the aim of restoring a consensus that has been disrupted."[24] Other critical theories, however, "have pointed to the role of empathy in motivating our desire to care for others," thus allowing us to broaden "our understanding of the role of emotion in world politics."[25] Can state agents and political leaders rely on emotions? Nel Noddings argues that "emotion affects our thinking and that, when feeling is recognized and acknowledged, thinking can be more free and authentic and, accordingly, moral imagination and moral conversation may both be enhanced."[26] The introduction of empathy into world politics, along with the evolution of human rights encourages other approaches and alternatives that can accommodate the affective aspects of the apology proc-

ess. One such approach is that suggested by Michael Walzer that valorizes our
ability to talk across cultures (thin morality) beyond our own culture and history
(thick morality). We can link our circumstances to the circumstances of others
elsewhere, at least some of the time, allowing empathetic communication.[27]
Thus, in spite of the particularities of cultures and differences a moral minimal-
ism is at work.

The new ideas and practices of apologies toward reconciliation rest upon
both well-established intellectual traditions and newer groundbreaking approaches that question the reified notions of state sovereignty, international security and reconciliation between nations. We could not have imagined the existence of the international regimes and institutions that are actively serving the
global commons if it were not for the accumulated wisdom of liberalism. One
can also argue that the advancement of human rights and conflict resolutions
have benefited from the observations and rediscovery of principles and practices
of peace building. In the same manner, the excavation of old ideas by critical
theorists, for example, the power of narrative or the counter-monument movement have been put to work in service of memorialization and reconciliation.
The ethic of apology I present here is informed by these traditions and seeks to
provide answers to some unanswered questions concerning the potentials and
limitations of political apologies.

An Ethic of Apology

The mode of apology and associated principles I propose derive from two
sources. One is internal to the normative and essential meaning of what we have
come to understand apology to mean. The other is external to that in the sense
that there are instrumentalist expectations of what an apology is going to accomplish. If I have offended a friend by insulting him publicly and I want to do
good by him, I will have to start by admitting my mistakes and the extent to
which I might have caused him pain. In other words, I begin the apologetic
speech act by taking stock of the wrong I have committed. This reckoning or
account of wrongdoing is naturally associated with the burden of regret about
my behavior and the betrayal of our friendship. The guilt and admission of
wrongdoing may restore the dignity of my friend, but the restoration of the
original moral order will require more apologetic steps. In order to mend our
friendship and redeem myself in the eyes of my friend, and possibly witnesses, I
need to take the apology further. I need to repent for my deed and express my
sincere remorse to my friend. I also need to make a promise to myself as well as
to my friend that I will change my offensive ways.

Acknowledgement and remorse therefore, are subsumed as part of any form
of apology, but an apology goes beyond that. It is aimed at seeking recognition
by the victim that the perpetrator is redeemed through repentance and meaningful deeds. In order to earn such recognition, one has to openly be accountable
and responsible for one's transgression and be prepared to pay one's debt. In

response to the demands of survivors and victims, those who apologize must also be prepared to confess the facts of the transgression or crime. Repentance and remorse then go beyond the first utterances of an apology to meet the mutual needs of reconciliation between perpetrator and victim. I thus suggest four criteria for a successful public apology that are necessary to bring about healing and reconciliation, namely: acknowledgement, truth-telling, accountability, and public remorse.[28] These are the minimal requirements for a successful apology by perpetrators of mass crimes and wrongdoing whether or not victims demand them and forgiveness is given. Let us consider each in turn.

An apologetic discourse commences with acknowledgement. It consists of a self-conscious process of assessing or estimating the damages one has committed. It is the act of reckoning. One should think that taking stock of wrongdoing should be an easy task and, therefore, a good place to start an apology process. We find so often this is not the case. The temptation by perpetrators to simply deny the facts or get by with partial truth often gets in the way of acknowledgement. Take the case of the apology by one of the alleged masterminds of the Killing Fields of Cambodia. When Khieu Samphan and Nuon Chea, two leading organizers of the Khamer Rouge genocide that slaughtered some 1.5 million people, came forth to apologize in 1998, the apologetic utterance of one of them, Khieu Samphan, was stunning. The Khmer Rouge leader told the press; "I would like to say sorry to the people. Please forget the past and please be sorry for me."[29] It is evident Samphan's offhand remarks do not take into account the colossal crime committed. Moreover it is a preposterous expression of denial and irresponsibility. When apology is given either voluntarily or on demand, there is the temptation to see acknowledgement as an end in itself rather than the first step toward reconciliation. Nevertheless, the simple recognition and public admission of a wrongdoing can be of crucial symbolic significance to those affected by past wrongs. Acknowledgement, in that context refers not only to the reckoning of damage done, but to recognition of the consequences of one's action to others, thereby acknowledging their humanity. Theologian Donald Shriver goes even further by contending that acknowledgement can effectively mend broken human relations if it derives from empathy when he notes that "acknowledgement of fellow humanity lays a groundwork for both the construction and the repair of any human community."[30]

Truth telling is the second important element of a successful public apology. Being transparent about the facts of the injurious event becomes essential to the apology in the eyes of the victim. The offending party may admit wrongdoing but not acknowledge the extent of the injury. The reasons for not accounting fully for the deeds of the past vary according to the willingness of the perpetrators to take full blame for the offenses in question. In apologies involving nation-states, requirements of declaratory apologies and official status are not conducive to openness and spontaneity. Consequently, in the affairs of state the performative use of power permits leaders to make vague and symbolic statements without cost or commitment. Sweeping declaratory apologies have been made recently. Recall the apology of French Jacques Chirac in 1998 that depicted the Dreyfus affair as a "judicial error" instead of an archetypal case of scapegoating. Or Tony Blair's both praised and ridiculed apology for the Irish Famine he attributed to British indifference, undermining its structural causes.[31] Detached public apologies, intentional or otherwise, prevent the offenders from telling the whole truth and facing up to the horrid details of what occurred during the period of the alleged wrongdoing. Partial truths and legal specifics pervade the language of the affairs of the state.

The third imperative of an apology proper involves the expression of remorse by the transgressor. The essence of remorse is regret for one's grievous actions, the wish that they did not happen, and the accompanying feeling of sorrow. The expression of collective sorrow on behalf of a people or its government seems to be an unattainable.[32] A remorseful apology can be extended from one individual to another but how can the same be extended to collectivities and nations? When the deputies of these collectivities are expressing public remorse are they merely performing rituals? While a leader can be personally remorseful for his actions, how can he or she express collective remorse?[33] The effectiveness of public remorse cannot be measured by a show of contrition alone, if one can determine this, but by its legal legitimation. So certain apologies satisfy both the legal-bureaucratic and the performative dimensions of public remorse such as the 1997 and 1998 consecutive apologies by Germany for the bombing and killing of more than 1,000 people in the Spanish town of Guernica in 1937, the horrors of which are immortalized by Pablo Picasso's painting. German President Roman Herzog first sent a message of atonement to survivors a day after the 60th anniversary of the bombing for what he called "the most terrible atrocities."[34] Exactly a year later the German Bundestag praised Herzog for apologizing and passed its own resolution of apology to the Spanish people.[35]

The last imperative in the evaluation of public apologies relates to making clear who the participants in an apology are and determining their accountability for wrongdoing. It is not always clear who exactly is apologizing to whom in many instances of public apologies. When Tony Blair apologized for the British role in the 19th century famine, whom was he addressing? The descendants of those who actually died? The survivors who fled, the Irish people, the present Irish leaders, or all the British people for sharing the shameful past? On the other side, on whose behalf was Blair speaking - his government, the English people today, or the British across generations? Such doubts call for clarification because only then can we address problems of responsibility. The notion of accountability in the apology framework presented here refers to who will morally be answerable for the damages or crimes committed. One can imagine a political identity as it relates to moral accountability, as James W. Booth does. Booth advances the notion of constitutional patriotism, which he links to "the idea of a community of memory, with debts to and inheritances from the past."[36] We will identify other such identities that come into being to morally account for grievous misdeeds.

Apart from these prerequisites for a successful apology, there are other conditions that contribute to this goal. First, an apology is affected by who initiates it, who responds to it, and who accepts responsibility. In recent instances of public apology, participants have included victims, perpetrators, activists, advocacy groups, and political leaders as individuals and as agents of the state. An ethic of apology should provide an alternative that surmounts the barricades of state sovereignty allowing civil society to participate. Transnational human rights activism has contributed to giving voice and empowering those individual and group victims that have been hitherto silent and weak in calling for redress against past justices.[37] Hence the moral practice of the apology project should first be based on a discursive and democratic space in which muted demands for justice by victims will find their voices. In order for an apology project to succeed, to heal and reconcile communities, an ethic of apology should take shape as an alternative to an ethic predicated only upon absolute sovereignty.

Second, questions of agency raise issues of power relationships, the most problematic of which is the asymmetrical relationship between the perpetrator state and its agents, on the one hand, and individuals and groups seeking the apology, on the other. When perpetrator states or their agents are not forthcoming about their past deeds victims are often too weak to press for justice. Consider the case of Germany, a Germany that has developed a most progressive culture of apology after the Holocaust, and its dealings with the Herero people of its former colony South West Africa, now Namibia. Germany finally accepted responsibility and apologized for the violent repression of the 1904 Herero uprising that cost between 45,000 and 65,000 lives.[38] The government ruled out reparations, however, arguing that it had given 500 million euros to Namibia in the form of aid.[39] Note the apology to the Hereros arrived decades after German apologies to victims of the Holocaust and half a century after reparations to Jewish victims and survivors had begun!

Overly emphasizing the performative acts of leaders undermines the extent to which victims, survivors, families of both, and their human rights advocates often engage in a protracted struggle for redress. The agency of victims is prominent in the initiative taken by individual citizens, advocacy groups and a few visionary political leaders. In the case of the Herero people of Namibia and their demand for apology and reparations from Germany, those who are politically active are the traditional leaders, commemoration committees, churches and individuals. The autonomy of such groups, however, has been contested by the "victim state," at one point. Reacting to an academic conference which dealt with finding ways of reconciling the Herero-speaking Namibians and Germany in November 2004, Namibia's Minister of Information Nangolo argued that "reconciliation negotiations should be a matter handled by the governments of one and the ethnic groups of another country."[40]

Third, the ethics of apology makes it necessary that participants in the apology project identify with each other morally, defying the conventional geopolitical map, constitutional communities, and generational divides. It also implies

that citizens assume political responsibility for past wrongs while resisting identification as guilty subjects. On this score most scholars seem to agree. Whether
the sentiment of guilt should be carried into politics, however, is a contentious
matter.[41]

Fourth, is the problem of proximity or distance between perpetrators and
victims. The temporal and spatial distances between perpetrators, victims, and
events of past wrongs raise complex issues of responsibility and eventually have
impact on the efficacy of public apologies.

Proximity and Responsibility

How can a state or its agents work toward doing good by the victims and their
representatives and move toward reconciliation? Can the distance between the
victims and those leaders who claim to represent collectivities in an apology
process be bridged? Such practical puzzles raise larger questions of representation, individual versus public morality, discourse ethics as they apply to world
politics and the role of language and performative ethics.

Public statements of remorse by leaders sometimes obscure the important
question of representation. They are rarely directly delegated by those very collectivities from where the regret is supposed to originate. When Polish President
Aleksander Kwasniewski apologized on behalf of the nation on the 60th anniversary of the massacre of thousands of Jews, he spoke as head-of-state and the
voice of his people. His apology was not directed to an undifferentiated audience, as is often the case of such rituals. Instead it was specific and representative of the two sides of an apologizing collectivity. The solemn gathering he led
was attended by some 3,000 people including families of the victims and high
Polish government officials. And Kwasniewski's language of remorse was to the
point: "as a citizen and as the president of the Republic of Poland, I beg pardon.
I beg pardon in my own name, and in the name of those Poles whose conscience
is shattered by that crime."[42] One can then ask if such apologies are legitimate
when they are so removed from the source of authority or from the people on
whose behalf the apology is being given. In the case of diplomatic contrition,
there is hardly any or no tradition in world politics where the people are informed of these actions in a transparent procedure. Does this shortcoming mean
that public remorse can only derive from executive authority and therefore lacks
democratic accountability? Executive leaders (heads of governments and states)
are normally given broad mandates to offer apologies as they enter into treaties
and agreements. Just the same, much as treaties go through a ratification process
in legislative bodies at home, formal apologies could carry more legal clout if
they were endorsed the same way. Related to the necessity of democratic legitimation is the importance of political action and initiative to tip the moral balance.

Posited against the dominant and prevailing perspectives through which we
view the world are the voices of those who challenge conventions with their

idealism. They raise unprecedented questions and call for actions that are extraordinary. Consider the following line of thought. In the discourse of apology can one speak of the unapologizeable? Albert Speer, the Nazi war criminal, once expressed that the scope of certain crimes, like the ones he was accused of, were such that they defy apology. Or apologies by themselves are not adequate enough for full redemption and forgiveness. A pure apology is by definition unconditional. Jacques Derrida speaks of forgiveness along the same lines demanding that forgiveness be pure. He asserts, "Forgiveness is not, it *should not be*, normal, normative, normalising. It *should* remain exceptional and extraordinary, in the face of the impossible: as if it interrupted the ordinary course of historical temporality."[43] But in relations between states, the politics of forgiveness as well as apology are aimed at maintaining the status-quo and normal relations, and as such make the acts less complete and pure.[44]

The ethic of apology proposed here then goes to some extent against the grain of established international relations and diplomacy. In fact it advocates the need to take risks in order to break a stalemate, disturb intransigent political positions, and search for breakthroughs in mending injured relations and restoring dignity. Imagine a Turkish Prime Minister in the near future stunning his nation and the world with the first utterance of apology for the 1915 genocide of some 1.5 million Armenians during Ottoman Turkish rule! Approximating the "exceptional" would require a degree of vulnerability - risking the cost of rejection, rebuff, and humility at the minimum in order to face up to one's responsibility.

At the core of an apology proper are the acknowledgement of a wrong and the expression of sorrow on the part of the offenders, ideally facing the victim. This direct confrontation demands humility. The ritualistic acts of bowing, kneeling, and prostrating in seeking forgiveness amount to humbling oneself while morally elevating the victim. It takes a great deal of courage to take that first step forward because the offender is taking risks that would be avoided if he or it, in the case of a corporate entity, chooses not to be repentant for the wrongdoing. For one thing, the apology may not be accepted and forgiveness is not readily given. There is also that risk of losing one's reputation or being tainted and publicly stigmatized as in the *Scarlet Letter*'s "A" - the "A" standing for apology, in this case.[45] Of course, this is not always the case, especially when we consider those whose apologies result in social acceptance, at least, or praise for their moral courage. But offering an apology always makes one vulnerable or invites reprisal. In certain legal systems the apologizer risks legal liability.[46]

A counterpoint is provided by Emmanuel Levinas in his idea of the ethical face. Levinas's ethical "face" provides a radical alternative to the more cynical world of *realpolitik* in which an apology by proxy is meant to amend wrongdoing. It offers a totally different alternative to third party intervention or political intervention whereby the perpetrator or the apologizer faces the Other with categorical vulnerability:

> There is first the uprightness of the face, its upright exposure, without defense. The skin of the face is that which stays most naked, most destitute. It is the most naked, though with a decent nudity. It is the most destitute also: there is an essential poverty in the face; the proof of this is that one tries to mask this poverty by putting on poses, by taking on countenance. The face is exposed, menaced, as if inviting us to an act of violence. At the same time, the face is what forbids us to kill.[47]

Proximity, i.e. being in the presence of the injured party, entails the risk of being vulnerable to the offended party. Levinas's notion of face in its "upright exposure," that simultaneously invites and forbids violence, subtly delineates this notion. We are extending the meaning of face-to-face presence to its metaphorical level, images of the sufferers or victims conjured up from memories and narratives, in apologies by proxy or when the apology itself is delivered by a delegate. We can imagine the apologizer facing an apparition who can be interchangeably indifferent, pathetic, haunting, or an accusing figure. Face can also imply a reflection of self as in a mirror. In contemplating an apologetic act, the apologizing subject is expected to seek self-knowledge and introspection in order to come clean, to be redeemed, or be restored into the community from which it has fallen. "Facing" is to look into one's conscience and through self-analysis perceive and admit culpability. It is in such context the question of proximity both literally and figuratively is related to the important issue of guilt and responsibility. In its responsibility to the Other's essential sensibility, Levinas's notion of the "face" reinforces two vital imperatives of a successful apology. The first is the importance of proximity between perpetrators and victims or between the wrongdoer and the injured. The other is the acceptance of total responsibility toward the Other in order to restore and reconcile.

On the question of guilt and responsibility, Karl Jasper's *The Question of German Guilt* remains relevant and insightful. An existential philosopher who narrowly escaped German concentration camps himself, Jasper outlines four levels of guilt that can help us clarify confusions concerning guilt and responsibility among individuals, groups or nations. The first, *criminal guilt*, will be determined by producing evidence against those who break the law. Following formal proceedings those found guilty pay the penalty. The second, *political guilt*, results from the actions of the citizens, the bureaucrats and the political leaders of a state. In this instance, everybody is co-responsible for the deeds of the state by virtue of citizenship.[48] The third, *moral guilt*, comes from either personal or spiritual complacency. According to Jaspers, "moral guilt exists for all those who give room to conscience and repentance."[49] The morally guilty are all those who knowingly or unknowingly, through apathy or timidity, would be complicit in all kind of crimes. Finally, *metaphysical guilt*, is that which extends beyond moral guilt to a transcendental level that gives a sense of solidarity with others. In Jaspers's words: "There exists a solidarity among men as human beings that makes each co-responsible for every wrong and every injustice in the world, especially for crimes committed in his presence or with his knowledge."[50]

Jaspers's category of guilt is useful in determining acknowledgement of and accountability for wrongdoing. We can also imagine a concentric circle of complicity and guilt corresponding to various levels of responsibility and appropriate apologies. Beginning with the most proximate parties of perpetrators and victims, guilt and responsibility can be extended to their families and communities, to the national level and finally to the international level where in fact we can all be implicated by virtue of our common humanity. The moral thread that ties the parties within each circle is the human empathy for each other, empathy that can be extended even to one's enemy. As Donald Shriver puts it, "understanding the humanity of enemies is another step toward entertaining the possibility of living with them as fellow human beings."[51]

An ethic of apology should be flexible enough to recognize the moral distance between an aggrieved individual, a survivor and the modern national state on the other. Different avenues exist for survivors of mass violence and for statesmen or governments to initiate a restorative act. This ethic should also accommodate the most proximate acts (i.e. fratricide) of reconciliation between perpetrators and victims, on one hand, the corporate apologetic modes, at the middle, and the most bureaucratic apologetic accommodation between two states in diplomacy.

The Political Calculus of Apology

In most cases of apology victims seek apology and compensation from the perpetrator-state responsible for the violence and the consequences. Thus an apology process cannot exclude the state from its moral discourse as the political calculus is unavoidably tied to the "high" politics of statecentric international order.

In defining the difference between personal apology and political apology we must determine whether emotions and emotional relationships can apply to international relations where dispassionate state interests are served, at least as realist international relations theory would have it.[52] Machiavelli's thoughts and writings articulate best the principal differences between individual and public morality by stressing that the agent of the public domain such as the prince has responsibility to not allow consequential harm to come to the larger community even at the expense of being cruel.[53] In Machiavelli's words:

> A prince, therefore, must not mind incurring the charge of cruelty for the purpose of keeping his subjects united and faithful; for, with a very few examples, he will be more merciful than those who, from excess of tenderness, allow disorders to arise, from whence spring bloodshed and rapine; for these as a rule injure the whole community, while the executions carried out by the prince injure only individuals.[54]

Standing Machiavelli's public morality on its head, in light of our discussion of the collective apology mode, the "prince" faces the imperatives of acknowledgment, accountability, and the pressures for remorse *post facto*, after negligence, short-sighted goals, inaction or other wrongdoing have brought injury to the larger community. We may ask what if the community of princes fails to act from excess of timidity, thereby allowing disorder and mass violence. Of course, this retort to Machiavelli's notion of public responsibility is valid *only* when we can extend the moral community from the immediate domain to the global community.

Remorse by Proxy

In spite of the gap between private and public morality, further reflections are needed on the nature and difficulties involved in the expression of public remorse in apology. We can begin by drawing out certain characteristics and problems associated with it. First, office-holders can not represent the body politics of emotions, turning atonement by proxy into a politically creative challenge. Second, public remorse needs to be on record to equal the sincerity of individual contrition. Third, it needs to address and influence the victim even when forgiveness is not forthcoming. Finally, public remorse directed toward reconciliation or seeking forgiveness needs to be publicly witnessed and politically reached.

In relations between the many to many, the language of apology is employed by functionaries who can tap into their private beliefs or allude to public morality in order to engage in public remorse. It is rather difficult to express genuine repentance in public communication, and even more untenable to separate the image-saving rhetoric of narrow political utility from the more serious contrition necessary for reconciliation.

In remorse by proxy, so to speak, leaders engage in both apologetic rhetoric and acts. Thus they render their apologies as office-holders and not as individuals. Also, while the expression of sorrow is a necessary ingredient for reconciliation in the interpersonal apology process, the dynamics of apology from many to many precludes this.[55] Tavuchis reminds us that "... sorrow is ruled out or, at best, perfunctory in light of the formal, official, and public discursive requirements of apology from the Many to the Many."[56] However, the negligible role of sorrow in collective apology does not make it an apology in name only. The practical and symbolic weight of a collective apology can only be judged by the remedial and reparative work it brings to society. What distinguishes interpersonal from collective apology is that interpersonal apology succeeds through sorrow and remorse. Tavuchis elaborates:

> Thus corroboration is a necessary but insufficient condition for an authentic apology between persons. In stark contrast, *although still within the conceptual purview of what is recognized as interpersonal apology*, the major structural

requirement and ultimate task of collective apologetic speech is to put things on record, to document as a prelude to reconciliation. And what goes on record ... does not necessarily express sorrow and, except in a pro forma fashion, need not in order to effect reconciliation between collectivities.[57]

This precise idea of putting things on record is perhaps among Tavuchis's most compelling ideas on the apology process. It resolves the problem of how to accommodate the lack of affectivity in public remorse by substituting commitment to some form of reparation for it. However, routinizing apology to the extent Tavuchis is advocating deprives it of its moral weight. The drawback of relying too much on such public documentation would also be the temptation to settle for less than what an open-ended approach to reconciliation might potentially lead to. The pressure to put tentative agreements on record could compromise the truth and full accountability for the injustice in question by leaving festering wounds unheeded. This tendency is more pronounced because perpetrator states are reluctant to take risks in a state-centric world that inherently fosters mistrust and insecurity. Yet groups and individuals do engage in dramatic acts of atonement for an increasingly growing global audience.

The language of remorse and repentance, freighted as it is with its religious connotations, is difficult to employ beyond the individual level of analysis. Marina Warner makes a major distinction between apologies that attract more cynicism, and deservingly so, and "public statements of responsibility and regret made by those involved directly with the injured."[58] Public leaders who make public apologies assume priestly roles and "their verbal retractions are magical, sacramental acts, designed to ease and soothe and purge hatred and grudge." However, the confessions of political leaders may turn out to be aimless when they assume a priestly role and apologize indirectly. In St Augustine's *Confessions*, his atonement "depended on the compact with a listening God." Warner's point that apologies do not work unilaterally is similar to Tavuchis's understanding that an apology is not a soliloquy.[59] A remorseful apology requires that it be direct, in the presence of the victim or her surrogate, and in the presence of witnesses or that it be on public record. I also contend the affective and performative dimensions of an apology are important for its success as well.

Cases regarding injustice and its redress most often involve "states" that have the power and organization to restore as they have the capacity to destroy efficiently. As such, the affairs of states are entangled with the lives of individuals and groups bringing up once again the perennial tension between public and private moralities. Our willingness to consider the power of public remorse in seeking reconciliation is influenced by the conflict or overlap between the two. Stuart Hampshire is one scholar who does not see walls between the two, asserting that private and public moralities do not have a "different set of prescriptions and they are not self-contained spheres of activities." Hampshire continues:

The claim is rather that the assumption of a political role, and of powers to change men's lives on a large scale, carry with them not only new responsibilities, but a new kind of responsibility, which entails, first, accountability to one's followers, secondly, policies that are to be justified principally by their eventual consequences, and thirdly, a withholding of some of the scruples that in private life would prohibit one from using people as a means to an end and also from using force and deceit.[60]

The premise of Hampshire's argument is that there is no neat and tidy moral theory that sets apart private life from the public, but there are degrees and balances that require attention in the differences between the two. Such a flexible perspective refuses to admit that there are barricades between private and public morality and thus permits an imaginative leap, for example, of agents of state engaging in extraordinary acts that we associate with private life. We can therefore imagine nations expressing guilt, forgiveness, apology and remorse by proxy.

Apology and Diplomacy

Apology, which is primarily an affective speech act, finds itself on strange grounds in a world that is driven by national self-interest. In a realist moral economy an aggrieved state like China appreciates compensation for damages and restitution. The apology part of getting things right is also weighed for its instrumental advantages. In other words, the restoration of national face has symbolic and instrumental value only as far as it serves the national interest. Apology in this sense is not redemptive and moral. The old truism on the distinction between the moral behavior of groups and moral behavior of individuals applies here. Theologian Reinhold Niebuhr made that distinction in his *Moral Man and Immoral Society* when he argued: "In every human group there is less reason to guide and to check impulse, less capacity for self-transcendence, less ability to comprehend the need of others and therefore more unrestrained egoism than the individuals, who compose the group, reveal in their personal relationship." [61] The "moral man" comes into being in his capacity to transcend self-interest, while the "immoral society" refers to nations and classes who often fail in their unjust self-assertion and selfishness to transcend rationalized self-interest.

One case that illustrates the limits if apology in a politically unstable context is the bizarre abduction incident that embroiled the two Asian countries of North Korea and Japan. When Japanese Prime Minister Koizumi was on a state visit to North Korea in 2002, its leader Kim Jong-il admitted that his country's special forces had abducted at least a dozen Japanese nationals during the 1970s and 80s "in a fit of patriotic overzealousness," as he called it. Kim not only apologized for the crime, he also promised "to indefinitely extend a moratorium on missile test launches, to respect international agreements on nuclear weapons inspections and to halt operations by spy ships in Japanese waters." In return the Japanese Prime minister praised the frankness of Kim's apology and extended a pet apology as Japanese prime ministers have done in the past. He expressed "deep remorse and heartfelt apology" for Japan's 1910-1945 colonial rule of the peninsula. Japan also agreed to extend economic aid, which is expected to be between \$5 and \$10 billion.[62] This case illustrates the limits of apology in a politically unstable context. North Korea's apologetic gesture and Japan's diplomatic response are both aimed at normalizing relations that fall short of resolving North Korea's nuclear threat, military posturing, and the unresolved consequences of Japan's war and colonialism of its Asian neighbors. The North Korean apology may have thawed the somewhat frozen relations between the two countries but failed to go beyond that. Apology toward reconciliation should by definition transcend normalization and the status quo. Normalization implies maintaining stability or legality. Reconciliation, on the other hand, demands extraordinary measures. Normalization settles for predictability in an otherwise uncertain environment while reconciliation, when grave injustices have been committed, requires political will and an extraordinary measures.

Hence hesitation about the utility of apology in a hostile international environment is understandable. One can argue that acting morally in an immoral or amoral society, to use Niebuhr's ethic, could be futile, even dangerous. In other words, how can a national leader conduct a foreign policy guided by moral choices in an international context of self-interest, nationalism and anarchy? Niebuhr's Christian pragmatism can perhaps provide an answer to this dilemma however paradoxical his ethical strategy is. One interpreter of Niebuhr's legacy finds the theologian's ethical theory to be built upon a deontological foundation of the law of love balanced against a pragmatism that operates best in a world of sin where an examination of the consequences is necessary in order to facilitate the cause of justice. If Niebuhr were alive today he would have perhaps applied the prescriptive role of the law of love to apologies to mend and heal as part of the permanent obligation of humankind. He would also have insisted for the examination of such initiatives case by case lest the consequences of these actions facilitate or hinder justice and peace.[63]

Cases of Apology by Proxy

Political apologies, apologies in which states have either a stake or when it is demanded of them, are varied according to the levels of transgression and the ends they are aimed at. A political apology may involve a simple diplomatic indiscretion or be a part of a conflict resolution process following a serious diplomatic crisis. A political apology is also associated with remedies and redress of large-scale historical injustice and violence. The following four chapters represent cases of political apology, both historical and contemporary, that together provide generalizeable observations about political apologies regardless of the scale of transgression or injustice. The selected cases will also permit us to explain how the scale of transgression affects the apology process. I start with the archetypal case of apology and reconciliation between Germany and Israel.

Notes

1.   In those days, the emperor's apology was his own with no pretense of popular representation.

2.   Bill Clinton's apology for the failure of Western powers to prevent the genocide in Rwanda was delivered in the staged presence of some survivors. It is an apology by proxy, a type of initiative for reconciliation that has raised questions as to its remedial powers.

3.   "Christian group retracing steps of Crusaders offers apology for killings." *The Vancouver Sun* (British Columbia), July 16, 1999, <http://web.lexis-nexis.com/>.

4.   David Lister, "IRA issues apology for civilian pain." *Times* of London, July 17, 2002.

5.   Rory Caroll, "Catholic unease at Pope's apology for church sins." *The Observer*, March 12, 2000.

6.   Political apology is a catchall term that involves the public directly or indirectly. As such the concept had lent itself to so many interpretations. In my 2002 article (*Apologia Politica*) I based my understanding on what Nicholas Tavuchis had already identified as "apology from the many to the many." With focus on state apologies in this work my understanding of state apologies I address the call made by Gibe and Roxstrom to take state apologies more seriously. Their examination of the place of state apologies within the purview of the development of international human rights is an important work. See Mark Gibney and Erik Roxstrom, "The Status of State Apologies," Human *Rights Quarterly* 23 (2001) 911-939. For collective apologies, see also the earlier remarkable volume by Roy L. Brooks ed., *When Sorry Isn't Enough* (New York: New York University Press, 1999).

7.   Elaine Ganley, "Chirac Acknowledges French Role in World War II Deportations." *The Associated Press*, June 17, 1995, http://web.lexis-nexis.com/. See also Allan-Gérard Slama, "An Apology Too Far?" *Le Point* (July 22, 1995), Reprinted in *World Press Review*, 42 (November 1995), 20.

8.   Nicholas Tavuchis's Mea *Culpa: A Sociology of Apology and Reconciliation* is the best work to date that provides a basic structure to the meaning of apology and its understanding at various levels of analysis.

9.   Tavuchis, *Mea Culpa*, 15-16.

10. Peter Brooks, *Troubling Confessions: Speaking Guilt in Law & Literature* (Chicago: Chicago University Press, 2000), 90.

11. Brooks, 92.

12. Marina Warner, "Sorry: the present state of apology," *Open* Democracy (July 11, 2002), <http://www.opendemocracy.net/debates/article.jsp?id=3&debateId=76&articleId=603> (July 7, 2003). Marina Warner's series of essays for the online forum, *Open Democracy*, are provocatively insightful in her exposé of the workings of the theater of power employing the rituals of confession and atonement.

13. It is worth noting that theorists such as Martha Nussbaum, Amelie Rorty and Ronald de Sousa have sought to rehabilitate the emotions in theories of rationality and action. Others like Alison Jaggar, Elizabeth Spelman and Michael Stocker have brought out the importance of emotions in guiding ethical and political interaction.

14. Dominick LaCapra, *Writing History, Writing Trauma* (Baltimore: John Hopkins University Press, 2001), ix.

15. For a description of a fieldwork among survivors of state terrorism in Chile, see Inger Agger and Soren Buus Jenson, *Trauma and Healing under State Terrorism* (London, Zed Books, 1996).

16. An excellent documentation of the origins and evolution of international human rights is Paul Gordon Lauren's *The Evolution of International Human Rights: Visions Seen* (Philadelphia: University of Pennsylvania Press, 1998).

17. John Torpey, "Introduction." In John Torpey ed. *Politics and the Past: On Repairing Historical Injustices* (Lanham, Md.: Rowman & Litttlefield Publishers, 2003), 5. Torpey's edited book, in addition to Elazar's *Guilt of Nations*, provides a solid theoretical foundation to deepen our understanding of the politics of reparations politics. Researchers ought especially look into Torpey's introduction and Olick and Coughlin's theoretical chapter in the volume.

18. See Nicolaus Mills, "The New Culture of Apology," *Dissent*, 48, no. 4 (Fall 2001), 113-16.

19. Michel-Rolph Trouillot, "Abortive Rituals: Historical Apologies in the Global Era." *Interventions*, 2, 2 (2000), 173.

20. See Jeffrey K. Olick and Brenda Coughlin, "The Politics of Regret: Analytic Frames," in *Politics and the Past: On Repairing Historical Injustices*, ed. John Torpey (Lanham, Md.: Rowman & Littlefield Publishers, 2003), 56.

21. See Erving Goffman, *Relations in Public: Microstudies of the Public Order.* (New York: Basic Books, 1971), 108-118.

22. Tavuchis, *Mea Culpa*, 8. Even though Tavuchis relied on Goffman's mode of apology for his own formulations, he differs with him on several grounds. For one, Tavuchis says that Goffman's "analytical focus is exclusively upon the offender and not on the relationship." Even more importantly Goffman fails to even mention "sorrow and regret" – notions central to Tavuchis formula. Tavuchis, 138.

23. Jurgen Habermas, *Between Facts and Norms: Contributions to a Discourse Theory of Law and Democracy* (Cambridge, Mass.: MIT Press, 1996), 182.

24. Jurgen Habermas, "Discourse Ethic," in *Moral Consciousness and Communicative Action* (Cambridge, Mass.: MIT Press, 1990), 67.

25. Neta C. Crawford, "Postmodern Ethical Conditions and a Critical Response." *Ethics and International Affairs*, 12 (1998), 139.

26. Ned Noddings, "Thinking, Feeling, and Moral Imagination," *Mid-west Studies in Philosophy.* Vol. 22: Philosophy of Emotions. Ed. Peter A. French and Howard K. Wettstein, University of Notre Dame, 1998, 135.

27. Michael Walzer, *Thick and Thin: Moral Argument at Home and Abroad.* Notre Dame: University of Notre Dame Press, 1994, 11.

28. See Girma Negash, "*Apologia Politica:* An Examination of the Politics and Ethics of Public Remorse," *International Journal of Politics and Ethics*, 2, 2 (2002), 121-125.

29. John Gittings, "Pol Pot men say sorry for killing fields." *The Guardian (London),* December 30, 1998.

30. Donald Shriver, *An Ethic for Enemies: Forgiveness in Politics.* New York: Oxford University Press, 1995, 8.

31. "France Atones for 'Dark Spot' of the Dreyfus Case." *The Independent (London),* January 9, 1998. See also "Blair admits British blame in Ireland's potato famine." *Calgary Herald* (Alberta, Canada), June 3, 1997.

32. Tavuchis explains that authentic expression of sorrow is possible in which "regret, gently but firmly, reminds us of what we were before we erred, what our place was, where we stood in relation to the other, and what we have lost," 20. For others, like Nigerian writer Wole Soyinka, remorse may be nebulous, "nebulous because one can only observe that an expression of remorse has been made. Is it genuine? Impossible to tell," in *The Burden of Memory, the Muse of Forgiveness*. New York: Oxford University Press, 1999, 34.

33. The same question can be raised about "forgiveness" by proxy. Can leaders of a corporate group or a state forgive on behalf of survivors, and victims both dead and alive?

34. "Germany's president conveys grief to survivors of Guernica attack." *Associated Press*, April 27, 1997.

35. "Germany apologizes for Spanish civil war bombing of Guernica." *BBC*, April 24, 1998.

36. W. James Booth, "Communities of Memory: On Identity, Memory, and Debt." *American Political Science Review*, 93, no. 2 (June 1999), 249.

37. Referring to the dominant statecentric system, Michael Shapiro observes that "although the dominant geopolitical map appears uncontentious and nonnormative, it constitutes what I am calling a moral geography, a set of silent ethical assertions that preorganize explicit ethicopolitical discourses." See Michael J. Shapiro, *Violent Cartographies: Mapping Cultures of War* (Minnesota: University of Minnesota Press, 1997), 16.

38. Frauke Roeschlau and Ralf E. Krueger, "German minister in emotional apology to Namibia's Herero," *Deutsche Presse-Agentur*, August 15, 2004.

39. "After German apology, Namibia's Hereros want a 'Marshall Plan'," *Agence France Presse*, August 19, 2004.

40. On the occasion of the centennial commemoration of the 1904 German-Ovaherero war, an international conference was held in Bremen, Germany, with members representing the two sides. Some of the Namibians objected that the subject had become solely academic and proposed that the conference address Germany's colonial injustices. Chief Riruako pointed out reconciliation would come from a genuine apology by Germany and its acceptance to compensate the descendants of the victims. The Ovaherero leader appealed to Germany to stop encouraging division within the Ovaherero people at the risk of promoting a second genocide for which they would be considered responsible. *All-Africa.com*, November 29, 2004, <http://allafrica.com/stories/printable/200411300778.html > (January 1, 2005).

41. Andrew Schaap points out that, in their responses to the 'German Question,' Karl Jaspers and Hannah Arendt agree in considering collective responsibility as political liability without imputing blame, but that the two philosophers go their separate ways concerning the sentiment of guilt in politics: "For Jaspers, a spreading consciousness of guilt through public communication leads to purification of the polity, but Arendt rejects guilt in politics, where publicity distorts it into a sentimentality that dulls citizens' responsiveness to the world." See Andrew Schaap, "Guilty Subjects and Political Responsibility: Arendt, Jaspers and the Resonance of the 'German Question' in Politics of Reconciliation," *Political Studies*, 2001, vol. 49, 749. Schaap sides with Arendt's conception of political responsibility in understanding and acknowledging past wrong through authentic political action and judgment for the sake of the world (political) rather than the self (legal/moral). 750-754. While Arendt's approach is dispassionately democratic and puts faith in "citizens' care for the world they share in common with others," it is as radically optimistic as Jasper's orientation is burdensome, weighing on the individual's feel-

ing of co-responsibility and shame regarding a people's commitment to amend past wrongs.

42. "Polish apology for Jewish massacre," *CNN*, July 10, 2001,<http://cnn.worldnews.printthis.clickability.com/pt/cpt?action=cp&title=CNN.com+-Pol...> (December 28, 2004).

43. Jacques Derrida, *On Cosmopolitanism and Forgiveness* (London: Routledge, 2001), 32.

44. Derrida admits he is torn between the "hyperbolic ethics" he would like to follow and the pragmatism required to make certain decisions in the process of reconciliation. Derrida, 51.

45. If you recall Nathaniel Hawthorne's classic novel *The Scarlet Letter*, about betrayal and shame in which a young woman in Boston has been found guilty of adultery and is forced to wear a scarlet letter A on her chest to indicate her shame. She is publicly dishonored, but eventually redeemed and forgiven.

46. There is a legal movement in the United States to encourage apologies in order to avert lawsuits and encourage settlement. Several states have enacted statutes to encourage and protect apologies. See Jennifer K. Robbennolt, "Apologies and Legal Settlement: An Empirical Examination," *Michigan Law Review*, December 2003, 102, i3, 460.

47. Levinas, *Ethics and Infinity*, 86.

48. Karl Jaspers, *The Question of German Guilt*. (New York: Capricon Books, 1961). 31-32.

49. Jaspers, 63.

50. Jaspers, 32

51. Donald Shriver, 8.

52. See Crawford, 139.

53. Niccolò Machiavelli, *The Prince and Discourses* (New York: Random House, 1950), 60.

54. Machiavelli.

55. Nicholas Tavuchis, *Mea Culpa: A Sociology of Apology and Reconciliation*, 100-104

56. Tavuchis, 104

57. Tavuchis, 109

58. Marina Warner, "Sorry: the present state of apology."

59. Warner, "Scene Two: St. Augustine's Confessions, *Open Democracy*, May 11, 2002, <http://www.opendemocracy.net/articles/ViewPopUpArticle.jsp?id=3&articleId=647 > (July 7, 2003).

60. Stuart Hampshire, "Private and Public Morality," in *Private and Public Morality*, ed. Stuart Hampshire (Cambridge: Cambridge University Press, 1978), 52.

61. Reinhold Niebuhr, *Moral Man and Immoral Society: A Study in Ethics and Politics*. (Charles Scribner's Sons, 1944), xi-xii.

62. Jonathan Watts, "North Korea apologises to Japan for bizarre tale of kidnap and intrigue." *The Guardian*, September 18, 2002.

63. Mark L. Hass, "Reinhold Niebuhr's 'Christian Pragmatism': A Principled Alternative to Consequentialism." *The Review of Politics*, 61, no. 4, Christianity and Politics: Millennial Issue I 9Autumn, 1999), 605-636.

Chapter 2

German-Jewish (Israeli) Relations: From Zealous Accountability to Belated Apology

Neither Israel, which is so terribly afflicted, nor the individual Jew, who in his flight from the Nazi concentration camps suffered a thousand deaths of fear, can utter the first word. We are the ones who must begin! – Eric Lüth and Rudolf Kustrmeier, founders of the Peace with Israel Movement.

One cannot overstate the great distance traveled by both Israeli Jews and Germans to come to terms with a bitter past so shortly after the Shoah. Just consider the present ties between the two that include scientific cooperation and cultural exchanges, Germany's committed military and economic aid since the 1950s, and the more recent increase of emigration of Israelis of German descent to Germany. The sixty years of relations between the states and the peoples of Germany[1] and Israel profile historic events and contingencies in the course of public apology and reconciliation. So do the actions of the individuals and groups who have played critical roles in that process. It would appear that the states of Israel and Germany now have normal relations, with diplomatic relations established since 1965. Yet the memories of the Holocaust remain malleable symbolic tropes for politics, identity and historiography in both countries. Were public apologies made? In what order and how completely were they made in the scheme of the apology process outlined above? How is remembrance related to reconciliation?

The German-Israeli case is permanently cast in the bitter memories of the German Nazi past and has been driven by the moral leadership and statecraft on both sides since the end of the war. In spite of reconciliatory advances by the governments and societies of both countries, the end of the Cold War ushered in renewed fears and anxieties. These were brought about by the specter of a pow-

erful Germany, the attention given by the media to the 50th anniversary of the
Holocaust, new questions about the German Fascist past, renewed anti-
Semitism, and Germany's balancing act in the Middle East, among other rea-
sons.

Accountability

The history of how both Israeli Jews and Germans related to the Nazi past and
toward each other provides a context for examining the anatomy of a public
apology that is epic in scope and in depth. But first, we need to identify the parties to that process, ideas and movements, the conjectures of history and the contingencies that intervened, as well as the discursive practices that characterized
the debates on dealing with the past. What makes the German-Israeli case outstanding is the fact that it is to date the most well-documented complex of activities by participants that lends itself to the study of the reconciliation process
including the apology imperatives of accountability, acknowledgement, truth-
telling and public remorse. Lessons can be learned from the experiences of perpetrators and victims alike and all those implicated in these essential practices.
Accountability can be assessed then by determining who came forth to assume
responsibility for the past, why, and how.

Reckoning and Accountability

Identifying who were the perpetrators and the victims and all the actors who
participated in every aspect of the reconciliation process is a difficult task. We
can perhaps divide participants in the apology process into two categories.
Among the more conspicuous in the first category are the main perpetrators –
the Nazi party leadership and those closely associated with the central command
that conceived, planned and carried out the war crimes. These were the high-
ranking officials, military leaders and industrialists 5000 of whom were prose-
cuted by the Western occupying powers following the Nuremberg Tribunal,
with 800 executed. In East Germany, the Soviets and purged German courts held
war crime trials in which 30,000 were tried and 500 were executed. Obviously,
the cleansing acts and the de-Nazification campaigns on both sides of the German divide were more about administering justice than beginning a reconciliation process and lasting peace. The simple dyad of perpetrators/victims does not
account for participants who collaborated with and accommodated the violence
of the perpetrators. One would face a similar difficulty sorting out who the victims were.

The first identifiable group among the victims could be the half a million or
so survivors of the Holocaust who settled or would eventually settle in Israel.[2]
The demand for compensation by Jewish groups at the end of the war also revealed all those dead or alive who lost their property as victims of the systemic
violence. While the focus of this study is on the victimization of Jews, more

recent studies are disclosing the victimization of other groups such as Gypsies and gays. Media attention was given to the demands for an official apology and compensation by such groups who have been dubbed the Nazis' forgotten victims.[3]

It was the activists individually and as a group who initiated and then advanced the demands of the victims for justice, restitution and apology. Demands for reparation to Jews came from Jewish leaders, scholars and researchers active in Britain and the United Sates, many of whom had escaped from German occupied countries.[4] Among these was Shlom Adler-Rudel, the Director of the Central British Fund in London, who on his own initiative sent memoranda to influential leaders describing Jewish conditions and proposing compensations to Jewish bodies and personalities. In the United States, the World Jewish Congress, the American Joint Distribution Committee and the American Jewish Conference were the important Jewish organizations active in the cause of post-war rehabilitation and compensation.[5]

One individual, who played a critical role in legitimizing reparation demands and moving them from individual legal claims to the more political collective claim on behalf of the Jewish people, was Dr. Siegfried Moses. Moses belonged to the Association of Central European Immigrants in Palestine, and in 1944 organized the Palestinian branch of the Council for the Protection of the Rights and Interests of Jews from Germany headquartered in London.[6] Although it was Georg Landauer who first formulated the Jewish national claims idea, Siegfried Moses "transformed the moral into legal claims."[7] Nana Sagi asserts that the Jewish claims presented to the allies in 1945 by Jewish groups and eight years later by the state of Israel owe a lot to Moses's booklet, "Jewish Post-War Claims," which laid the ground for collective claims.[8] Influential personalities and groups might have advanced the cause and demands for justice and reparations, but it is the early ideas and movements that laid the foundation for the historic decisions and the political constructions yet to come.

Ideas and Movements

The two constitutive ideas that would soon hatch results turned out to be *national* claims and Zionist ideology and politics. These made the construction of a modern national Jewish identity possible. Elzar Barkan considers the idea of *national* claim to be a unique idea and the most novel aspect of the restitution demands:

> By reinforcing the demand for a Jewish state, it dovetailed with Zionist ideology and politics. As World War II was winding down, the national claim for reparation emerged as a dual demand: first, that the Jewish community as a whole be considered the primary victim and, by moral imperative, the rightful beneficiary of compensation for confiscated heirless and communal Jewish

property; and second, that restitution be directed toward the building of a Jewish state.[9]

While nationalism and nationalist movements gave the participants the direction and drive for reconciliation to succeed, the German case depicts a complex apology dynamic in which grassroots participation and government initiatives from above worked to initiate an apology process.

Historical Conjectures

The post-war global power and national configurations that had a lasting impact
on the Israeli-German case include the division of Europe and Germany, the
beginning of the Cold War and the establishment of Israel followed by the Palestinian diaspora. These were historic junctures that were to shape the apology
of the many to the many in which states and their agents play the leading roles.
So, if one wants to assess who was accountable in terms of coming to terms with
the consequences of the Holocaust, the domestic and foreign policies of the Federal Republic of Germany (West Germany before reunification), the Democratic
Republic of Germany (East Germany then), Israel and the United States all came
into play.

The mediation of states and their state agents in this epic political apology
raises questions of discontinuities and tensions between morality and politics.
Since the end of World War II German governments have been most accountable in the apology process. *Realpolitik* considerations on the part of the states
of West Germany and Israel are what would lead toward eventual rapprochement and normal relations. In those "new" regimes, the pursuit of their respective national interests took precedence over issues of morality and justice.[10] The
improvement of "Germany's image in the wake of a heightening East-West conflict" was understandably in the best national interest of the war-torn Germany
just as it was in the Israeli interest "to put the young Jewish nation onto a stable
economic footing."[11] As the first Israeli ambassador to the Federal Republic of
Germany, Asher Ben-Natan, explained, "Adenauer had come to realize quite
early that a reconciliation with the Jewish people carried great significance for
reasons of foreign policy – in order to improve the standing of the Federal Republic and its relationship to the Western powers – as well as for aspects of domestic politics, based on moral motives."[12]

George Lavy asserts that the Reparations Agreement with Israel concluded
by Chancellor Adenauer demonstrated that the German leader and his closest
aides "acted sincerely out their consciences and in that made themselves into the
conscience of the people. For Adenauer political advantage only played a sub-
sidiary part."[13] In view of such an appraisal, one can deduce from Adenauer's
actions and words the trademarks of political expediency mediated by private
morality. We are hard pressed however to reach easy conclusions when it comes

to the gaps between statecraft and morality in the foreign policies of Germany and Israel.

Consider, for example, the initial distance between their peoples and their governments in the wake of the Reparation Agreement in both Israel and Germany. The Israeli government insisted on receiving reparation payments from Germany without having to go through direct negotiations. The question of whether Israel should negotiate the reparations directly with Germany divided the Israeli people. Those who were vehemently opposed to dealing directly with Germany after the abominable crime of the genocide stressed the collective guilt of the Germans and preferred instead "a thousand-year proscription placed upon Germany, just as had been the case with the 500 year ban on the Jews following their expulsion from Spain."[14]

The decision by the Israeli government to approve direct negotiations was followed by a tempestuous debate inside the Knesset with protest and demonstrations outside, including the stoning of the parliament. There was also a marked opposition to the agreement in Germany, in spite of the full endorsement of SPD (the Social Democratic party). Fear of an indefinite demand of reparations to Israel was registered in the public opinion at the time.[15] In response to this opposition, German negotiators requested and the Israelis confirmed that there would be no more claims with the signing of the agreement. This politics of doing justice demonstrates the disparity, more than anything else, between the convictions and moral disposition of individuals and groups, on the one hand, and the responsibilities and sense of obligation of office holders, on the other. The stories of moral agency on the statecraft track are worth revisiting.

The Lead of Moral Agents & Contingencies

The measure of accountability in dealing with the common Nazi past is first to identify who comes forth to claim or counter-claim, to negotiate the representations of the past, to atone for sins committed, to deal with reparations (if that is possible), to apologize publicly (even when it is not accepted), and in the process, to redefine moral identities.

In the debates surrounding the question of whether or not Israel should carry out direct negotiations with Germany concerning reparations, David Ben-Gurion, one of the founders of Israel and the premier of Israel, assumed a role in favor of the negotiations in the face of bitter opposition. Ben-Gurion's arguments rested on the obligations of leaders to the "never again" core logic of the Jewish state and on a *realpolitik* calculation of the importance of a future Germany. Ben-Natan recounts:

> He spoke of the duty to those murdered to make a strong and prosperous state out of Israel that should prevent for ever a repetition of the Holocaust. He quoted from the Bible, "Thou shall not murder and at the same time inherit", but he also asserted that Adenauer's Germany and that of the Social Democrats

was not identical with Nazi Germany. Another argument that he later frequently repeated emphasized the Israeli interests in establishing connections
with a Germany that one day would be an important part of a Europe that was
unifying itself.[16]

This momentous step involved much more the future than the memory of
the past. Ben-Gurion's position that parallels Adenauer's in Germany reminds
us once again of the difficulty of separating private from public acts and applying moral criticism to the intentions and actions of political leaders. On the face
of it both leaders were praised for their political pragmatism. How would one
weigh Ben-Gurion's decision to overlook the sentiments of the Jews against
those who were opposed to receiving reparation payments that they considered
to be "blood money" and to dealing with Germans whom they collectively held
as guilty of genocide?

Correspondingly, how would one judge Adenauer for holding a view that
Germans were responsible but not collectively guilty for the heinous crimes? In
light of our focus on the apology process, Adenauer's choice of reacting expeditiously to reparation demands and laying the grounds for normalization instead
of dealing foremost with the bitter past raises further questions of political effectiveness and moral yardsticks. Without alluding to any grand theory of ethics
and international affairs at this point, and by simply examining the biographies
of the likes of Ben-Gurion and Adenauer some scholars reveal insights on how
such statesmen made the difficult choices of reconciling power and principle.
Such an approach is pursued in *Ethics and Statecraft* edited by Cathal J. Nolan.[17]
In explaining Adenauer's decision to rearm post-war Germany, Carl C. Hodge, a
contributor to the Nolan collection, has this to say about Adenauer's moral practice:

> Adenauer approached democratic governance as a call to political trusteeship.
> Fortified by a Weberian ethic of responsibility, he assumed a mandate to inter-
> pret for himself the best interests of the German people and to seek public ap-
> proval at the end of his term for the consequences rather than the intentions of
> his actions. Adenauer's personal definition of politics spoke of "the art of real-
> izing that which is recognized as ethically responsible."[18]

Human agency in international affairs played significantly in the rapprochement between Germany and Israel is unmistakable. Statesmen like Adenauer and other protagonists of history stood against the uncertainties and large
events of their time, moderating and sometimes shifting the directions of the
winds of change. The War and its unforeseeable outcomes, the realignments of
power, and the unpredictability of fast moving and uncontrollable events are the
contingencies that make up the rest of the narrative.

While the creativity and deeds of the larger historic figures are best remembered in shaping the substance and the direction of change, surmounting the
contingent events, accidents and follies, there are others who grapple and some-

times fail in dealing with those contingencies. In most cases, the constraints on leaders and politicians issue from a renewed politics of memory including geo-political and regime changes. The pre-election political strife in the Spring of 2002 between the Jewish community in Germany and the Free Democrats (FDP) are illustrative of such constraints.

The crisis began when Juergen Moellemann, deputy head of the FDP, sought to admit the Syria-born Greens member Jamal Kasli into the Liberal party. Public outcry forced the withdrawal of Karsli's application. It prompted Moellemann to say that the behavior of the German Council of Jews, Deputy Michel Friedman and Israeli Minister Ariel Sharon inspired anti-Semitism.[19] Consequently leaders of the FDP had to issue a statement saying the party "disapproves and regrets" the remarks made about Israel and about Jewish leaders in Germany by one of their top officials. The statement, however, fell short of a formal apology from Moellemann. On and on went the cycle of recriminations.[20] These verbal low-intensity wars are the reflection of the politics of memory and the reactions to new events and uncertainties among contending interests.

Generational differences, the re-unification of Germany, and the Israeli-Palestinian conflict were pivotal in German politics and the definition of its national identity. Take for instance the drama surrounding Ignatz Babus, the venerated Jewish leader, in his sunset years. It was Babus who reacted vehemently to Martin Walser's "the memory of the Holocaust has been overworked" speech. Babus was fearful towards the end of his life that the third German generation after the Shoah would feel less responsible for Nazi crimes and the rise of anti-Semitism. Ever conscious of people's selective historical amnesia, he wished to be buried in Israel for fear that his grave would become a rallying point for neo-Nazi protest in Germany.[21]

Accountability is determined by the nature of the discursive practices of the Israeli Jews and Germany in their 60-year relations. The ritualized public discourse between Israel and Germany is often framed in a victim/victimizer dichotomy, a simplified model that undermines full accountability. In reality, the debates and issues surrounding post-Shoah reconciliation bring out uncertain and not fully identifiable relationships while implying unexpected others. Take for example the 1985 international furor over the planned visit by President Reagan and Chancellor Kohl to a German military cemetery in Bitburg where members of the SS were buried. Reagan's decision to go ahead with the visit and his clumsy explanation that "the German soldiers interred at Bitburg 'were victims, just as surely as the victims in the concentration camps" turned sorrow into outrage, as Newsweek reported.[22] It went on to say that "Reagan succeeded in offending Jewish memories of the Holocaust not once but three times – first when the White House announced his intention to visit the cemetery at Bitburg, then by drawing a crude parallel between the German war dead buried at Bitburg and Jewish Holocaust victims, and finally by belatedly adding a tour to the site of a World War II concentration camp to his itinerary in Germany."

In order to calm the furor, the normally unrepentant Chancellor Kohl said it was the Germans' duty to keep alive the memory of the full dimension of the holocaust. Kohl, in the presence of survivors, many of whom had traveled from Israel, spoke of Germany's historical responsibility. He said, "a people that escapes from its history gives itself up."[23] In Israel itself, President Chaim Herzog said that President Reagan had been "ill-advised in visiting a cemetery in which the SS are buried."[24] Ironically Reagan's words and actions were intended to be part of a gesture of reconciliation with West Germany that backfired instead, inviting reproaches from American Jews, Israelis, and World War II veterans.

The most memorable reproaches came from Nobel for Peace Prize winner Elie Weisel who lectured Reagan that he should find another way to commemorate Germany's suffering in the war. Referring to the cemetery in Bitburg, Weisel beseeched Reagan: "That place, Mr. President, is not your place. Your place is with the victims of the SS."[25] The discursive practices represented in these debates were highly ritualized and therefore would have ever diminishing relevance to the lives of Jews, Israelis and Germans removed from the Shoah by three generations and to the apology and reconciliation process.

Yet, the accountability imperative was met by the readiness of the German leadership to step forward and assume responsibility to pay for the consequences of Nazi crimes and the war. It is indeed remarkable that Adenauer's achievement of the Luxembourg restitution agreement came ahead of a clear acknowledgement of the war crimes, of telling the truth about them or seeking justice, and certainly far ahead of putting remorse as part of public record.

From Denial to Acknowledgement

The history of restitution and reparation says a lot about the commitment of successive German governments to accept responsibility for the violence and ghastly deeds of the Nazis, but at the outset it falls short of meeting the acknowledgement imperative one would expect. While the accountability demands identifying *who* should be answerable and who should be party to the apology process, acknowledgement seeks to determine *who* comes forth to accept and admit wrong-doing. An apology proper customarily begins with the acknowledgement of wrongdoing voluntarily or an admission of guilt if accused or charged. An acknowledgement implies making public one's guilt, however grudgingly, or even against one's will. The affective and discursive distinction Tavuchis makes between giving an account or excuse and seeking forgiveness and redemption, helps us sort out the self-serving discharges from wrongdoing of the 'excuse-me' variety from the more sincere commitment to acknowledge offense and to express sorrow. The former act is dismissive and detached while the latter is responsible and engaged.[26] An apology proper, according to Tavuchis, "requires *not* detachment but acknowledgement and painful embracement of our deeds coupled with a declaration of regret."[27]

Here there seems to be a compromised approach to an apology, one that is commensurate with conflict resolution and statecraft and less with a more permanent reconciliation. The German-Israeli case brings to our attention the distinction between simply bearing responsibility and moving beyond that towards making peace and reconciling. Assuming responsibility can simply be interpreted as a matter of settling an account in the legal sense, perpetrators of a crime can distance themselves from the crime, blame others, or dilute their responsibility but sharing it with undefined others.

Although we were able to identify the parties and subjectivities of the apology process in assessing accountability, our focus was primarily on the special relationship between West Germany (later Germany) and Israel and the central role played by the reparations in Germany, Israel and elsewhere. A full appraisal, however, would require us to apply an apology mode or criteria to what has transpired between Germans, Israelis and Jews in the wake of the atrocities of World War II. An "apologizable" discourse did not begin in earnest until 1951. Against that criterion, therefore, important actions and speech acts will be weighed and put in sequence in order of importance.

As it turned out, the silence was broken by the German side, but only after Israeli Prime Minister David Ben-Gurion pointed out that Israel would not end the state of war with Germany as others had, because Germany had failed to denounce Hitler's war against the Jews. In reaction to that challenge, Eric Lüth and Rudolf Küstermeier, founders of the Peace with Israel Movement, did not wait for the German government to respond to Ben-Gurion, but instead proposed reconciliation with the Jews and with Israel. After six years of silence concerning the past between both Germany and Israel an apologetic call is made. In Lüth's words:

> What we all can do, the way in which we can all make a beginning, is to speak to the Jews in Germany and in Israel. Neither Israel, which is so terribly afflicted, nor the individual Jew, who in his flight from the Nazi concentration camps suffered a thousand deaths of fear, can utter the first word. We are the ones who must begin! We must say: We ask Israel for peace … We must set an example, which at the same time should be a sign that we are prepared to wage the struggle against the remnants of antisemitism with the same passion and uprightness with which we will fight any new antisemitism. We must link this call for peace … with an expression of grief for the six million innocent victims and of thanks for the incalculable good that the Jews have done in the service of mankind and in Germany.[28]

The call by these individual leaders launched an apologetic discourse, by naming the crime and the victims, and by the urgency of their apology, accompanied by an expression of grief. It has all the elements of an acknowledgement, however cursory the account of the crimes committed. The response from the government came in the words of Chancellor Adenauer about a month later, in a now famous speech before the Bundestag on September 27, 1951, offering material restitution:

> The Federal Government and with it the great majority of the German people are aware of the immeasurable suffering that was brought upon the Jews in Germany and the occupied territories during the time of National Socialism ... unspeakable crimes have been committed in the name of the German people, calling for moral and material indemnity ...The Federal Government are prepared, jointly with representatives of Jewry and the State of Israel ...to bring about a solution of the material indemnity problem, thus easing the way to the spiritual settlement of infinite suffering. They are profoundly convinced that the spirit of true humanity must once again come alive and become fruitful. The Federal Government consider it the chief duty of the German people to serve this spirit with all their strength.[29]

Adenauer's statement amounts to an acknowledgement of the national sins of the past and along with it assumptions of certain obligations and responsibilities towards Israel and the Jewish people. Yet Jeffrey Herf points out the shortcomings of that statement which in fact amounts to less than full acknowledgement: "He spent more time exculpating the majority of Germans than enumerating the specifics of the crimes of the Nazi regime."[30] He further attributes the failure to identify the perpetrators to the passive reference to "suffering brought upon the Jews in Germany," and in the phrase "in the name of the German people" has the effect and intent of distancing the criminal acts of the Germans of the Nazi period. Finally, Herf concludes, Adenauer's "acknowledgement of the burdens and obligations of the past and his effort to soften the blow to the national psyche remained enduring features of Adenauer's public discourse regarding the Nazi past."[31] What seems to be a contradiction here can only be explained by the consciously created boundaries between individual and public responsibility and a leader's pragmatic act ahead of the assumption of collective moral responsibility by a popular majority.

A decade later, Chancellor Erhard, under whose clock normalization between Israel and Germany was established, made similar gestures to acknowledge the burdens of the past, in a speech in New York: "Germany will ...continue to make good [for] the injustice which has been committed in its name, to make amends to the victims as far as one can atone through material compensation."[32] Erhard's tone of reconciliation and commitment to reparations is no different from Adenauer's. The central themes of discourse on the shared past have been, in broad terms, the accountability of the new German state for the consequences of the world war, the acknowledgement of the crimes committed by the Nazi regime and of Jewish victimization, and the need for atonement through material compensation. Leading up to and after normalization, including full diplomatic relations between Israel and Germany, there was a recognizable shift in semantics when German leaders spoke about the Nazi past. On the first state visit to Israel by a German chancellor in June 1973, Erhard's successor,

Willy Brandt, acknowledged the special relations with Israel, redefined now "as normal relations with a special character." Brandt's explanation of that special relationship was poignant:

> The recognition of our responsibility of /for/ our crimes was the decisive act of inner freedom for us, without which external freedom would have been unreliable. The thirteen years of horror will not be forgotten. German-Israeli relations must be seen against the grim /background/of the National Socialist terror regime. This is what we mean when we refer to our normal relations with a special character. (Deutschland-Berichte, July 1973)[33]

In that speech Brandt also spoke about learning lessons from the past and not being a captive of it. His certainty about not becoming "captives of the past" at this point in the relations between Israel and Germany would change later to a more remorseful discourse, but at this stage the cautiousness of diplomatic language prevailed. The German leadership had to balance its relations with the Arab states while remaining committed to Israel's right to exist. Hence the language of reconciliation towards Israel had to be re-framed according to the new freedoms and constraints in the wake of normalization. By the 1980s and thereafter, the rhetoric of remembrance and reconciliation, having been used by different parties to different ends, had lost its potency and become banal. Björn Krondorfer claims that the prevailing discourse "which has hardly changed in the decades since the war, has attained a ritualistic quality that is static and conservative rather than creative and transformative."[34] While the bottom line for the Christian Democrat chancellors since Adenauer has been to accept responsibility, remembrance was something they would rather forget. Chancellor Kohl's favorite theme was said to be: "the time has come to replace sombre remembrance by reconciliation." In 1985, at the height of the Bitburg scandal, Kohl shifted his rhetoric to the importance of memory at his visit to the death camp of Bergen-Belsen, where he underscored "the Germans' duty to keep alive the memory of the full dimension of the holocaust."[35]

In Adenauer's historic address to the Bundestag in 1951 while launching the restitution agreement, and the subsequent statements made by successive chancellors of Germany in dealing with the Nazi past, one finds the voices of three post-Shoah generations representing divergent views and feelings about guilt and responsibilities. According to Christian Pross, Germany had three clearly disparate generations: "1) the generation of the perpetrators, those who, in one way or another, witnessed it -- a generation one might call the generation of actors; 2) the generation of their children, a generation one might, with notable exceptions, as a whole classify as one of silence; and 3) the generation of *their* children, a generation one might look upon as that of inquiry."[36] Yet the realities reflect a more complex web of reactions and attitudes overlapping generations that were no doubt influenced, among other things, by the knowledge of Nazi crimes, the need for normality, ideological persuasion, and above all by political considerations. Representative of the first generation is Adenauer's approach to dealing with the past, which was to start with the pragmatic decision of paying moral debt through restitution while admitting wrongdoing. Adenauer's declaration of guilt - his acceptance of the burdens of Nazi crimes was part of a negotiation in the secret contacts between Germany and Israel.

Among the circumstances that broke the silence of the second generation was an unexpected media event in 1979. The telecast of an American television drama series, *Holocaust*, stirred up debate about guilt, memory and justice relative to the genocide among a German population, two-thirds of whom were born after the war years. The nine-part series that told the story of the genocide, through a fictionalized single family, summoned positive reactions from the majority of Germans particularly from the Jewish community. West German author Eugen Kogon, who spent seven years in Buchenwald, thought "it was essential for young people to see this film so they understand a subject that is still largely taboo in the schools and many homes of Germany – East and West."[37]

An examination of an apology process can be so concentrated on what the perpetrator does or says that it could undermine the agency of the victims or the recipients of the apology. In what we were able to consider so far with respect to accountability and acknowledgement, we have not identified the real and potential beneficiaries of restitution, reparations and other ways of doing justice. Considering victims of mass violence, one should start first with those victims who did not survive. What justice or reparation can be rendered to the dead? In primordial and Old Testament systems of justice, vengeance and retributions were deemed proper in the name of the victimized.

In more recent times we have pursued retributive justice while at the same time we have built a consensus toward new ways of prosecuting crimes against humanity and rendering justice. Who spoke in the victims' defense in the case of Germany? The victors of the war assumed this role in holding the Nuremburg Tribunals that carried out retributive justice, however symbolic. Donald Shriver comments: "However necessary were the symbolic retributions handed out by the Nuremberg court against leading Nazis, its judges had to peer down the slope toward other candidates for 'justice' who were too numerous for courtrooms or jails, too ambiguously 'criminal' for confident prosecution, or too necessary to the immediate rehabilitation of a devastated society to be prudently removed from it."[38]

In spite of the legal flaws, politically expedient decisions, and their uncompleted tasks, the International Military Tribunal and the successor trials brought Nazi crimes to the center of public memory, discourse and public policy. The prosecution of Nazi political criminals, besides setting a precedent for judging crimes against humanity, brought to light the loci of accountability, acknowledgements of wrong-doing, confessions and remorse. They also legitimized further demands for restitution, reparation and apology.[39] Michael R. Marrus reminds us of the importance of Nuremberg in disclosing so much about Nazism and the Holocaust: "More than many of the organizers even hoped, Nuremberg was a voice for history – in the form of thousands of documents on the Third Reich assembled by the court and released for the scrutiny of historians and writers with every possible viewpoint."[40]

Yet another measure of "doing good by the victims" is the degree of benefit from restitutions and reparations. The praise for the 1953 agreement and Adenauer's role in it, along with the figures of how much money Germany has paid in reparations to Jews and other victims since then are often quoted in the press. The rhetoric of *Wiedergutmachung* (to make good again) highlights the intent and law of the restitution but overshadows the difficulties and, in some historians' view, the almost scandalous struggle of surviving victims to receive their payments.

Describing the encounters between persecutors and victims in the 1950s, Christian Pross wrote: "The German people did not like the victims, and they certainly did not like paying for them. Reparations were a burdensome duty imposed by the victors."[41] That original reluctance to pay reparations and the bureaucratic and political obstacles which followed would eventually be overcome. For example, in the year 2000, Germany created a special fund to pay up to 5 billion U.S. dollars to nearly a million survivors who worked as slave and forced laborers under the Nazis. This fund was called "Remembrance, Responsibility and the Future," and was promoted by Chancellor Gerhard Schroeder who argued that it was "a moral imperative" for industry and government in Germany to provide the unique fund.[42]

What can the dead of the Holocaust gain from an apology? What would appease their souls – a decent burial, prayers for their souls, memorials, commemorations, remembrance? Survivors, however, can make their wishes known. They can also leave a will. Recall Babus's wish to be buried in Israel so that Neo-Nazis could not make a scene at his grave. It is usually survivors and the families of the dead who care to remember and decide how to remember. In the case of aggrieved nations or peoples, memorials have an added importance. They do not want atrocities to be forgotten nor repeated again. They want moral debt to be paid and this is one way of doing it. In former traditional societies where past influences still linger today, the importance of upholding the spirit of the dead remains. We would not want our dead to turn in their graves. Nor would we want their innocence and sacrifice to be forgotten – if they were indeed victims or heroes.

Now we come to the benefits for the perpetrators. We will start with those who got away with murder. There are those who paid their dues -- served sentences etc. Many benefited from quiet amnesties and the miscarriages of justice. It is German leaders like Adenauer, however, who redeemed Germans and Germany by doing the following. 1) With allied encouragement, moving away from placing collective guilt on Germans as a nation and emphasizing individual guilt instead. This involved one time justice via Nuremberg and successive trials, and deNazification campaigns. In this way, the German leadership wanted to redeem itself in the eyes of world public opinion and to be accepted as a new democratic European country. 2) Embracing the Marshall Plan and reconstruction in order to fight a new war against the Soviet camp. 3) Transformation of Germany into a normal nation by making reparations, assuming responsibility for the past, achieving peace with Israel and Jews everywhere (while aware of the importance of American Jews), rearming and building their economy without threatening Europe.

Statecraft and Morality

Reparations as economic leverage are similar in some ways to blood money passed between feuding tribes to keep temporary peace. It can be a dispassionate exchange between parties bent on making peace and equilibrium rather than bringing justice to bear upon past misdeeds. Postwar settlements, treaties and diplomacy were part of a new power realignment shaped by the dictates of the victors and the beginning of an ideologically-split world. Thus, under the emerging global order *moralpolitik* took a back seat to *realpolitik* when the leaders of a war-torn Germany and an emergent Israel were bound by the consequences of the Holocaust and by what needed to be done to come terms with it.

The pragmatic leadership that came out of necessity in Germany as well as Israel chose to assume accountability first and to come to full acknowledgement of wrongdoing later, a position which was reinforced by the fact that it was easier not to grapple with the recent horrors of the war and the genocide. Much of what is known now about the psychological states of both victims and victimizers was dictated by shame and guilt. It was better and easier to avoid and not come to terms with such memories. Or the choice was to take some responsibility and move on as soon as possible. Hence it made sense in both Israel and Germany that the states and their agents assume the leading role to come to terms with the past and move on with the rebuilding of state and national identities.

State agency in an apology process that involves the eventual reconciliation between peoples would sound odd by today's measure when individual activists and transnational organizations are playing the leading roles in such movements. In the state-centric international politics of postwar years, it makes perfect sense for leaders to pursue their respective national interests even when public opinion lags behind the choices they make. The leading precepts in those years, as they continue to be with believers of neorealism today, were sovereignty, national security and national interests. The pragmatic leaders of those years like Adenauer and Ben-Guirion could only go as far as giving moral justifications for their statecraft but could not pursue *moralpolitik*. It is interesting to note that Ben-Gurion was able to communicate to Israelis who did not want to open direct negotiations with Germans on moral grounds by couching his support for those negotiations on the moral necessity of the survival of Israel. International law was also at the time more state-centric than it is today, considering that the Nuremberg trials set a precedent for judging a crime against humanity just as the reparations to Israel were outside of the jurisdiction of international law as the recipient state did not exist at the time the crimes were committed.

The history of reparations and restitution by the Federal Republic of Germany, and the successor Germany, illustrates the failure to meet the acknowledgment imperative at the outset, but says much about the commitment of successive German governments to be accountable for the deeds and consequences of Nazi crimes.[43] For Adenauer, reparation "was an acknowledgement of the 'special relationship' to the past, while moving away from guilt. Restitution was conceived by the Germans not as an admission of guilt but as a goodwill measure. Indeed for the first generation after the war there was little evidence of public guilt."[44] Reckoning with the Nazi past did not become part of the public discourse until an open society was promoted and established by Western allies and German leaders of the following generation. The debates on what to remember and forget about the Holocaust, the testing of the imperative of truth-telling, were not in motion until the 1980s and thereafter.

Debates on History and Memorialization

How Germans on the one hand, and Israel and Jewish groups on the other, consciously related to their respective pasts rested upon the truth they found in the narratives and testimonies of survivors, perpetrators, as well as the works of those who made it their mission to expose what transpired in Nazi Germany and the occupied territories. Among the observers of collective memory are academics, mainly historians, who take part in debates from time to time to maintain historiographical consensus, and in some cases in the re-writing of history. Historical revisionism often brings forth debates beyond academic circles because it provides a site that relates the collective memory of a people to its identity.

As Daniel Levy points out, "collective memory itself has become a contested terrain where groups self-consciously struggle to re-shape their national pasts to suit their present political views for the future."[45] For Germany and Israel, both of them nations reborn and born respectively after the war, the truths about the Holocaust became defining elements of their national identities. When Daniel Goldhagen's *Hitler's Willing Executioners*, appeared in 1996 it re-evoked old ideas of "collective guilt," "national character," "eternal anti-Semitism," ideas avoided by the Federal Republic of Germany since the end of the war. Pivotal to the rejection by most scholars of Goldhagen's book was his assertion that "the perpetrators were motivated to take part in the lethal persecution of the Jews because of their beliefs about the victims, and that various German institutions were therefore easily able to harness the perpetrators' pre-existing antisemetism once Hitler gave the order to undertake the extermination."[46] Levy concludes that he is "less interested in the historical accuracy of

Goldhagen's thesis than in the initially vehement reaction to it by historians and other intellectuals, and the gradual public acceptance of Goldhagen among some circles of the German left."[47]

In a way, such occasional historiological storms have brought knowledge and facts about the Nazi crimes, or at least provided critical tests of the record. The Nuremberg trials, memoirs, works of fiction and popular culture in the form of films and television drama have added to the truth-telling process. In this particular case of reconciliation, a truth and reconciliation commission like South Africa's was not formed and not yet conceived. It is highly hypothetical to imagine such a commission having held open hearings in which former Nazis would have confessed their crimes before victims and survivors. It is even more farfetched to imagine such a degree of cooperation by both perpetrators and survivors. Vindication was sought by the victors of the war and the survivors only through the prosecution of the Nazi leadership. Whatever degree of reconciliation was sought in Germany, it advanced through responsibility minus a full dispensation of justice. The telling of the truth about Nazi crimes turned out to be a prolonged process revealed in the politics and aestheticization of memories.

Memory, Truth and Aestheticization

As in most other cases of mass injustice, the issue of evidence of the Nazi crimes and how they should be remembered has been central to the imperative of truth-telling as part of the reconciliation process. The country's Nazi past has been to a great extent part of the reconciliation discourse in West Germany, a practice that was first forced by Allied powers and then encouraged by democratic politics and a freer media. In East Germany, however, such public debate was delayed for 44 years until the unification. To begin with, the documented accounts of what transpired in the war years have been unraveled with the details and magnitudes of the genocide and other war crimes only to be questioned by holocaust-deniers.

For victims and sympathizers, the fear of forgetting in the face of waves of anti-Semitism has been a constant in German politics. In response to the wishes of Jewish leaders who called for sanctions and punishment for those who repeat the "Auschwitz" lie, the Social Democrats passed a bill that made it an offense to refute or belittle the murder of six million Jews by the Nazis.[48] Perhaps the personal accounts and memoirs of survivors and perpetrators of the Holocaust were the most pervasive testimony in the truth-telling process. Reliance on memory and memorials, however, has its own power as well as problems. Let's start with the debate about memorials.

With the end of the Cold War and the reunification of Germany that came soon after, Germans embarked upon what they called *Vergangenheitsbewälti-gung*, or confrontation with the past.[49] This we can say marked the beginning of seriously addressing the truth-telling imperative. The debate among German historians over the issue of "normalizing" German history began in earnest around the mid-1980s. Normalizing German history or treating the impact of Hitler and the Third Reich in a detached fashion is at the center of the debate about history or *Historikerstreit*.[50] The revisionism of neoconservative historians was countered by philosopher Jürgen Habermas who demanded a continuing and open confrontation with the Nazi past.[51] Habermas argued that the burden of the past "was a debt-producing, incorrigible legacy to the community's collective memory and identity and one to be sheltered from the erosion of time, forgetting and normalization."[52]

Following the publication of Daniel Goldahagen's *Hitler Willing Executioners: Ordinary Germans and the Holocaust* (1996), another round of academic debate stirred up questions of public memory and national identity. The aforementioned Goldahagen's thesis is that the Holocaust had more to do with the pervasive anti-Semitic and eliminationist German culture than with obedience to authority. That particular assertion seems to have advanced truth-telling to the extent that it engaged many Germans in public debate across generational and ideological lines. The Nazi legacy once again embroiled intellectuals and politicians a few years later, when a soul-searching debate about remembrance took the center stage.

The question of what kind of memorial would be suitable for the Holocaust was tossed around from the late 1980s onwards, but it was not until the elections of 1998 that it became highly politicized, when Chancellor Helmut Kohl proposed a national holocaust memorial in Berlin. The remarks by German writer Martin Walser on the planned Holocaust memorial provoked a public storm in 1998 for instance. In an award ceremony in his honor, Walser said that the history of the Nazi extermination camp Auschwitz was being used as a "moral cudgel" to hammer home "(German) disgrace for current-day purposes."[53] The immediate reactions to Walser's statements are indicative of the distance and the depth of historic wounds unattended. It is at once a reflection of the sensibilities of the parties involved, the contested representation of the Holocaust and the domestic politics of post-Cold War Germany.[54] Such factors as the changing demography of German Jews, the rise of Eastern Europe, anti-Semitism in the new Germany, the Israeli-Palestinian impasse and the generational divisions among the descendants of the Holocaust emanate from the globalization of issues and the changing configurations of power.

Martin Walser's *faux-pas* touched sensitive nerves of national identities-in-the-making bringing to the surface not only repressed attitudes towards Jews, but raising old debates on German accountability. When Walser accused his detractors of using the Holocaust as a "moral cudgel," he was also asserting his own understanding of personal and public forms of commemoration."[55] At the center of this particular protest, however, is his condemnation of the planned Holocaust Memorial that he thought to be an inadequate representation of the past. Underlying his criticism, also shared by other critiques, is a new critical alternative to a "monumental" memorial - one that calls for a "dialectic process of commemoration" and that will concentrate on "remembering" rather than "ritualising."[56]

In an important work on the Holocaust, James E. Young identifies the challenge faced by a younger generation of artists and architects as they articulate the Holocaust memory. First, Young observes, they must devise ways to express memories of a catastrophe they have not lived through but have only gained knowledge of through a myriad of narratives including, films, television dramas, novels, photos and survivor memoirs. Second, they must find a way to formulate a memorial act that is "anti-redemptive" and that avoids at all times "the aestheticization of the Holocaust."[57] Speaking for those who were members of the commission designing Berlin's "Memorial for the Murdered Jews of Europe," Young describes a concept of memorialization that would address certain vital questions, such as:

> What are the national reasons for remembrance? Are they redemptory, part of a mourning process, pedagogical, self-aggrandizing, or inspiration against contemporary xenophobia? To what national and social ends will this memorial be built? Just how compensatory a gesture will it be? How antiredemptory can it be? Will it be a place for Jews to mourn lost Jews, a place for Germans to mourn lost Jews, or a place for Jews to remember what Germans once did to them? These questions must be made part of the memorial process, I suggested, so let them be asked by the artists *in* their designs, even if they cannot finally be answered.[58]

When Kohl proposed a national memorial in Berlin, his idea was attacked by both the right and left among Germans, but it was eventually approved by the Bundestag. To appease those who were dismayed by the original design of concrete pillars, including Chancellor Schroeder, a compromise was made in the design of the memorial by adding to it a research center so that "education rather than remembrance alone should be at the heart of the project."[59] The eventual outcome of this debate on memory and memorializing embraces the idea of confronting the past, the collective responsibility of ensuring that the horrors of the Holocaust are not repeated, and redefining the role of the new Germany in Europe and the world.[60] The responsibility taken by unified Germany to take advantage of the horrors of the past as lessons for a more tolerant and democratic Germany does perhaps best address the truth-telling imperative.[61] According to this plan, German students can learn to respect ethnic and religious diversity, transforming "the meaning of citizenship into a multicultural enterprise within the narrative of their nation."[62]

After decades of emotional debates on how Germany could remember Holocaust victims, the German parliament approved the national Holocaust memorial designed by an American architect. The debate about what would be an appropriate memorial accentuated the differences between those who wanted to remember and those who wanted to forget, as well as between those who wanted to freeze the past and those who felt responsibility to it. Peter Eisenman's design is a compromise of the two tendencies – between those who wanted a monument to permanently allay their fears of "forgetting" and members of the younger generation who preferred a more interactive representation that will continue to educate the public.

The latter, counter-monumentalists, accused the former that underneath their preference for commemorative markers was their desire to forget. Such a counter-monumentalist is architect Daniel Libeskind, who designed Berlin's new Jewish Museum. Libeskind's architectural representation of the violent excision of the Jews from German history is represented in the architecture of the museum by the use of negative space as an expression of absence and void. Libeskind says, "Only through acknowledging and incorporating this erasure and void of Berlin's Jewish life can the history of Berlin and Europe have a human future."[63]

The inauguration of the Memorial to the Murdered Jews of Europe took place in Berlin on May 10th 2005. The last in a series of ceremonies observing the 60th anniversary of the end of the war, this event stirred up old debates, emotional reactions, and new reflective criticisms. The ceremony itself that brought together leaders and dignitaries including Chancellor Gerhard Schroder was not without historic irony. The monument had been erected on the very grounds of the chancellery and ministries of the Third Reich, with Hitler's underground bunker only a few meters away.[64] Undoubtedly the opening of the memorial represents a historic juncture, the reaching of a consensus among the postwar German elite on how to commemorate the horrible past. It is only appropriate that a German parliamentary leader speaks to that consensus six years after the German Bundestag had passed a resolution to build the permanent memorial for the Murdered Jews of Europe after a bitter debate in and outside parliament. Wolfgang Thierse, president of the German parliament, declared at the dedication ceremony: "Today we are opening a memorial that commemorates the worst, the most atrocious of the crimes committed by Nazi Germany the attempt to destroy a whole people."[65] Thierse went on to say, "The horror touches the limit of our comprehension. ... This memorial acts on the limits of our comprehension." He continued, it will serve "as a place of memory" for generations, helping them "to face up to the incomprehensible facts." [66] Anticipating criticism, Thierse also defends the abstract form of the memorial: "The Nazi regime's systematic murder of Europe's Jews remains something difficult to comprehend. For this reason, we chose an abstract monument."[67]

The starkly abstract nature of Architect Eisenman's design lent itself once again to emotional reactions by Germans and Jews alike on that day of commemoration. The monument consists of a gravestone-like maze of 2,711 concrete slabs of uneven heights spread over five acres of land in the heart of Berlin. To this memorial field an underground Information Center is added. Visitors are expected to roam among these gray stones for full effect, as did one of the first dignitaries to visit the memorial, President Moshe Katsav of Israel, two weeks after the opening of the memorial. Those counter-monumentalists who supported an abstract representation of the Holocaust that avoided an attempt of being redemptive and aestheticized might have won the day. By virtue of the visceral reactions to the memorial and the new and old criticisms, Eisenman's concept of memorialization meets James Young's point about raising vital questions concerning the ends of the memorial even when they may not all be answered. The open-ended aspect of the architecture is reflected in the new and longstanding criticisms of the memorial.

Among the most serious criticisms of the memorial is one that charged the abstract character of the monument as somehow trivializing remembrance by not telling the full story of the war crimes.[68] Paul Spiegel, president of the Central Council of the Jews in Germany expressed that sentiment by emphasizing the importance of the information center and the hope "that some will make the effort to go beyond their own experience and to look for the facts." The memorial, he said, "would have been better if it would have addressed the motivations of the perpetrators."[69] The same Jewish leader raised a second criticism brought up by others and that is, the memorial omitted non-Jewish victims like gypsies, homosexuals and other victims of the Holocaust. Spiegel said that the omission of non-Jewish victims suggested "a hierarchy of suffering."[70] The main objection to the memorial in the last six years came from conservatives like the former Chancellor Helmut Kohl who held that the memorial was so large and central to German public space that it would hold Germany as captive of its memories. The most scathing criticism, however, is neither political nor ideological, but aesthetic. An American art critic who was present at the dedication ceremony found the postminimal design of the memorial too sterile, soul-less and cold. The effect of entering Eisenman's memorial, the critic writes, is "less visceral than dryly intellectual."[71] The defenders of this now yet-to-be famous site are many, beginning with Eisenman himself.

In rebuttal to the arguments that the memorial was an incomplete statement in so far as it did not address the motivation of the perpetrators and had omitted the representation of non-Jewish victims, architect Eisenman responds: "It is clear we won't have solved all problems. Architecture is not a panacea for evil. Nor will we have satisfied all those present today, but this cannot have been our intention."[72] Eisenman's best defense and one that had won the approval of the majority of the political elite is the fact that the memorial is intended to become part of daily life to Germans, Berliners in particular, and that it is meaningful to generation of Germans who were not directly affected by the Holocaust. As Eisenman points out: "There is nothing of the museum about it. You don't have to know about the Holocaust to experience it … If some people tell me it's not Jewish enough, and others say it's not appropriate for the Jews, then I think I've got it right. The fact is there is no possibility to describe the horror of the Holocaust."[73] Berliners have already appropriated the public space for their individual use. Just days after the opening of the memorial came reports of teenagers jumping from the memorial concrete slabs and engaging in unruly conduct. Swastika graffiti had to be removed from the slabs before the visit by Israeli president Katsav. Eisenman is not worried about the monument being defaced as log as it merges with daily life in Berlin. He says, "It is a great place for skateboarding. ... I don't care if people scratch its surface; at least it will show that they feel something. That's what it's all about."[74] While irreverent visitations live up to Eisenman's concept of an open memorial, Herr Thierse's more serious interpretation of openness dignifies Eisenman's design, that is in fact a "remarkably open monument, not a place for collective memory but somewhere allowing individuals to face up to their individual thoughts."[75] Perhaps the remarks made by Dagmar von Wilcken, the designer of the monument's information center, come closest to the anti-monumentalist vision that the memorial's main task was to keep alive the discussion about one period of German history. Von Wilcken asserts: "It is not a thing that says we have apologized and now it's over."[76] Will such a discussion carry on from generation to generation? Will the Holocaust be forgotten or will the newer German generations begin to believe it took place elsewhere? Such are the perennial questions of anxious survivors of the Holocaust.

If the so-called Third Generation rejects the imposition of an institutional memory, such as the one caste in stone in the new massive Memorial, and instead prefers individual discovery of one's history, the problem of maintaining collective national memory remains unresolved. Marian Marzynsk, a survivor, bluntly expresses the wishes of many survivors: "I wish there would be no celebration of the end of World War II, no finishing touches, no government-designed memorials. My unreasonable request to the German people would be to live in a permanent state of guilt, if such a thing exists."[77] Such a wish for a collective guilt has been resisted by the war generations and those that followed while the consensus for a collective responsibility solidified. But there is such a thing as a collective responsibility to remember, not one that derives from guilt but one that comes as the result of authentic political action and judgement for the sake of the world (political) rather than the self (legal/moral), as Hannah Arendt maintains. It is significant that the most moving voice of the memorialization on the day of the dedication of the Memorial to the Murdered Jews of Europe comes in the person of Van der Linden of Australia, a survivor, who has the last word: "I am the voice of the lucky few. I am a witness ... I have learned that hatred begets hatred. I have learned that we must not be silent." She goes on to say that she does "not believe in collective guilt," and that today's German young can not be blamed for the sins of their seniors but she adds, "you can hold them responsible for what they do with the memories of their ancestors' crimes."[78]

Testimony to the commitment to the collective responsibility of Germans by the Adenauer generation and subsequent political leaders, is President Kastav's visit to the new memorial and his joining with German President Horst Koehler to create a joint fund to build upon the 40 year diplomatic relations between the two countries, among other things, to assist exchange of scientists, artists, and young people. Against this evidence of normalization however, are the realities of the rise of anti-Semitism and the ever present fear of historical amnesia. While the two presidents reaffirmed the responsibility that the Holocaust must never be forgotten, the Israeli president made a point of reminding the press of a recent poll that suggested 50 percent of Germans under the age of 24 did not know the meaning of Shoah (Holocaust).[79]

Truth-telling, Testimonies, and Fiction

Truth-telling is best served by the voices of those who lived the experience. The next best recourse for bringing out the truth would be through the testimonials of witnesses. Such is the value of the documentary *Shoah* (1985) by French filmmaker Claude Lanzmann, which sets out to discover the past through the witnesses' and survivors' testimonies. Lanzmann insists his film is not a documentary and that it should not be viewed as being about the *Shoah*. The film could be viewed from several vantage points including the historical and aesthetic perspectives, but Dominick LaCapra observes that *Shoah* is probably best viewed as "neither representational nor autonomous art but as a disturbingly mixed generic performance that traces and tracks the traumatic effects of limit-experiences, particularly in the lives (or afterlives) of victims." [80] It is clear, however, that Lanzmann crafted his film in such a way that witnesses testify even when they do it in secret, to add to the authenticity of telling the truth. Indeed some of the witnesses gave testimony on condition that they were filmed secretly, off camera.[81]

The truth of what is remembered reaches a crucial stage as third generation Germans and Jews grapple to come to terms with it in their own way and as the last of the Holocaust survivors are passing on. Individual memories in Germany and Israel are related to national memories in these successive generations and those memories have traditionally been preserved by the official guardians of history in the history books, museums, national holidays and the like. In postwar East-Central Europe and to a lesser extent among third generation artists in Germany, fiction and poetry led the way as custodians of memory and truth-telling.[82] Perhaps encouraged by the postmodernist challenges to epistemology and/or the elevation of language and discourse to give voice to long-silenced peoples, such as the literature of dissent has brought to Central and Eastern Europe, fiction has come to the forefront with a vengeance, sometimes to the detriment of truth-telling.

When *Fragments: Memories of a Childhood, 1939-1948* by Benjamin Wilkomirski was first published in 1995, the graphic description of a child's experience in a concentration camp at first aroused sympathetic emotions and drew literary praises. As it turned out, three years later both the identity of the writer as well as his memoir were in question when a Swiss writer wrote an expose claiming that Wilkomirski was not who he says was and he had been to the concentration camps only as a tourist. In fact, he was born in Switzerland in 1941 as Bruno Grosjean, to be later adopted by the Doessekker family.[83]

Omer Bartov gives a redemptive interpretation of this fact-fiction hullabaloo by suggesting three explanations. First, Wilkomirski/Doessekker may have imagined himself as a child during the Holocaust, "transforming a second-generation Swiss into a Jewish victim" and identifying with the victims of genocide, thereby shattering "the limits of identity and truth." Second, he earnestly "believed himself to be that child, creating for himself a fictitious – but for him entirely real – world of memories." Finally, Wilkomirski could be that child who was provided with a false identity by Swiss officials who issued the adoption papers.[84] Whatever one wants to believe, the Wilkomirski case raises serious questions of representation in the case of the Holocaust, as articulated by Bartov:

> Can we say that the Holocaust is a case in which the rules of representation operate differently, in which what is allowed, indeed, what has been almost taken for granted in recent times, should be forbidden? And if the Holocaust *is* placed beyond the rules and conventions of representation, does this also imply that it is beyond history? Would this not lead us down the perilous path of dehistoricizing the Holocaust and thereby transforming it from a concrete past event into an increasingly malleable myth? Is this not the surest way of ultimately detaching the Holocaust from human experience and morality by making it disappear into the mists of mythology, incomprehension, and ineffability?[85]

It is reasonable to assume that problems of representation can arise in how we deal with all traumatic events. In the historic efforts of South Africa's TRC, similar crises of public memory and agency arose along with all the other shortcomings of the Commission's work, not in the least, accusations of a perpetrator-oriented amnesty process, all of which may have eluded representation. Nevertheless the narrative voices of post-apartheid literature have complemented what was not fulfilled by the victims' voices in the reconciliation process.

One such work is Antjie Krog's *Country of My Skull: Guilt, Sorrow, and the Limits of Forgiveness in the New South Africa.* Based on her Truth and Reconciliation Commission radio report, the Afrikaner poet and journalist both documents and reflects upon the stories told by victims and perpetrators at the commission's hearings. The strength of Krog's narrative lies in her allowing the people to speak for themselves while complementing it with personal reflections and reconciliatory insights. The empowering value to the victim of telling one's story is demonstrated by one such narrative:

> Nomkephu Ntsatha: "They took a wet sack and put it over my face. They suffocated me. While they were doing that, my child was crawling on the floor. They gave her a toilet bag to play with. They slapped me. They sat on my stomach. They took my baby's blanket and stifled my face."
> It is dark when the last woman finishes testifying. Some of the commissioners have already left to catch their planes. The cold of the wet night is seeping up through the cement floor. The women of Mdantsane slowly get up. They fold

their blankets, they smile, they congratulate one another … no rain, no power
failure, no men, could silence their stories today.[86]

Atonement and Remorse

Among the most moving pleas for forgiveness is one dramatized by a dying
Nazi German, in Simon Wiesenthal's *Sunflower*, who pleads with the protago-
nist survivor: "I know that what I have told you is terrible. In the long nights
while I have been waiting for death, time and time again I have longed to talk
about it to a Jew and beg forgiveness from him …" After having listened in silence to the dying SS soldier for many hours, the Jew simply walks out.[87]
Wiesenthal raises a moral question at the end of the story on behalf of the pro-
tagonist: "Was my silence at the bedside of the dying Nazi right or wrong?" And
to the reader Wiesenthal poses the following challenge: "You, who have just
read this sad and tragic episode in my life, can mentally change places with me
and ask yourself the crucial question, 'What would I have done' ?"[88] The second part of the book is made up of the invited responses from eminent individuals.

    Wiesenthal's parable poses difficult ethical questions about forgiveness. On
the other hand, apologies, whether on demand or voluntarily given, present a
different set of problems. Just as genuine forgiveness demands a degree of moral
imagination and self-knowledge; apology requires the same if it is aimed at reconciliation. While remorse is associated with individual repentance, in political
apologies the language of apology is employed by office-holders who can tap
into their private beliefs, or allude to public morality and therefore engage in
public remorse. It is somewhat difficult to read repentance in public communication, and even more untenable to separate the image-saving rhetoric of narrow
political utility from the more serious contrition that yields lasting restoring
power. Recently the Norwegian parliament authorized compensation of 20,000
kroner (3,280 dollars) to Norwegian children born out of laisons between Nazi
soldiers and Norwegian women.[89] Many of the war children were victims of
lifetime abuse, put into institution and scorned by society. In spite of its symbolic value, the weight of the compensation remained ambiguous. According to
the committee chairman, Finn Kristian Marthinsen, "compensation is a deep
apology from society to victim."[90] On another occasion the same legislator concludes: "We are saying 'we're sorry about what happened' but we can't pay
compensation to match what you suffered because we can't estimate it."

    When Helmut Schmidt, West German chancellor from 1974 to 1981 said, in
a speech at Auschwitz-Birkenau: "the crime of Nazi fascism and the guilt of the
German Reich under Hitler's leadership are at the basis of our responsibility,"
his remarks were reconciliatory and remorseful. They spoke loudly of normalizing German-Polish relations but were "strangely silent about the fact that
Auschwitz-Birkenau was above all a death camp in which the Nazis had murdered 1.5 to 2 million Jews.[91] One can observe a similar political string attached

to the apologetic acts of Schmidt's predecessor, Willy Brandt. Considering Brandt's commitment to *Ostpolitik* and diplomatic success in Eastern Europe and the Soviet Union, would we doubt the sincerity projected by one most memorable image of remorse, that of the chancellor getting on his knees to express remorse and desire for atonement at the memorial for Jews killed in the Warsaw Ghetto?

The inadequacies of the German apologies in regard to the public remorse imperative are twofold. First, the leaders engaged in both apologetic rhetoric and acts, and as in most political apologies, they were carrying out an "apology by proxy", one could say. Thus they rendered their apologies as office-holders and not as individuals. Secondly, while the expression of sorrow is a necessary ingredient for reconciliation in the interpersonal apology process, the dynamics of apology from the many to the many preclude this.[92] Tavuchis reminds us that "... sorrow is ruled out or, at best, is perfunctory in light of the formal, official, and public discursive requirements of apology from the Many to the Many."[93] The restitution to Israel and the Jews and other legislative and juridical acts that dealt with Nazi crimes would be the only ones that would pass as public remorse on record. Those would remain weighty in their reconciliatory powers. Yet the speech acts and performatives of remorse and repentance, with religious connotations sometimes, are essentially personal, used by individual leaders in the public space. Those extraordinary acts, like Willy Brandt's, have the potential to tip the moral balance and are weightier than putting remorse on public record.

A most original atonement is one continued by third generation Germans who are seeking reconciliation through unpaid service. These are young Germans volunteering to work as guides at death camp memorials and other memorial centers, at homes for the disabled and the like, in countries that suffered under the Nazis. The program that enlists such a service called Action Reconciliation has been in existence for 35 years, although now it is not exclusively related to the consequences of the war. The German founder of the organization, Reverend Lothar Kreyssig, appealed in 1958: "We ask the peoples who suffered violence at our hands to allow us to perform a good deed in their countries with our hands and resources, to erect a village, a settlement, a hospital, or whatever they request, as a sign of atonement." [94]

Public remorse and the reckoning of it on record is the ultimate test of apology and reconciliation. Public remorse has been late in coming in Germany having been subject to *realpolitik* cynicism and ideologically based debates. In the relations between Israel and Germany, gestures of sincere apology and public remorse have not been recognized so far for their worth because the rituals and symbolic gestures of reconciliation between the two have been normalized since diplomatic relations were established in 1965. Nevertheless, the images of public remorse such as Willy Brandt falling on his knees in 1970 in Poland to pay tribute to victims of the Warsaw Ghetto, or the laying of wreaths by German Chancellor Schroeder and Israeli Prime Minister Barak at the Sachsenhausen death camp in 1998, remain as important symbols of reconciliation. It is the leaders' commitment politically to not repeat the past and to prove their genuine remorse through political, legislative and juridical action that makes remorse morally public and publicly moral.

What is notable about this case also is the order in which the reconciliation process took place, with accountability coming first. The accountability of Germany to the Jewish Diaspora and Israel, at least in material terms, was addressed at the outset. We can also draw other conclusions from this archetypal case of atonement. The Holocaust and its aftermath intimately brought together perpetrators and victims thereby defining the identities of Germans and Jews, and of the New Germany and Israel. Also in this case the historic weight of events like the occupation by the Allied Powers, the Marshall Plan and reconstruction, the Cold War and the creation of Israel had an impact on the progress or setbacks of the apology process. History as well as "remembering and forgetting," or rewriting history, shaped the pragmatic and political partnership of Israel and Germany. The German and Jewish peoples not only reached an unprecedented stage of reconciliation but they were also active agents in the process.

Notes

1.   In this section of the analysis, Germany refers to West Germany or the Federal Republic of Germany and the unified Germany after 1990. Reference to the old East Germany or the Democratic Republic of Germany will so be indicated.

2.   Elazar Barkan, *The Guilt of Nations: Restitution and Negotiating Historical In justices* (New York: W. W. Norton & Co., 2000), 8. Barkan's work contributes toward a better understanding of the reconciliation process by examining the role of restitution in past injustices. For Barkan even apology becomes part of a restitution mosaic calling for the need to rectifying past injustices.

3.   "Gay activists press for German Apology," *The Independent (London),* November 1, 1997), 12.

4.   Nana Sagi, *German Reparations: A History of Negotiations* (New York: St. Martin's Press, 1966), 14.

5.   Sagi, *German Reparations,* 15

6.   Sagi, 17.

7.   Barkan, *The Guilt of Nations,* 4-5.

8.   Sagi, German Reparations, 20. Also see George Lavy, *Germany and Israel: Moral Debt and National Interest* (London: Frank Cass, 1966), 1 and Barkan, *The Guilt of Nations,* 4-5.

9.   Barkan, *The Guilt of Nations,* 5.

10.   Amnon Neustadt in *Thirty Years of Diplomatic Relations between the Federal Republic of Germany and Israel* (Tribune Books, 1995), 115.

11.   Neustadt, "The Main Pillars Towards Understanding."

12.   Asher Ben-Natan, "Bridges Over Many Chasms: Thirty Years of Giving and Taking," in *Thirty Years of Diplomatic Relations between the Federal Republic of Germany and Israel* (Frankfurt: Tribüne-Books, 1995), 33.

13. George Lavy, *Germany and Israel: Moral Debt and National Interest.* (London and Portland: Frank Cass, 1966), 12.

14. Ben-Natan, "Bridges Over Many Chasms," 34.

15. A poll by Allensback Institute in September 1952 indicated that only 11 per cent of the total population expressed themselves in favor of unrestricted reparations; 24 per cent endorsed them in principle, but found the sum too high; 44 per cent declared the reparations superfluous; and 21 per cent expressed no opinion. See Kenneth M. Lewan, "How West Germany Helped to Build Israel," *Journal of Palestinian Studies* 4 no.4 (Summer 1975), 55.

16. Ben-Natan, 34.

17. Joel H. Rosenthal in Nolan, "Forward: Biography, Ethics, and Statecraft," in *Ethics and Satecraft: The Moral Dimension of International Affairs*, ed. Cathal J. Nolan (Westport, Conn.: Praeger, 1995), xi-xvii.

18. Carl C. Hodge, Konrad Adenauer, Arms, and the Redemption of Germany," in *Ethics and Statecraft*, ed. Cathan Nolan, 155.

19. Debra Cole, "Anti-Semitism charges spark new struggle over German identity," *Agence France Presse*, May 30, 2002, and "German political party 'regrets' official remarks about Jews," *Deutsche Presse-Agentur*, May 31, 2002.

20. "German political party 'regrets' official remarks about Jews."

21. Eliahu Salpeter, "What will German Jewry look like in the next century?" *Financial Times (Israel)*, August 17, 1999.

22. "Judgement at Bitburg," *Newsweek*, April 29, 1985, 14.

23. Abba Tomforde, "Khol says Belsen is never-ending shame," *The Guardian (London)*, April 22, 1985.

24. Tomforde, "Khol says Belsen is never-ending shame."

25. "Judgement at Bitburg."

26. Nicholas Tavuchis, *Mea Culpa: A Sociology of Apology and Reconciliation* (Stanford, Cal.: Stanford University Press, 1991), 17

27. Tavuchis, *Mea Culpa*, 19

28. Eric Lüth, *Wir Bitten Israel Um Frieden!* Hamburg 1951, 7. The declaration continues: " We must with inner conviction connect the appeal for peace that we direct toward Israel, with the sorrow for six million innocent victims and with appreciation for the immeasurable good the Jews, in the service of humanity including in Germany, have performed. We must not forget these thanks, for thereby we also remit some of the guilt that exists toward the dead." Translation by Valdis Lumans.

29. Rolf Vogel, *The German Path to Israel: A Documentation.* (Chester Springs, Penn. Dufour Editions, 1969), 33.

30. Jeffrey Herf, *Divided Memory: The Nazi Past in the Two Germanys* (Cambridge, Mass.: Harvard University Press), 282.

31. Herf, *Divided Memory*, 282-283

32. Ludwig Erhard, Address to the Council on Foreign Relations in New York, June 11, 1964. In *Common Values, Common Cause: German Statesmen in the United States American Statesmen in Germany 1953-1983 Statements and Speeches* (New York: German Information Center, 1983), 62.

33. Lily, Gardner Feldman, *The Special Relationship between West Germany and Israel.* (Boston: George Allen & Unwin, 1984), 169.

34. Björn Krondorfer, *Remembrance and Reconciliation: Encounters between Young Jews and Germans* (New Haven and London: Yale University Press, 1995), 24.

35. Krondorfer, *Remembrance and Reconciliation*, 24. Also see Michael Wolffsohn, *Eternal Guilt? Forty Years of German-Jewish-Israeli Relations* (New York: Colombia University Press, 1993), 211.

36. See Christian Pross, *Paying for the Past: The Struggle over Reparations for Surviving Victims of the Nazi Terror* (Baltimore, Md.: The John Hopkins University Press, 1998), 195.

37. Michael Getler, "Holocaust: A Shock to West Germans," *Washington Post* (January 24, 1979).

38. Donald Shriver, *An Ethic for Enemies: Forgiveness in Politics* (Oxford, N.Y.: Oxford University Press), 81-82.

39. See Miriam J. Aukerman "Extraordinary Evil, Ordinary Crime: A Framework for Understanding Transitional Justice," *Harvard Human Rights Journal* 15 (Spring 2002), 47-48; and Martha Minow, *Between Vengeance and Forgiveness: Facing History after Genocide and Mass Violence* (Boston: Beacon Press, 1998), 8.

40. See Michael R. Marrus, "The Nuremburg Trial: Fifty Years After," *American Scholar* 66, no. 4 (Fall 1997), 569-570.

41. Christian Pross, 3.

42. William Drozdiak, "Retribution for Nazi suffering: Germany creates special fund to compensate forced labourer and slaves," *The Montreal Gazette,* section B, July 18, 2000.

43. See *Censoring History: Citizenship and Memory in Japan, Germany, and the United States,* ed. Laura Hein and Mark Selden (Armonk, N.Y.: M.E. Sharpe, 2000). Hein and Seldon argue that "At first West Germans under Konrad Adenauer, chancellor from 1949 to 1963, avoided reflection on the past by arguing that their still fragile democracy could not withstand honest remembrance of the Nazi era. (Adenauer combined that policy with the partially contradictory one of supporting financial restitution to the state of Israel)," 30.

44. Barkan, *The Guilt of Nations*, 15

45. See Daniel Levy, "The Future of the Past: Historiographical Disputes and Competing Memories in Germany and Israel," *History and Theory*, 38, no. 1 (Fall 1999), 52.

46. Daniel Jonah Goldhagen, *Hitler's Willing Executioners: Ordinary Germans and the Holocaust* (New York: Alfred A. Knopf, 1996), 463.

47. Levy, "The Future of the Past," 56.

48. Anna Tomforde, "Right Wingers Oppose Holocaust Bill," *The Guardian (London),* March 14, 1985.

49. See Gregory Wegner, "The Power of Selective Tradition: Buchenwald Concentration Camp and Holocaust Education for Youth in the New Germany," in *Censoring History,* 229.

50. Daniel Levy, "The Future of the Past," 56.

51. James W. Booth, "Communities of Memory: On Identity, Memory, and Debt," *American Political Science Review*, 93, no. 2 (June 1999), 252-255.

52. Booth, "Communities of Memory: On Identity, Memory, and Debt," 255. See also Wegner in *Censoring History,* 226.

53. Debra Cole, "Anti-Semitism charges spark new struggle over German identity," *Agence France Presse*, May 30, 2002.

54. For a discussion of Martin Walser's controversial speech see Alexander Mathäs, "The Presence of the Past: Martin Walser on Memoirs and Memorials," *German Studies Review* 25/1 (2002), 1-22.

55. Mathäs, "The Presence of the Past," 3.

56. Mathäs, 10.

57. James E. Young, *At Memory's Edge: After-Images of the Holocaust in Contemporary Art and Architecture* (New Haven, Conn.: Yale University Press, 2000), 191-199.

58. Young, *At Memory's Edge*, 197.

59. Wegner, 229.

60. Girma Negash, *"Apologia Politica*: An Examination of the Politics and Ethics of Public Remorse in International Affairs," *International Journal of Politics and Ethics* 2, no. 2 (2002), 125-127.

61. In "The Power of Selective Tradition: Buchenwald Concentration Camp and Holocaust Education for Youth in the New Germany," in *Censoring History*, Gregory Wegner reports his experience of five days as a participant-observer with a group of German teenagers and their teachers at the Buchenwald concentration camp, 226-257.

62. See Lauren Hein and Mark Selden, "The Lessons of War, Global Power, and Social Change," in *Censoring History*, 31

63. Carollee Thea, "The Void: Daniel Libeskind's Jewish Museum as a Counter Movement," *Sculpture* 19, no. 9 (November 2000), 38.

64. Roger Boyes, "Germany Finally Admits the Holocaust to Its Dark Heart," *The Times (London)*, May, 11, 2005.

65. Richard Bernstein, "In Berlin, A Nation Bares Its Shame," *The New York Times*," May 11, 2005.

66. Bernstein.

67. Tony Paterson, "Germany Unveils Monument to Its National Shame," *The Independent (UK)*, May 11, 2005.

68. There were also other controversies surrounding the conception and construction of the memorial. For example, it was discovered that the stones of the concrete slabs were sprayed with counter-graffiti chemicals produced by Degussa, a German company that succeeded a group that produced the poison gas for Auschwitz death camp.

69. Eetta Prince-Gibson, "Europe's Jews Remembered at Berlin memorial," *The Jerusalem Post*, May 11, 2005.

70. Richard Bernstein, "Berlin Holocaust Memorial Opens," *New York Times*, May 12, 2005.

71. Christopher Knight, "A Gray Grid Forms an Intangible Holocaust Memorial in Berlin," *Los Angeles Times*, June 25, 2005.

72. Jeffrey Fleishman, "Permanent Memory of Holocaust Opens in Berlin," *Los Angeles Times*, May 11, 2005.

73. Roger Boyes, "Germany Finally Admits the Holocaust to Its Dark Heart."

74. Tony Paterson, Germany Unveils Monument to Its National Shame."

75. Roger Boyes.

76. Tony Paterson.

77. Marian Marzynski, "Good Guilt in Germany," *Washington Post*, May 28, 2005.

78. Jeffrey Fleishman, "Permanent Memory of Holocaust Opens in Berlin."

79. "Israel and Germany Create Fund to Improve Relations," *Deutsche Presse-Agentur*, May 30, 2005.

80. Dominick LaCapra, "Lanzmann's 'Shoah': here there is no why," *Critical Inquiry*, 23, o. 2 (Winter 1997), 232.

81. Shoshana Felman, "In an Era of Testimony: Claude Lanzmann's Shoah," *Yale French Studies* 0, issue 97, 50 Years of Yale French Studies: A Commemorative Anthology. Part 2: 1980-1998 (2000), 108. It is the impression of Professor Tom Butler that the

effectiveness Lanzmann's picture comes from the fact that "memory was always conveyed at ground level. His shots seemed to be made consciously from the ground of memory. "Personal communication, November 2004.

82. Richard S. Esbenshade, "Remembering to Forget: Memory, History, National Identity in Postwar East-Central Europe," *Representations* 0, Issue 49, Special Issue: Identifying Histories: Eastern Europe Before and After 1989 (Winter, 1995), 74.

83. Omer Bartov, *Mirrors of Destruction: War, Genocide, and Modern Identity* (Oxford, N.Y.: Oxford University Press, 2000), 224-225.

84. Bartov, *Mirrors of Destruction*, 225.

85. Bartov, 227-228.

86. Antjie Krog, *Country of My Skull: Guilt, Sorrow, and the Limits of Forgiveness in the New South Africa* (New York: Random House, 1998), 249-250.

87. Simon Wiesenthal, *The Sunflower* (New York: Schocken Books, 1976), 57-58.

88. Wiesenthal, *The Sunflower*, 98-99.

89. As a matter of policy, Hitler encouraged soldiers to have children by Norwegian women to breed his dream race of a superior Aryan nation.

90. "Norwegian Parliament Backs Compensation for Wartime Victims," *Deutsche Presse-Agentur*, March 18, 2005.

91. Jeffrey Herf, *Divided Memory*, 346.

92. Tavuchis, *Mea Culpa*, 100-104.

93. Tavuchis, *Mea Culpa*, 104.

94. Action Reconciliation / Service for Peace (*ARSP*) was founded in Berlin at the1958 synod of the Protestant Church by individuals who had belonged to a small resistance group during the Nazi regime called the "Confessing Church". During a discussion of Protestant leaders about their position on chaplains within the German army and the question of nuclear armament on German soil, Reverend Lothar Kreyssig presented a "Call for Peace" and urged the delegates to support his plan. A majority of the delegates supported Kreyssig's plan and Action Reconciliation was born. Thirteen years after his original vision in 1945, it finally became a reality. Web site: http://www.asf-ev.de/usa/.

Chapter 3

A Political Calculus of Apology: Japan and Its Neighbors

Many have asked me whether I am still angry with the Japanese. Maybe it helped that I have faith. I had learned to accept suffering. I also learned to forgive. If Jesus Christ could forgive those who crucified Him, I thought I could also find it in my heart to forgive those who had abused me. Half a century had passed. Maybe my anger and resentment were no longer as fresh. Telling my story has made it easier for me to be reconciled with the past. But I am still hoping to see justice done before I die.

Maria Rosa Henson, *Comfort Woman*[1]

These are the concluding thoughts in a memoir by one of the comfort women who were forcibly taken as sex slaves by the Japanese army in World War II. Her words reveal a remarkable capacity of human forgiveness as well as a yearning for justice. Most of the so-called comfort women like her have now reached the mature ages of 70s and 80s. Such a dying wish for justice makes their claims all the more morally potent and transhistorical.

As the last demanding voices for justice or calls for apology and reparation are fading, a new generation of activists has taken up the banner in Korea, China, the Philippines, Taiwan, Singapore, and in Japan itself, with the emergence of a universal norm of human rights. On the other side of the equation is the Japanese political elite, barely removed from the first generation of Japanese leaders who survived the Tokyo Trials, and those who received the blessing of the American occupation powers to build a stable and peaceful Japan. The following pages will focus on the reluctance and political calculus of the Japanese political elite in response to the rising calls by its neighbors and the international community for an apology and compensation for Japan's war crimes.

Reluctance to Acknowledgement

The wounds of the last world war have provoked continuous minor crises since the 1960s. As recently as 2001 there was the shocking story about Korean protestors who ritually chopped off the tips of their little fingers in protest against Japanese Prime Minister Koizumi's visit to the shrine honoring the dead together with his refusal to order revisions of middle-school history textbooks that gloss over Japan's incriminating history of war and colonialism.[2] Two years later the Chinese government delayed high-level diplomatic visits of Japanese officials until a "good atmosphere" had been created by Japan. The "bad atmosphere" had been instigated by the visits of Prime Minister Junichitro Koizumi in October 2003 to the Yasukuni Shrine - the memorial for Japan's war dead. This is the controversial shrine where 2.5 million Japanese dead, including fourteen Class A war criminals, are worshipped and commemorated.[3] Visits by Japanese Prime Ministers since the 1970s have brought protest against the violation of religion and state as well as protests from Asian countries that see the shrine as a symbol of Japanese militarism and ultra-nationalism. The festering anger by surviving victims and their advocates only intensified with the continued reluctance of the Japanese authorities to acknowledge alleged wartime crimes perpetrated by the Japanese military. More recently visits to the shrine by Japanese officials have been followed by a routine press release from the Japanese government expressing profound remorse and sincere mourning for all victims of the war.

The slow-in-coming acknowledgement of guilt on the part of the Japanese can be attributed to several factors, beginning with the nature of the Japanese defeat. The aftermath and trauma resulting from the Hiroshima and Nagasaki nuclear bombings, the first and last use of such weapons that killed 100,000 civilians in each city, understandably created a culture of victimization. Those horrors along with the Tokyo War Crimes Tribunal supervised by the Americans, which brought swift justice to leading Japanese war criminals, and the associated disarming treaties, have laid to rest Japan's imperial past - at least as far as the Japanese political elite were concerned. Hence, in response to some of the first demands for apology and redress, the Japanese government's pet answer was that Japan had settled its obligations through several of the treaties it had signed since the end of the war. One such treaty was the Treaty of Basic Relations Japan and South Korea signed in 1965. Under that treaty, Japan promised to provide South Korea with a grant of 300 million dollars to be distributed over a 10-year period and also a long-term and low interest 200 million dollar loan extended by the Overseas Economic Co-operation Fund of Japan.[4] For over twenty years until the 1965 agreement, the normalization talks between Japan and South Korea had provoked strong emotions in both countries. The credit, grant and loans received under that treaty were "for claims made for debt owed, unpaid wages, savings held in Japan, and other specific damages."[5]

Thus it was easy for Japanese leaders to hide behind such treaties and declare that they had no obligations toward their Japanese neighbors, and thereby exonerate themselves from any responsibility. Also, because of their sense that they had paid the price, strongly reinforced by the trauma of Hiroshima and Nagasaki, the Japanese elite, unlike their German counterpart, were unburdened by a sense of guilt for Japan's war crimes. Furthermore, the events and the memories thereof were far removed from the daily lives of the Japanese since most of the horrendous war crimes took place far away from home. For the Japanese leaders as well as the Americans who had forced their surrender, stability had priority over any dispensation of apology and compensation at the end of the war and the beginnings of the Cold War.

A secondary factor that contributed to Japanese reluctance to acknowledge wartime wrongs was the carryover of virulent Japanese nationalists as represented by unrepentant social conservatives and the revisionist right. The fact that General Douglas MacArthur chose to spare Emperor Hirohito from being brought to trial, and the emperor's refusal to acknowledge Japanese wrongdoing, have contributed to a continuation of the prewar mentality.[6] Even wartime leaders resumed leadership in post war Japan; as Shuko Ogawa points out:

> Significantly, of the seven Class A war criminals (those tried for the crime against peace of waging an aggressive war) sentenced to death at the Tokyo War Crimes Tribunal, only one, wartime Foreign Minister Koki Hirota, was a civilian. Thus, the mindset of civil servants and emerging political figures was changed little as they set about the task of reconstructing the country. Mamoru Shigemitsu, another wartime foreign minister who was sentenced to prison at the Tokyo War Crimes Tribunal, later even re-emerged to serve as foreign minister in 1954.[7]

Conservative members of the Japanese political elite, mostly present in the Liberal Democratic Party (LPD), the party that had dominated Japanese postwar governments, had for the most part downplayed and denied Japanese complicity in such war crimes as the Nanjing Massacre and the exploitation of "comfort" women. Japanese right-wing revisionists and conservatives inside and outside of the LDP argued that Japan had already apologized and paid for the war damages. Further, social conservatives were unwilling to admit to any wrongdoing because they believed "children should be allowed to have pride in their country, and thus not be overexposed to Japanese wartime atrocities."[8]

The politics of denial and the status quo was established from the very beginning with the silence of returning soldiers and wartime censorship. That status quo was enabled by a silent generation ready to forget the war and a younger generation protected from the harsh truths of the war atrocities. Finally, Japanese reluctance to come to terms with the war and apologize to their neighbors can be tied to an identity crisis of the new Japanese generation caught between the influences of neonationalist revisionism and the pressures of globalization. The young also happened to be the innocent consumers of commodified images of Japan and thus could not be in tune with the long-seated grievances of neighboring countries.[9]

When the Japanese authorities were finally coming around to acknowledge some of the crimes perpetrated by the Japanese military, their admissions came out only in fits and starts. In 1992, after fifty years of denial, the Japanese government finally admitted its involvement in the comfort women system. The system involved an organized racket by the Japanese army that forced approximately 200,000 women from China, Korea, the Philippines and other Asian countries into sexual slavery to serve the Japanese Imperial Army between 1931 and 1945. Euphemistically called "comfort women," or *Jugun Ianfu*, these women were forced to have sex on the average of thirty to forty men a day. They were raped, tortured, mutilated and sometimes killed in the process. The Japanese authorities acknowledged Japanese government involvement only after incriminating documents were uncovered and made public.

According to new findings, the Japanese government, not private businesses, ran and regulated these comfort stations.[10] A statement by the Chief Cabinet Secretary in 1993 announced the findings of a government study in which it hedges on its admissions to Japanese culpability: "The then Japanese military was involved directly in the establishment and management of the comfort stations" and also the transfer of comfort women. The recruitment of the comfort women was conducted mainly by private recruiters who acted in response to the request of the military.[11]

After years of hedging on the part of Japanese authorities, the momentous acknowledgement of the country's guilt in World War II came from Prime Minister Tomiichi Murayama, on the morning of the 50th anniversary of Japan's surrender. He told journalists that Japan had followed a "mistaken national policy" of "colonialism and aggression" that had caused "tremendous damage and suffering to the people of many countries." His admission to Japanese guilt of "aggression," which had never been admitted by any Prime Minister before, brought praise from the West. His choice of the term "apology" or *owabi* instead of the habitual "regret" was also significant.[12] On its worth as an expression of public remorse, I will return to later. Muruyami's apology paved the way for Japanese leaders to soften the diplomatic discourse in the steps to be taken for normalization and cooperation between Japan, the two Koreas and China.

When President Kim Dae Jung of South Korea visited Japan in 1998, a joint declaration read: "Prime Minister Obuchi regarded in a spirit of humility the fact of history that Japan caused, during a certain period in the past, tremendous damage and suffering to the people of the Republic of Korea through its colonial rule, and expressed his deep remorse and heartfelt apology for this fact. President Kim accepted with sincerity this statement of Prime Minster Obuchi's recognition of history and expressed his appreciation for it."[13]

The acutely sensitive issue of the demands of the "comfort women" was not brought up on such occasions. In fact, every postwar Japanese government "has resisted pressure to issue a formal apology, always limiting Japanese responsibility for what happened to comfort women by oblique references to 'pain' caused during the 'troubled' period of World War II."[14] Yet, in an indirect acknowledgement of the crime, the Japanese government helped found the Asian Women's Fund in 1995, a semi-autonomous organization funded privately, to provide atonement money. The government committed to assist AWF in operational costs as well as fund-raising and claimed to have begun disbursing the funds. With each atonement payment, a letter of apology was attached from the Prime Minister who extended his "most sincere apologies and remorse to all the women who underwent immeasurable and painful experiences and suffered incurable physical and psychological wounds as comfort women."[15] Seeking direct and official apology from the government, only a few "comfort women" have come forward to accept the token of sympathy. In the mean time, in the Japanese parliament, the Diet, a bill "to promote the settlement of the issue of the victims forced into becoming wartime sex slaves" was introduced in 2001 and reintroduced several times but failed to win support.[16]

Amnesia and Truth-telling

Even though the government's rhetoric has become more transparent and factual in its acknowledgement of Japan's wartime wrongs, the resistance to coming clean with the truths about the consequences of Japanese occupation and war has continued. As recently as the 1980s, Japanese authorities were resistant to popular demands for dealing with the past in neighboring Asian countries and reacted slowly and only when the governments of those countries were willing to bring up the issues defying delicate bilateral relations. For example, in 1982, Chief Cabinet Secretary Kiichi Miyazawa made a statement on the issue of revisionist history textbooks indicating that Japan would attend to the problem in the spirit and respect of the 1965 joint communiqués with ROK and China. In that spirit Miyazawa declared: "Recently, the Republic of Korea, China, and others have been criticizing some descriptions in Japanese textbooks. From the perspective of building friendship and goodwill with neighboring countries, Japan will pay due attention to these criticisms and make corrections at the Government's responsibility."[17]

Another side of Japan's reluctance to telling the truth was the pressures of a countervailing democratic movement represented by Japanese groups and citizens, with their counterparts in Korea, China and elsewhere, who were all determined to reveal the horrific facts of the war. The impact of these grassroots pressures was evident in the government's response to challenges arising from new exposures on the extent of wartime atrocities regarding the "comfort women." No sooner had the Korean government demanded that attention be paid to this issue, the Japanese government had embarked on its own investigation, including hearings by former military personnel and Japanese and U.S. archives, and had begun reporting its findings in 1992.[18]

The government's move came in response to the activism of South Korea Professor Yun Chung Ok, the South Korean Church Women's Alliance, the Seoul District Female Students' Representative Council, and other regional groups. It is Professor Yoshimi Yoshiaki's discovery of incriminating documents in the Library of the National Institute for Defense Studies and the publication and public exposure of those documents that forced the Japanese and other accommodating Asian governments to advance the cause of the aggrieved "Comfort women."[19]

One of the developments towards more transparency on the part of the Japanese government was support of historical research and documentation. In preparation for the fiftieth anniversary of the end of World War II, Prime Minister Tomiichi Murayama announced the establishment of an Asian Historical Document Center "to enable everyone to face squarely the facts of history."[20]

A culture war of sorts may also have contributed to this dialectic of truth-telling. Yamatani Tetsuo's 1979 film, *An Old Lady in Okinawa: Testimony of a Military Comfort Woman*, that was based on the first publicly identified "comfort women" may have encouraged activists to heighten the world's awareness of the plight of "comfort women." On the revisionist side, a 1998 Japanese film, *Pride: The Fateful Moment*, a sympathetic film about General Hideki Tojo, a war criminal executed following the Tokyo War Tribunal, became a box-office hit that year despite the protest of Japan's neighbors. Shortly after, a comic book with a similar revisionist vein had a runaway sale. The book depicted the Japanese army as the liberator of Asia from Western colonialism, which suggested that the Rape of Nanjing was exaggerated, Tojo was unfairly treated, and that Taiwanese women willingly became sex slaves for the occupying Japanese army.[21]

A resurgence of nationalism manifested in right-wing revisionism of Japan's history has become increasingly vocal since the 1990s. Such organizations as the "Committee for the Examination of History" and the "Group for the Creation of New History," are influential in the right-wing factions of the leading parties, especially in the LDP. These groups shared the views that alien influences via the American conquest/occupation distorted the Soul of Japan, and therefore Japan had to re-evaluate its history, and they argued that Japanese militarism and colonialism was in fact beneficial to Asia. They also entertained the ideas of constitutional changes and reclaiming the history curricula in schools to instill Japanese pride in the young.[22] Ever sensitive to the awakening of Japanese nationalism, the failure by the Japanese government to silence the neonationalist voices in Japan has brought loud protests from the governments and peoples in the Koreas, China, Taiwan and elsewhere. During the 2001 ceremony marking the anniversary of the unsuccessful Korean uprising of 1919 against the Japanese colonial rulers, South Korean President Kim Dae-jung called on Tokyo "to maintain a correct perception of history." It is the activists in Korea who shouted the loudest against "the refusal of Japanese authorities to ban a controversial junior high school history textbook that glosses over the abuses perpetrated by the colonial regime during its 35-year occupation of the Korean peninsula." Critics have charged that the failure to effectively screen the school textbooks is related to the possible intimidation of Japanese authorities by the extreme right-wing activism.[23] Government's official position on the history textbooks in response to criticisms is predictable and proforma. In an official statement, the government declared: "During the process of the recent authorization of textbooks, various concerns have been expressed from neighboring countries. However, the authorization was carried out impartially based on the Regulations of Textbook Authorization, including the Course of Study and the 'Provision Concerning Neighboring Countries'."[24] The Asian neighbors were outraged that the Japanese government gave approval to a middle-school textbook written by scholars who defended Japan's record in the last world war. The South Korean government first lodged a complaint and then recalled its ambassador from Tokyo. The high-profile dispute over the textbooks was considered a setback to South Korean-Japan relations by officials in both countries after the Japanese government had apologized in 1998 "for inflicting 'great suffering' on Koreans under colonialism."[25]

The battle over history textbooks for middle-schools underscored Japan's struggle to redefine its identity. It also reflected the gulf between the nationalists who want to preserve the right to interpret Japan's history and those who wanted Japan to come to terms with its past and by so doing become a "normal" member of the international community. Revisionist historians like Professor Nobukatsu Fujioka, a key member of the Japanese Society for History Textbook Reform, argued that "the goal of history education as laid down by Japan's Education Ministry is to deepen the love of children towards Japanese history. Comfort women would not help to foster love towards one nation." Thus, in the textbook the Society produced, the issue of wartime sex slaves was totally omitted and, as a result of pressure from the government, four of the other seven textbooks approved by the education ministry also have dropped references to comfort women. The book made no apologies for the annexation of Korea. Moreover the term "war of aggression" was omitted. It would seem that in avoiding asking for a full re-write the government had given it a tacit blessing.[26]

The retreat of government officials, in spite of the more apologetic earlier pronouncements, was what intensified the protest from countries like South Korea. The government of President Kim Dae Jung in Seoul issued a statement describing the textbooks as "rationalizing and beautifying Japan's past wrongdoings based upon a self-centred interpretation of history."[27] In 2001 Foreign Affairs Makiko Tanaka commented: "The tense atmosphere and concern in the ROK over this issue has been conveyed repeatedly to Japan in various forms, and as the person in charge of foreign affairs I take this matter seriously."[28] In the meantime, an ethnic Korean living in Japan initiated the publication of a book on the sexual slavery to enlighten readers and Japanese teachers. It was a translated version of a 2000 publication of the Korean Institute of the Women Drafted for Military Sexual Slavery by Japan.[29] Individuals and groups in Japan, with support from activists in the region and the world at large, have gradually made gains in pressuring the powers that be to be more transparent and truthful about Japan's wars and their consequences.

Extracted Accountability

One way of assessing the extent of accountability accepted by successive Japanese governments is by the measure of the distance traveled between the reckoning of wrongs and the eventual redress and compensation for those wrongs. One would think acknowledgement should precede accountability as the perpetrator state needs to admit wrongdoing before acting on what it would be responsible for. As it turns out, in such war crimes the perpetrator can hurriedly make a settlement ahead of acknowledging fully the crimes committed and before the specificities thereof are exposed. Postwar Germany more or less defied any artificial sequencing of the order of the apology mandates of acknowledgement, accountability, truth-telling and public remorse. Chancellor Adenauer initiated and pummeled through the German political process, the landmark reparation legislations of the 1950s that set the stage for restitution to Jews and Israelis for decades. Reparations came in short order before the truths of the Holocaust were unveiled layer by layer and definitely before the national debates that allocated responsibilities or guilt, and it was even longer before remorse entered the national public discourse. Japan by comparison did not earnestly take up the thorny issues of dealing with its wartime past until almost forty years after the Germans did.

If we consider Japan's postwar beginnings, which unlike Germany were not impacted by deliberate policies of denazification and democratization by Western Allies, it is easy to appreciate the political consensus that emerged and its reinforcement of the already existing political culture and thereby the reluctance to be accountable for wrongdoing. There is no evidence of guilt among the survivors of the Tokyo War Crimes Tribunal. Moreover guilt as in the Judeo-Christian tradition is less known in Japan than the idea of shame and letting down one's group. Also authoritarianism rooted in its feudal roots, respect to elders and authority grounded in Confucianism, and the notion of *wa* or cultivating harmony with others can explain the moral minority in Japan who raised soul-searching questions about Japan's past. In Germany, the open debates on reparations and public remorse were facilitated by a diversity of opinions, not to mention the debates between the two ideological blocks on the right and the left. Whereas the demand for justice and reconciliation, in Japan, originates mostly outside the political circles.

Legal recourse for reparations and apology has been initiated by individuals and groups and increasingly encouraged by Asian countries and the international community. Chinese Liu Lianren filed a lawsuit against Japan demanding 20 million yen in compensation and an official apology from the state for being abducted from his home and forced to work in a Japanese coal mine. At the end of the war Liu Lianren ran away and hid in the mountains for 13 years unaware that the war had ended. In ordering the state to pay damages, Judge Seiichiro Nishioka said that the state "should be held responsible for Liu's suffering as a fugitive after the war. He said the state had failed in its duty to protect the rights of Liu, who was brought to Japan at the Japanese government's behest."[30] In the end it was a bittersweet victory, considering that Judge Nishioka rejected the claim by the plaintiff's lawyers for compensation for wartime forced work. In dismissing the claim, he said that the Meiji Constitution absolved the state of liability for damages and international laws do not support individuals for seeking reparation for suffering during wartime. It was that same court, in 1998 that recognized the state's exploitation of "comfort women" and ordered payment of 900,000 yen in compensation to nine former Korean sex slaves – a ruling that was overturned later. Included among those seeking legal redress from the Japanese state are Japanese nationals - the so-called war orphans who had been separated from their parents and had lived in Chinese foster homes for decades. The government was accused of failing to bring them to Japan and to assist them even after they were finally settled in Japan. This is just one of several far-from-settled cases demanding apology and compensation.[31]

To employ Karl Jasper's ethical mode of responsibility in which he makes a distinction between criminal, political, moral and metaphysical guilt requiring different forms of accountability, Japanese leaders had difficulty in assuming political guilt let alone in considering moral culpability. One creative approach Japanese authorities have resorted to is to set up outlets such as the Asian Women's Fund to deal with reparation demands while at the same time allowing the state to skirt around direct state responsibilities. As the press release from Chief Cabinet Secretary Hidenao Nakagawa states, "the government of Japan is painfully aware of its moral responsibility regarding the issue of the 'wartime comfort women' and has been dealing sincerely with this issue through the fund."[32] The government touts the fact it is meeting its moral responsibility to the "comfort woman" through atonement projects in the Netherlands, the Philippines, Korea, Indonesia and Taiwan since the establishment of the Asian Women's Fund in 1995.[33]

As we have seen, among the factors that inhibited Japanese political leaders from making either major concessions or aggressive initiatives to make comprehensive settlements with classes of war victims, is the convenient belief that treaties reached between Japan and the allies and between Japan and Korea have settled all claims of compensation. Although North Korea, China, the Philippines and Taiwan are not party to any treaty with Japan, Japanese authorities have broadly cited previous treaties to deny compensation to claimants. The two major treaties Japanese courts have taken shelter under are the Allied Treaty and the Korean Treaty. The Allied Treaty's disclaimer reads:

> Except as otherwise provided in the present Treaty, the Allied Powers waive all reparations claims of the Allied Powers, other claims of the Allied Powers and their nationals arising out of any actions taken by Japan and it nationals in the course of the prosecution of the war, and claims of the Allied Powers for direct military costs of occupation.[34]

In the same way the Korean Treaty states:

> The High Contracting Parties confirm that the problems concerning property,
> rights and interests of the two High Contracting Parties and their peoples (in-
> cluding juridical persons) and the claims between the High Contracting Parties
> and between their peoples, including those stipulated in Article IV (a) of the
> Peace Treaty with Japan signed at the city of San Francisco on September 8,
> 1951, have been settled completely and finally.[35]

Japanese authorities have been using such provisions to show claims have
been settled. According to Parker and Chew, "neither treaty addresses private
claims but only claims in which states are the parties. According to these treaties, the parties have agreed not to take up additional state claims against the
other parties."[36] In response to condemnation of Japan in regard to the status of
the comfort women, the Japanese delegate takes issue with the concluding observations of the Committee on Economic Social and Cultural Rights of the UN
Economic and Social Council, by stating, "With regard to the issues of reparation, property and claims relating to the last war including the issue known as
'wartime comfort women,' the Government of Japan has sincerely fulfilled its
obligations in accordance with the San Francisco Peace Treaty and other relevant treaties and agreements."[37] And from there the delegate simply asserts Japan's commitment to fully support the Asian Women's Fund and thereby expresses "its sincere sentiment."[38]

Non-governmental organizations and advocates of victims have resorted to
putting pressure on their governments to be more representative of their demands to remedy past injustice. For example, the Korean Council for the
Women Drafted for Military Sexual Slavery by Japan demanded in August 2003
that the government "officially declare that comfort women were not included
among the benefactors of the 1965 Korean-Japan Agreement which concluded
the compensation issue for Japan's longtime occupation of the Korean peninsula."[39] The pursuit of "ultimate ends" by groups in civil society like the Korean
women stands in clear contrast to the standard practice by Japanese politicians to
weigh on the side of an "ethic of responsibility," as Max Weber posited it in his
"Politics as a Vocation." [40] Two hundred Koreans who were once forced laborers and comfort women felt so strongly about their government's indifference to
their legal claims against Japan to such an extent that they expressed their intention of giving up their Korean citizenship.[41]

The legal claims of some lawsuits made so far are complex and some have
tenuous standing in international law. The guarded jealousy of state sovereignty
weighed against the ambiguities and the weaknesses of international law make
the struggle of groups and individuals seeking justice exceedingly difficult even
as international public opinion is changing. Japanese courts seem to be under
more pressure to work with existing international law and are seeking the legis-
lation of new municipal laws to aid them in dispensing justice as the claims are
multiplying. As Laura Hein explains:

> Clearly, some of the most recent rulings demonstrate, however, that judges feel
> real discomfort about just dismissing the claims, given how much the plaintiffs

had suffered at the hands of wartime officials. The growing confusion and angst revealed in these judgments suggest a shift in attitudes among jurists, although this change of heart has not yet been reflected in most of the rulings.[42]

When ten Chinese filed lawsuits in 1999 seeking redress from the Japanese government for war crimes committed by Unit 731, a biological warfare unit, the Tokyo District Court dismissed their demand for a formal apology and 1000 million yen from the state. At the same time, the court acknowledged the claim by the wartime victims and their families and "urged the government to apologize to the people of China to establish peace and friendly relations with its neighbor."[43] In other words, the court's argument is that apology should be given to the nation at large but not the victims themselves. Judge Ko Ito's conclusion was that "the payment of redress for wartime suffering is a political issue and should be negotiated on the diplomatic level between the states involved and dealt with by a peace treaty."[44]

Considering the various defenses of the legally embattled Japanese state, groups and individual claimants have devised varying legal strategies or have tried in some cases to create a common front. South Korean, Japanese and Dutch civic groups sought compensation in 1999 for their sufferings under hard labor in Siberia and the Dutch East Indies. The three groups reached an agreement to cooperate in demanding compensation at first, but they soon developed separate legal strategies. The Japanese groups wanted a joint appeal to the U.N. Human Rights panel, while the Dutch group sought for Japan to recognize individuals' right to seek compensation.[45]

As a final resort, war victims have turned to bringing their lawsuits against Japan to the United States on the assumption that their cause will receive wider global attention and that the United States provides a better climate for such cases. In 2000, fifteen former sex slaves from South Korea, China, Taiwan and the Philippines filed a class-action lawsuit against the Japanese government in a federal district court in Washington D.C. A month earlier, Chinese nationals sued Japanese companies in California for wartime forced labor. The plaintiffs are allowed to file lawsuits in the United States under the Alien Tort Claims Act under the 18th century American law that permits foreign citizens to sue other foreign citizens and entities for international law violations. A year later, 30 surviving former sex slaves filed another lawsuit against Japan in a U.S. court. In both cases, the U.S. government sided with Japan, arguing that the courts do not have jurisdiction and that Japan had already addressed issues of compensation in postwar treaties. [46]

As the international human rights campaign has been moving in the direction of intolerance to crimes against humanity, the Japanese government has been under pressure to cope with these challenges for redress. Demands for reparations and apologies for past injustices have become, in John Torpey's words, "a major preoccupation of the one-time victims (or their descendents), of their societies more broadly, and of scholars studying social change as well."[47] Former sex slaves and their advocates have advanced their cause by any means including the arts. Testimonial narratives, exhibitions of art works by victims and symposia are among these.[48] Even a bill was introduced in the U.S. Congress expressing "the sense of Congress that the Government of Japan should formally issue a clear and unambiguous apology for the sexual enslavement of young women during colonial occupation of Asia and World War II, known to the world as "comfort women", and for other purposes."[49] The Japanese government has systematically countered and responded defensively to every allegation at all international forums.

Remorse in Private and Public Space

An expression of remorse for injury is at the core of an apology for reconciliation. While such an expression can easily be communicated between individuals, how can an expression of collective sorrow on behalf of a people or its state be attainable? Japanese authorities have employed legally adept language in many responses to lawsuits, charges of neglect and amnesia for its war crimes. However, since the mid-1990s, expressions of sorrow and regret have progressively become more explicit in their apologetic discourse.

A month before the 50th anniversary of the war's end, on a state visit to China, Prime Minister Tomiichi Murayama set the tone for what was yet to come, the most credible apology to war victims. During that official visit he made a claim that Japan had in fact been remorseful all along. In his own words: "Japan has been thus working to forge bonds of mutual understanding and confidence with other Asian peoples, based on the profound remorse for its acts of aggression and colonial rule of the past."[50] An editorial opinion in the *Asahi Shimbun* had a different take on the character of public remorse undertaken by the Japanese: "The Japanese perception of the war in the post war period has been anything but commendable. While supporting the pacifism enunciated by the Constitution, the Japanese have been apt to forget their position as aggressors in the war that they waged for their own purpose." That same editorial calls for the Diet to adopt, on the historic 50th anniversary of World War II, a no-war resolution "making clear to the world Japan's remorse for the war and its commitment to peace."[51] Prime Minister Murayama also took advantage of the 50th anniversary to officially establish the "Asian Women's Fund" to atone for the so-called wartime comfort women who, in his words, "suffered emotional and physical wounds that can never be closed," recognizing that "the scars of war still run deep in these countries to this day."[52]

The most dramatic of expressions of remorse from the Japanese was given by Prime Minister Tomiichi Murayama on August 15, 1995. A culmination of his efforts and those of the Socialist Party he belonged to, his speech, choice of words, and the setting were indeed significant. In his nationally televised speech from his home, Murayama said:

> During a certain period in the not too distant past, Japan, following a mistaken national policy, advanced along the road to war, only to ensnare the Japanese

people in a fateful crisis, and, through its colonial rule and aggression, caused tremendous damage and suffering to the people of many countries, particularly to those of Asian nations. In the hope that no such mistake be made in the future, I regard, in a spirit of humility, these irrefutable facts of history, and express here once again my feelings of deep remorse and state my heartfelt apology. Allow me also to express my feelings of profound mourning for all victims, both at home and abroad, of that history.[53]

Murayama's acknowledgement of "aggression" and his use of the term "aggression" had no precedent in past apologetic statements from government officials. Moreover his using of the word "apology" (*owabi*) instead of the overused term of "regret" (*hansei*) received much attention, as it was an expression of deeper remorse.[54] But another observation about the speech is that it was delivered at his residence for a national television audience right before attending the official ceremony commemorating the 50th anniversary of the end of the war. Delivered at a private space separated from the official site of the ceremony threw doubt on the authoritativeness of the apology. A more sympathetic interpretation of the choice of site would say "by separating the speech from the ceremony ... Mr. Murayama gave his words much more of the force of the state" since the commemorative ritual was for the Japanese where sympathies were being extended to Japanese victims of the war.[55] No Japanese politician would fail to acknowledge Japan's enormous loss from the Hiroshima and Nagazaki bombings inhibiting any unconditional remorse for Japan's war crimes. Nonetheless, the private venue of the apology and what seemed like a personal contrition might have diminished the efficacy of Murayama's apology. The only other avenue to deliver a legitimate apology could have come from the Japanese parliament, the Diet.

After much debate and contention among the major political parties, the Socialist Muruyama failed to persuade the Liberal democrats to pass a resolution similar to the one he was able to deliver two months later. The resolution that was passed by the National Diet was remorseful but not explicitly apologetic. It was more a "carefully crafted ambiguity than a sincere apology," as one reporter called it.[56] The resolution read: "Solemnly reflecting upon many instances of colonial rule and acts of aggression in the modern history of the world, and recognizing that Japan carried out those acts in the past, inflicting pain and suffering upon the peoples of other countries, especially in Asia, the Members of this House express a sense of deep remorse."[57] The reactions to the bill inside Japan and in the neighboring countries were negative. Opposition parties either boycotted or opposed the compromise made with the right-wingers of the Liberal Democratic Party. Incidentally, the text used regret or soul-searching *hansei* instead of *owabi* or *shazi* contrary to President Murayama. The feeble apology actually angered the neighboring countries. One diplomat described the root of that anger as "Japan's determined wriggling not to face up to its guilty past."[58] The Japanese have continuously been touting Murayama's 1995 speech every time international questions are raised over Japan's recognition of its own history. Yet Murayama's famous pronouncement has not been endorsed by the Diet to this day.[59]

As if it were waiting to happen again, a diplomatic crisis between Japan and its neighbors emerged in April 2005 over the same unresolved historical legacies of World War II. Although the conflictual issues were the same as the past, the diplomatic disputes escalated fast endangering regional stability. Tens of thousands of Chinese demonstrators took to the streets in several cities on April 9 in response to the approval by the Japanese government of school textbooks that allegedly glossed over wartime atrocities against China and Korea by the Japanese. In some cases protestors threw rocks and bottles at the Japanese Embassy and the ambassador's residence. A week later close to 20,000 protestors marched in Shanghai and Shenyang damaging the Japanese consulates there. Japanese demands for apology and compensation for the rampages were addressed through legal compensation although most of the damages remained unrepaired, their relations even more so. [60] What precipitated the latest outbreak of hostilities in China and the other neighboring countries are not only the history textbook issue and the visits of the Yasukuni Shrine by Prime Minister Koizumi and other politicians, but the new campaign by Japan for a seat in the Security Council of the United Nations.

In the hopes of improving relations with Japan's neighbors that have recently been chilled, Prime Minister Koizumi used the Asia-African Summit meeting in Indonesia as a forum to express that "In the past, Japan, through its colonial rule and aggression, caused tremendous damage and suffering to the people of many countries, particularly to those of Asian nations." It was a speech reminiscent of that made by the then Prime Minister Tomiichi Murayama marking the 50th anniversary of the end of World War II. The speech went beyond placating Japan for its wartime sins and seemed to reaffirm Japan's unique qualification as a viable member of an enlarged Security Council. He said: "With feelings of deep remorse and heartfelt apology always engraved in mind, Japan has resolutely maintained … its principle of resolving all matters by peaceful means, without recourse to use of force." In the same speech Koizumi goes out of his way to point out both the importance of a reformed UN that reflects global realities and Japan's past contributions toward global development and assistance.[61] Unfortunately, on the same morning that Koizumi apologized, some 80 MPs of the ruling Japanese political party paid homage to the controversial Yasukuni Shrine that also honors 14 Class A war criminals.[62] Prime Minister Koizumi has been visiting the same shrine outraging the neighboring countries since 1991.

When Chinese president Hu Jintao and Prime Minister Junichiro met the day after the Japanese mea culpa, President Hu reminded the public that apologies for war crimes have to be backed up by actions. The actions to be taken on the part of Japan are not evident although the Chinese president made it clear that Tokyo should refuse to support any moves toward independence by Taiwan.[63]

In this latest conflict between Japan and its neighbors, one thing seems to be clear. The recipients of these occasional apologies by Japan seem to be tired of the preforma of apologies. Murayama's apology of 1995 cannot be topped in the sincerity of language. So what do the new Japanese leaders have to offer? As South Korea's president Roh Moo-hyun put it succinctly: "We call on Japanese leaders not to make new apologies but to take action suitable to the apologies already made." He went on to say that these apologies by Japan cannot be taken seriously, when in fact Japanese politicians continue to do things that "are not consistent with the spirit of apology and penitence."[64] What the Chinese consider as solid evidence of remorse would be, among other things, an end of Koizumi's visits to the Yasukuni's Shrine.[65] Thus Japanese apologies are being scrutinized for their substance and form. Once again questions have to be raised as to why the Japanese will not deliver an unequivocal apology once and for all, when in fact they have contributed so much to the economic health of their neighbors. These puzzling contradictions remain. Japan's acknowledgments of the war crimes committed in its name come out grudgingly, if they come at all. At the same time it prides itself of a pacifist constitution. According to Andre Schmid, "When you're speaking in Japanese there are definite hierarchies of how you express your remorse, and terms used have always been of a low level, and done in the passive voice which neglects to say who did the acts."[66]

The Political Calculus of Apology

We concentrated in this chapter on the responses, initiatives and resistance on the part of the Japanese state to demands by victims and advocates for an official declaration of remorse and compensation. Thus an apology process cannot exclude the state from its moral discourse as the political calculus is unavoidably tied to the "high" politics of the statecentric international order.

Measured against the straightforward criteria of success in an apology process, postwar rapprochement between Japan and its neighbors has been an abysmal failure.[67] The Japanese leadership has been slow to acknowledge the brutal consequences of its colonialism and imperialist wars while at the same time downplaying war atrocities including the exploitation of sex slaves. Unlike Germany, which was left with the burden of guilt after the war, the legacies of Hiroshima and Nagasaki were responsible for a culture of victimization that was to reinforce the reluctance of the new Japanese elite to acknowledge guilt for Japan's own crimes. Along with postwar policies and the Cold War, that same culture conspired to insulate Japanese leaders from the Asian cries for apology and compensation. Denial politics and new revisionist interpretations of Japanese history have exasperated any efforts to tell the truth about Japanese war crimes. The official history of Japan's role in World War II and its earlier history stand in marked contrast to the grievances and claims of its Asian neighbors. Thus, the first acknowledgements of Japanese wartime excesses and remorseful pronouncements by government officials were not to be heard until the late 1980s and 1990s, and only after grassroots pressures from within Japan and from its Asian neighbors. Successive Japanese governments responded through selective accountability, careful contrition and contradictory languages of apology as the international challenges grew.

In the apologetic discourse involving Japan and its neighbors there is a continuous muddle between private and public accountability. Did the Prime Ministers, Murayama or Koizumi engage in personal repentance or as deputies of their state? Their apologies do not seem to be delegated even as they address distant victims and their representatives.

The discursive distance between victims and perpetrators is far and wide considering that the crimes perpetrated are geographically removed from the Japanese public space and memories. The victims could not face the perpetrators in the way they were accommodated in the dramatic truth commissions in Argentina, Chile, East Germany and South Africa. Thus the unraveling of the truths about war and colonial atrocities has been revived by individuals and groups who seek proximity with a faceless state in their pursuit of justice. The mostly Asian victims of Japanese-induced crimes seek both apology and reparation. They want at once an apology that stipulates proximity and genuine sorrow, and reparation that is not aloof but authoritative. These demands have precipitated schizophrenic reactions so it seems from political leaders who are caught between a rock and a hard place – between representing empathy for themselves and the peoples they represent and the sanctified interests of the state in a statecentric moral order. In 1985 the Japanese Prime Minister with a number of his ministers made an official visit to the Yasukuni Shrine, the memorial for the Japanese war dead but also the resting place for the so-called "Class-A war criminals." The uproar that followed prevented the Prime Minister from making a similar visit the following year. Years later, in 2002 and again in 2003, Prime Minister Junichiro Koizumi defiantly visited the shrine by claiming that he would honor the Japanese war dead and at the same time apologize for the victimization of Asians.[68]

The difficulty for deputies in the apology process derives from the inherent conflict between the universal norms on reconciliation, bringing new ethical sensibilities, and the established habits of state sovereignties. This persistent conflict questions the efficacy of speech acts that pass as public remorse. Therefore, unless public apologies are put on record, which once again reinforces the power of institutions and legality in statecentric international law, the efficacy of public apologies are undermined by both victims and perpetrators. That is why the failure of the Japanese Diet to deliver a forceful statement of public apology and an authorization of comprehensive reparation settlements represents the weak side of the Japanese political calculus.

The political calculus of apology between Japan and its neighbors, other than reconciliation, is more discernable as they have to do more with normalization and power politics.[69] The Japanese wish to deal with past wrongs just enough to maintain the status-quo on bilateral relations with these countries, although historically sensitive issues of revisionism and new fears of militarism have precipitated habitual setbacks. Japan desires to become a normal state that would enable it to be a member of the U.N. Security Council and play a role of global leadership in peacekeeping and other areas. Japan is also taking into account its special relations with China marked by mutual economic gain as well as potentially dangerous power rivalry in the region. By avoiding to reach more comprehensive settlements of grievances with its neighbors, Japan would be undermining its long-term interests.

Notes

1.   Maria Rosa Henson, *Comfort Woman: A Filipina's Story of Prostitution and Slavery under the Japanese Military* (Lanham: Rowman & Littlefield Publishers, Inc, 1999), 91. This personal account is a powerful testimony to the suffering, shame and resilience of survivors of the sex slavery. Another testimonial document is *Comfort Women Speak: Testimony of Sex Slaves of the Japanese Military*, ed. Sangmie Choi Schellstede (New York: Holmes & Meier 2000) that includes three United Nations reports.

2.   "Koreans Slice Their Fingers in Anti-Japan Rite," *The New York Times*, August 14, 2001.

3.   "Unambiguous apology needed," *The Japan Times*, November 5, 2003, <http://www.japantimes.co.jp/cgi-bin/getarticle.p15?rc20031105a1.htm> (February 4, 2004).

4.   *Agreement between Japan and the Republic of Korea Concerning the Settlement of Problems in Regard to Property and Claims and Economic Co-operation*, June 22, 1965, International Legal Materials, 5, 1 (January 1966).

5.   George Hicks, "The Comfort Women Redress Movement," in *When Sorry Isn't Enough*, ed. Roy L. Brooks (New York: New York University Press, 1999), 114.

6.   Shuko Ogawa, "The Difficulty of Apology: Japan's Struggle with Memory and Guilt," *Harvard International Review* (Fall 2000), 43.

7.   Ogawa, "The Difficulty of Apology," 43.

8.   Ogawa, 42.

9.   Aaron Gerow, "Consuming Asia, Consuming Japan: The Neonationalistic Revisionism in Japan," in *Censoring History: Citizenship and Memory in Japan, and the United States*, ed. Laura Hein and Mark Selden (Armnok, N.Y.: M. E. Sharpe, 2000), 92-93.

10.   Christine Wawrynek, "World War II Comfort Women: Japan's Sex Slaves or Hired Prostitutes?" *New York Law School Journal of Human Rights*, 19, 3 (Summer 2003), 913.

11.   The Ministry of Foreign Affairs of Japan. "Statement by the Chief Cabinet Secretary Yohei Kono on the result of the study on the issue of "comfort women," Statement by the Chief Cabinet, Secretary, August 4, 1993, <http://www.mofa.go.jp/policy/women/fund/state9308/html> (February 9, 2004).

12.   Edward W. Desmond, "Finally, A Real Apology," *Time*, v. 146, August 28, 1995, 47.

13.   The Ministry of Foreign Affairs of Japan, "A New Japan-Republic of Korea Partnership toward the Twenty-first Century," Japan-Republic of Korea Joint Declara-

tion, October 8, 1998, <http://www.mofa.go.jp/region/asia-paci/korea/joint9810.html> (February 9, 2004).

14. Harry Sterling, "Japan Refuses to Face Up to its History." *The Toronto Star*, January 8, 2001, first edition.

15. The Ministry of Foreign Affairs of Japan, "Recent Policy of the Government of Japan on the Issue Known as "Wartime Comfort Women," June, 2001, <http//www.mofa.go.jp/policy/women/fund/policy0011.html>. (February 9, 2004). Also see Junichiro Koizumi "Letter from Prime Minister Junichiro Koizumi to the former comfort women," The Ministry of Foreign Affairs of Japan, Year of 2001,<http://www.mofa.go.jp/policy/women/fund/pmletter.html> (February 9, 2004).

16. Tomiko Okazaki. Comment by Upper House lawmaker from Minshuto. *The Asahi Shimbun*, August 9, 2002, Financial Times Information.

17. The Ministry of Foreign Affairs of Japan. "Statement by Chief Cabinet Secretary Kiichi Miyazawa on History Textbooks," August 26, 1982, <http://www.mofa.go.jp/policy/postwar/state8208.html>

18. The Ministry of Foreign Affairs of Japan, "On the Issue of Wartime 'Comfort Women'," August 4, 1993, <http://www.mofa.go.jp/policy/postwar/issue9308.html> (February 9, 2004).

19. Hicks, "The Comfort Women Redress Movement," 115-119, in Brooks.

20. The Ministry of Foreign Affairs of Japan, "Statement by Prime Minister Tomiichi Murayama on the 'Peace, Friendship, and Exchange Initiative'," August 31, 1994, <http://www.mofa.go.jp/announce/press/pm/murayama/state9408.html> (February 9, 2004).

21. Jonathan Watts, "Japan reclaims 'war hero'." *The Guardian* (London), December 23, 1998.

22. "Hearts and Minds: Three Questions for Japan." *Korea Times*, June 28, 2000.

23. Michael Millett, "Japan's Take on History Upsets Neighbours." *Sydney Morning Herald*, March 3, 2001.

24. The Ministry of Foreign Affairs of Japan, "Comments by the Chief Cabinet Secretary, Yasuo Fukuda on the history textbooks to be used in junior high schools from 2002," April 3, 2001, <http://www.mofa.go.jp/announce/announce/2001/4/0403.html> (February 9, 2004).

25. Paul Shin, "Japanese textbook offends Koreans." *Chicago Sun-Times* (Associated Press), April 10, 2001.

26. Kwan Weng Kin, "Japan Wages War of Words." *The Straits Times* (Singapore), May 6, 2001.

27. Harry Sterling, "Whitewashing history: Japan refuses to come to grips with its military past." *The Gazette (Montreal, Quebec)*, May 28, 2001.

28. The Ministry of Foreign Affairs of Japan, "Comment by Minister of Foreign Affairs Makiko Tanaka on the official Stance Conveyed by the Government of the Republic of Korea on the Decision to Authorize Japanese History Textbooks," May 8, 2001. <http://www.mofa.go.jp/announce/2001/5/0508.html> (February 9, 2004).

29. "Ethnic Korean Leads Publication of Book on Comfort Women Issue in Japan," *Korea Times*, April 8, 2002.

30. "Family Wins 20 Million Yen for Laborer's Time on Run," *Japan Times*, July 13, 2001.

31. "Second Wave of War Orphans Hits Government with Lawsuits," *Japan Times*, September 25, 2003.

32. The Ministry Foreign Affairs of Japan, "Press Statement by Chief Cabinet Secretary Hidenao Nakagawa on the Asian Women's Fund," September 1, 2000, <http://www.mofa.go.jp/policy/postwar/state0009.html> (February 9, 2004).

33. The Ministry of Foreign Affairs of Japan, "On the Completion of the Atonement Project of the Asian Women's Fund (AWF) in the Netherlands," July 13, 2001, <http://www.mofa.go.jp/policy/women/fund/project0107-1.html> (February 9, 2004).

34. *Peace Treaty between Japan and the Allied Powers*, East Asian Studies Documents, <http://www.isop.ucla.edu/eas/documents/peace1951.htm>, (January 3, 2005).

35. *Agreement on the Settlement Problems Concerning Property and Claims and on Economic Cooperation, June 22, 1965, Japan-Korea*, 583 U.N.T.S., 260.

36. Karen Parker and Jennifer F. Chew, "Reparations: A Legal Analysis," in *When Sorry Isn't Enough*, ed. Roy L. Brooks (New York: New York Press), 142.

37. United Nations Economic and Social Council, Committee on Economic, Social and Cultural Rights, 29th session, *Comments by States parties on concluding observations: Japan*, November 29, 2002, Summary Record of the 43rd Meeting, E/C.12/2001/12, November 29, 2002. <http://www.unhchr.ch/tbs/doc.nsf/(Symbol)/E.C.12.2002.12.En?Opendocument > (January 3, 2005).

38. United Nations Economic and Social Council. Comments by state parties.

39. "Comfort Women Seek Justice Apart from 1965 Korea-Japan Agreement," *Korea Times*, August 14, 2003.

40. For a criticism of Max Weber's most influential essay, "Politics as a Vocation," see Peter Johnson, *Politics, Innocence, and the Limits of Goodness* (London: Routledge, 1988), 150-152. Johnson says "Weber's belief that the problem of political morality is a choice between Christ and Caesar is too simple and reveals a romantic conception of man as isolated, individual chooser," 151.

41. "Comfort Women Seek Justice."

42. Laura Hein, "War Compensation: Claims against the Japanese Government and Japanese Corporations for War Crimes," in *Politics and the Past: On Repairing Historical Injustices*, ed. John Torpey (Lanham, Md.: Rowman & Littlefield, 2003), 133.

43. The Unit 731 biological warfare unit is "known for its germ warfare experiments on Chinese, the 1937 Nanjing Massacre and indiscriminate bombing over a safety zone during the 1937-1945 war." See, "Court Rejects Chinese War Victims' Damages Case." *The Japan Times*, September 22, 1999, <http://www.jpantimes.co.jp/cgi-bin/getarticle.p15?nn19990922a5.htm> (February 4, 2004).

44. "Court Rejects Chinese War Victims' Damages Case."

45. "War Victims Unite Efforts to Win Redress from Japan," *The Japan Times*, February 12, 1999, <http//www.japantimes.co.jp/cgi-bin/getaarticle.p15?nn19990212a3.htm> (February 4, 2004).

46. "Former Sex Slaves Seek Justice in U.S.," *The Japan Times*, September 17, 2000, <http://www.japantimes.co.jp/cgi-bin/getarticle.p15?nn20000917a1.htm> (February 4, 2004). See also "Ex-comfort Women Sue Japan in U.S. over Sex Slavery," *Japan Economic Newswire*, September 18, 2000.

47. John Torpey, *Politics and the Past: On Repairing Historical Injustices*. Ed. (Lanham, Md.: Rowman & Littlefield, 2003), 1.

48. " 'Comfort Women' Exhibit Visits U.S.'," *The Japan Times*, December 28, 2000.

49. House Concurrent Resolution 195; 107th Congress, 1st session, July 24, 2001.

50. The Ministry of Foreign Affairs "Remarks by Prime Minister Tomiichi Murayama during His May 1995 Visit to China,", May 4, 1995, <http://www.mofa.go.jp/announce/press/pm/murayama/china.html> (February 18, 2004).

51. "No-war resolution can help Japan chart future course," *Asahi News Service*, March 6, 1995, http://web.lexis-nexis.

52. The Ministry of Foreign Affairs of Japan, "Statement by Prime Minister Tomiichi Murayama on the Occasion of the Establishment of the 'Asian Women's Fund'," July 1995. <http://www.mofa.go.jp/policy/women/fund/state9507.html> (February 9, 2004).

53. The Ministry of Foreign Affairs of Japan, "Statement by Prime Minister Tomiichi Murayama 'On the Occasion of the 50th anniversary of the War's End," August 15, 1995. <http://www.mofa.go.jp/announce/press/pm/murayama/9508.html> (February 18, 2004).

54. Edward W. Desmond, "Finally, a Real Apology," *Time*, 146, August 28, 1995, 47.

55. Sheryl WuDunn, "Premier of Japan Offers 'Apology' for its War Acts," *The New York Times*, August 15, 1995, Section A.

56. Ben Hills, "Japan Expresses Remorse but Ducks Apology for War," *Sydney Morning Herald*, June 8, 1995.

57. The Ministry of Foreign Affairs of Japan, "Prime Minister's Address to the Diet," June 9, 1995, <http://www.mofa.go.jp/announce/press/pm/murayama/address9506.html> (February 18, 2004).

58. Kevin Rafferty, "Japan's 'Feeble' War Apology Angers Neighbors," *The Guardian (London)*, June 10, 1995.

59. Kwan Weng Kin, "Japan wages war of words," *The Straits Times (Singapore)*, May 6, 2001.

60. "China Says Apology for Anti-Japan Protests Not An Issue," *Financial Times*, June 16, 2005.

61. "Koizumi Issues Rare War Apology," *The Japan Times*, April 23, 2005.

62. Malaysian Lawmakers Demand Apology from Japan Over War Crimes," *Japan Economic Newswire*, April 25, 2005.

63. Audra Ang, "Chinese, Japanese leaders fail to reach settlement in dispute over Tokyo's wartime past," *The Associated Press*, April 24, 2005.

64. "South Korean President Demands Actions "Suitable" to Past Japan's Apologies," Financial Times, May 6, 2005.

65. "Waiting for May; Anti-Japan Protests in China," *The Economist*, April 30, 2005.

66. Steven Edwards, "60 Years, and Still No Shame: Failure to Atone for Wartime Atrocities Diminishes Japan," *National Post*, April 13, 2005.

67. An excellent source on reactions by the Japanese elite, personal testimonies, narratives and legal and political analyses is Roy L. Brooks's *When Sorry Isn't Enough: The Controversy over Apologies and Reparations for Human Injustice* (New York University Press, 1999). Also, see my brief analysis on Japanese-Korean rapprochement in "*Apologia Politica*: An Examination of the Politics and Ethics of Public Remorse in International Affairs," *International Journal of Politics and Ethics*, 2, no. 2, 128-130.

68. The Ministry of Foreign Affairs of Japan, "Statement by Chief Cabinet Secretary Masaharu Gotoda on Official Visits to Yasukuni Shrine by the Prime Minister and Other State Ministers on August 15 of this year," August 14, 1986, <http://www.mofa.go.jp/policy/postwar/state8608.html> (February 9, 2004). See also The Ministry of Foreign Affairs of Japan, "Observation by Prime Minister Junichiro Koizumi on the Visit to Yasukuni Shrine," April 21, 2002, <www.mofa.go.jp/announce/pm/koizumi/observe0204.html>. (February 9, 2004). See also The Ministry of Foreign Affairs of Japan, "Address by Prime Minister Junichiro

Koizumi at the 58th Memorial Ceremony for the War Dead," August 15, 2003, <http://www.kantei.go.jp/foreign/koisumispeech/2003/08/15skiji_e.html> (February 9, 2004).

69. Jean-Pierre Lehmann argues for a combination of genuine contrition on the part of Japanese leaders with intense dialogue between the peoples of Japan and its neighbors, beyond the state-to-state apparatus, which would establish trust and confidence between the alienated nations. He writes, "Prime Minister Junichiro Koizumi could go to Nanjing and, as German Chancellor Willy Brandt did when he came to the Warsaw ghetto memorial, kneel and beg forgiveness." He also suggests, writing in 2002, "a schedule over the next 10 years to bring together representative across the spectrum of Japanese society and their counterparts from China, South Korea and other Asian countries that were victims of Japanese aggression to engage in open discussion and confidence building." Jean-Pierre Lehmann, "Japan in the Global Era: How to avert the risk of war with China." *The Japan Times*, June 17, 2002, 16th in a series, <http://www.japantimes.co.jp/cgi-bin/getarticle.p15?eo20020617jl.htm> (February 4, 2004).

Chapter 4

Voices and Silences in Mourning Rwanda

But I, the one of the middle of a life, I have always waited, hovering invisible above my skeleton exposed to the curiosity of the crowd.

Phalène des Collines by Koulsy Lamko

A Rwandan queen raped and murdered in the Rwandan bloodbath of 1994 returns as a moth to the crime scenes and the gravesites in search of recognition. In *Moth of the Hills*, Chadian novelist Koulsy Lamko gives voice to victims and survivors who have been silenced, restoring thus the dignity denied them by their victimizers. The narrative is an attempt to come to terms with the 1994 genocide in the Land of A Thousand Hills through the representational exploits of a queen who has been ravaged and killed in the "holocaust," but has now returned as a moth to haunt the Rwandan grave-sites seeking reckoning and justice. This moth's eye view of post-genocide Rwanda objectifies the violent events as the apparition hovers above the wasteland mockingly, so it seems. The novel alludes to both the historical and structural ravages of the country's violent history. It represents a complex of multinarratives of the Rwandan violence and trauma adding to other accounts made by international journalists, diplomats and aid workers.

Lamko's story is one among the middle voices, as Ronald Barthes would conceive it, between perpetrators and victims, all making truth claims at different levels.[1] There are other narratives on the genocide and the resulting trauma, in the form of testimonies, historiography, and political discourse of apology and restoration. I examine here the apologies given to endeavor to come to terms with the horrible past on the part of all implicated in a concentric circle of com-

plicity, beginning with the survivors at the center and spiralling out to the perpetrators, bystanders, witnesses, and beyond that to the international community –
and us. I will look into several narratives on the truth of what transpired in 1994
in Rwanda; what is acknowledged; who came forth to be accountable, if remorse
was expressed; and finally into the nature and extent of the apologies and restorative actions taken so far. Besides exploring the facts, the silences, misrepre-
sentations, subjective fragmentation and incomplete mea culpa, we will also turn
to Koulsy Lamko's narrative, a sample of the new imaginative constructions,
more specifically the reenactments represented by the African artistic project:
"Writing as a Duty to Memory."

Memory, Warnings, the Genocide, and Aftermath

The new Genocide Memorial Center on the Gisozi hillside opened its doors to
visitors on the tenth anniversary of the first day of the mass slaughter in
Rwanda, April 6, 1994. The first area or zone of this memorial is named "Before
Genocide" providing an interactive guide to Rwanda's history including Belgian
colonialism and its divide and rule policy that contributed to the mutual alienation of the Tutsi and Hutu peoples.[2] The violence in the spring of 1994 in
Rwanda was not the only bloodshed in modern Rwanda's history. There were
others, like the mass violence against the Tutsi inspired by the 1959 Hutu Revolution, but in its scope and magnitude and the systematic approach chosen by the
perpetrators to carry out the extermination of a people, in this case the Tutsis
and the Hutus who tolerated them, it characteristically constitutes a genocide.[3]
The inception and the development of the violence that swiftly degenerated into
the last horrific crime against humanity of the twentieth century was all the more
shocking in that it was predictable.

In October 1990, the invasion of the Rwandan Patriotic Front (RPF) from
neighboring Uganda was condemned and interpreted by Hutu extremists as an
eminent threat to inflict Tutsi domination over the majority once again. For the
next three years Hutu president Habyarimana held back on power sharing and
the establishment of a multi-party democracy. During that time the Rwandan
army armed and trained a civilian militia known as *Interahamwe* ("those who
stand together"). At the same time politicians and journalists were being perse-
cuted, and thousands of Tutsis killed in separate incidents while ideologues of
Hutu extremism spread the virus of hatred. In November 1992, a prominent
Hutu intellectual Dr. Leon Musegera appealed to the Hutus to send the Tutsis
"back to Ethiopia" via the rivers.[4] A year later when the RPF guerrillas reached
the outskirts of Kigali, the Rwandan government appealed for help from the
French. It is here one can observe the replay of neocolonial politics. Even
though Rwanda had been a Belgian colony and the Belgians had provided military and other aids to Rwanda, the French had also been active in providing
military hardware since the 1970s to counter the Anglophone influence of such

countries as Uganda. In 1990 when the RPF invaded Rwanda and the Belgians stopped military aid to the embattled regime, the French were eager to oblige and "Rwanda's Hutu regime was happily sucked into the Francophone orbit."[5] Against the tides of geopolitical intrigues, refugee formation, and the rise of xenophobia a peace settlement was in the making to resolve the deepening conflict between the Rwandan government and the RPF rebels.

After months of negotiations in Arusha, Tanzania, the Rwandan government and RPF signed a series of agreements and a peace accord. Habayarimana agreed to political power sharing with the RPF and the Hutu opposition. He also consented to the integration of the Rwandan army (FAR) and the Rwandan Patriotic Army (RPF military wing) according to a 60-40 percent formula. While all the workings of a peaceful settlement were theoretically in place, two sets of circumstances, one that could have been avoided and the other unexpected and unforeseen, derailed the possibility of a peaceful outcome and consequently set Rwanda on a deadly and tragic course.[6]

The installation of the transitional government was supposed to take place after a deployment of UN peacekeepers and the withdrawal of the French forces. As it turned out the peacekeepers never arrived in time, the French troops remained and the proposed Transitional Government was never formed. Other explosive points of the agreements, such as the replacement of ethnic identification documents, were never implemented. During those months President Habyarimana delayed the setting up of a power-sharing government, militia training intensified, and the extremist radio stations began broadcasting virulent propaganda exhorting attacks on Tutsis. Most representative of what could have been done to avert the pending massacre is the now famous fax sent by UNAMIR commander General Romero Dallaire informing headquarters of the intelligence he had gathered about systematic plans by Hutu extremist groups to exterminate the Tutsis. His plan to seize a cache of weapons identified by an informant was not accepted, and his request for the protection of that informant was denied by his superiors in the Department of Peace Keeping Operations at the UN, including Kofi Annan, who did not share Dallaire's sense of urgency. In 20/20 hindsight, most critics find it incredulous that the UN bureaucrats missed the opportunity to avert disaster.[7]

Other unforeseen circumstances may have also contributed to the disastrous political outcome. One such impact was the interethnic conflict and violence in neighboring Burundi. In fact the politics of Burundi – a country with a similar ethnic makeup of a Hutu majority and a dominant Tutsi minority – has been intertwined with Rwanda's history and destiny. In 1993 Burundi's instability spilled into Rwanda. Soon after Melchior Ndadaye, a Hutu, won the presidential election, defeating the incumbent Pierre Buyoya. Tragically, Tutsi officers assassinated the newly elected president in an abortive coup d'état, setting off a cycle of violence first aimed at the Tutsi, followed by harsh retaliation by the Tutsi-dominated military. Before the dust settled, an estimated number of

50,000 to 100,000 people were killed with some 600,000 Hutu refugees who left Burundi. Of those, it is estimated that 375,000 entered southern Rwanda. The assassination of Ndadye, the Hutu refugee influx, and the inaction by the UN in regard to the crisis in Burundi were to have dire consequences for Rwanda. As Arthur J. Klinghoffer points out, "the Rwanda-Burundi relationship was truly symbiotic, as the dramatic events of April 6, 1994 were later to prove"[8] On that fateful day all the contingent, surreptitious but unheeded factors came to a head precipitating the genocidal violence.

The second zone of the new Kigali memorial and museum is called "Warnings" depicting the horror that could have been avoided, with displays of a copy of Dallaire's famous fax and a quotation from Colonel Bagosora vowing to prepare for an "apocalypse." "At the top of a stairwell," journalist Rory Carroll describes, "is a stained glass window depicting dark brooding clouds of midnight blue."[9] These displays stir memories of a dreadful beginning. When an aircraft transporting the Rwandan and Burundian presidents from the Dar es Salaam summit was struck by missiles over Kigali, all hell broke loose. In the controversy over who shot the missiles, the Rwandan government and the Hutu extremists blamed the RPF for carrying out the deed and the UNIMAR Belgian peacekeepers for not preventing it. When the killing began that first night, it was the political leaders in the opposition or those seen as sympathetic to the RPF who were targeted, beginning with Hutu moderates. In the following days, the victims of the killings were randomly selected to be Tutsis. Militiamen carried out the attacks at roadblocks taking the law into their hands. Hutus were being coerced into killing Tutsi or being killed themselves. The Tutsis in Kigali were an easy target having been located by the February 1994 city census. Deadly was the vengeful exhortation by Radio-Télévision Libre des Mille Collines aimed at the well-disciplined militia and the unruly lumpen classes and peasants to go on a rampage of killings. Provoked to popular anger "the military, the militiamen, and peasants launched the *gukora*, a code word meaning literally 'to work,' used for the first time in 1960 by PARMEHUTU. In this context, the word's meaning is to rob the Tutsi of his property or to kill him."[10]

The inexplicable crimes that took place in late Spring and Summer of 1994 have been recounted in a variety of ways. In one such account the use of barriers and roadblocks effectively brings home to the reader the predatory nature of the war criminals as the victims met their inescapable fate. Paved roads, dirt roads, even footpaths were blocked by the army, militia, communal police, neighborhood protection groups and local peasants. The fleeing people had to show their national identity cards at these roadblocks. In the absence of ethnic identification, physical characteristics were put to use. The Tutsis were almost always robbed and killed brutally. According to one account culled from witnesses: "often the condemned had to pay for the quick death of a bullet, whereas the less fortunate were slashed with machetes or bludgeoned to death with nail-studded clubs."[11] Refugees who survived the massacre had to bribe those manning the roadblocks. In some cases they were forced to bludgeon Tutsi captives to death in order to move on. Compelling those whose life was spared to kill the captives was intended to ritually blur the boundary between "genocidaires" and the innocent among the Hutu and to make the innocent Hutu morally complicit in the genocide.[12]

"The Genocide" is the third zone of the new memorial of the genocide. It is a passageway of horrific images in photo stills and film clips reflecting unflinchingly the events of 7 April 1994. In a glass case the weapons of mass murder such as machetes, clubs and guns are displayed along with video playbacks of survivors telling the harrowing tales of rape and mutilation.[13] Between the extremes of abstraction and tourist voyeurism lies the acknowledgement and appreciation of a horrendous past that is likely to induce in us an empathic disturbance of the type LaCapra speaks of.[14] Any of the stories of the brutality of the genocide as told by survivors suffice to provoke our commiseration with the victims. One such story is that of the massacre of the people in Cyahinda who had taken refuge in a church as described by a survivor:

> Here it was completely full of people, and they shot into this dense crowd with machine guns. A lot of people died here. There are no bullet holes on the walls, because the crowd was so dense that the bullets went into their bodies. Even if the bullets passed through one person's body, they went into the body of another person. The assailants with guns then forced their way into the Church through the main doors and the doors on the right side. Others, armed with machetes, clubs, and spears, followed close behind. The violence was so extraordinary in scale and ruthlessness that a witness, hiding in her home and watching from the window, rubbed her eyes in disbelief and asked the person with her, "Do you see what I see?"[15]

Among such testimonies by survivors are the individual stories of women who lived to tell the horrors of sexual violence:

> Josepha was thirty-eight years old and living in Shyanda commune, Butare prefecture, in 1994. Her family was attacked by the militia in April 1994 and many were killed. She hid in the sorghum fields, but was caught by the militia. They hit her over the head, and took her by the arms and legs and threw her in the air. She fell on the ground on top of some broken bottles. Then two of the militia raped her. One of them has not been arrested and continues to live in Butare. Josepha said, "rape is a crime worse than death." She has not returned to her land or her house, but stays in a camp for widows with her one surviving daughter.[16]

These voices reveal the preoccupations of the *genocidaires* that were both sexual and ethnic in character.[17] Testimonies of such victimization were used later to set the precedent of adding rape to crimes against humanity in the Rwandan Tribunal. In 1997, the International Criminal Tribunal of Rwanda brought charges of rape and genocide against Jean-Paul Akayesu who was convicted, making the first case "in which rape – one of the most ancient of war crimes – would be held by a court of law to be an act of genocide and a crime against humanity."[18] A full account of the genocide would include an acknowledgement of those murdered, the traumatized survivors, the perpetrators, the individuals, and the groups and nations who stood by idly during the course of those crimes.

Many individuals failed to assist victims, even clergymen and organized Christian groups that belonged to the Roman Catholic Church and the Church of England. A few days after the killings had begun; Catholic bishops stated their support of those who were carrying out the killings.[19] Even more shocking, as more is known about the perpetrators and the collaborators, is the extent of the participation of Churches in the genocide.[20] There were nevertheless stories of courageous members of the clergy, of sisters who chose to stay with their brothers and sisters in danger and eventually died with them.[21]

"Responses" is the name of the fourth zone of the Kigali memorial and it focuses on "the heroism of those who hid fugitives, resisted death squads and retained their humanity, at a time of disparity."[22] Determining who in the international community stood by while a genocide was in progress in Rwanda has to include the decision by the United Nations to disengage its peacekeeping forces. After the killing of Belgian peacekeepers in the first days of the genocide, Belgium withdrew from the United Nations peacekeeping force. The evacuation of the nationals of other countries followed soon after. The slow and hesitant reaction of the international community is best characterized in the refusal by the United Nations Human Rights Commission to discuss the crisis when the first reports of mass violence and killings were coming in. Eventually, urged by Canadian delegates and following a hearing in May 1994 and also a special report, the Commission accepted the designation of the killings in Rwanda as genocide, and the appropriateness of establishing an international tribunal.[23]

In the UN Security Council debates on how to respond to the violence, there were divisions among members between those who wanted full withdrawal of peacekeeping troops, those who wanted to reduce the force and those who wanted to authorize a robust force that would stop the violence and restore order. The U.S. was for full withdrawal while other UNSC members, including France, New Zealand, and non-aligned countries supported a Chapter VII mandate authorizing the use of coercive force. However, under pressures from the international human rights community, the U.S. adopted the position of retaining a token force in Kigali, and finally on April 21st the UNSC voted to reduce the size and mandate of UNAMIR. When the violence intensified, the Secretary-General wanted the council to reconsider its decision. Following yet more debates on the size and contribution of troops, on May 17th the UNSC passed Resolution 918 authorizing an increase of the UNAMIR to 5,500, short of a Chapter VII authorization to use force capable of stopping the genocide. In spite of its support of the resolution, the Clinton Administration "went out of its way to hamper implementation by proudly applying its new PDD 25 criteria. ... it insisted that only a small fraction of the troops be dispersed immediately," that the SG report back to UNSC with a plan of operation before deployment; and ascertain that the UN did not enter into situations that it could not handle. [24] Even more outrageous is the fact that "the Pentagon effectively blocked the provision of promised vehicles and equipment for weeks."[25]

Trauma

What can it be like to be a survivor of the Rwanda genocide? In this more conscious age of therapy, we tend to question the silent denials of trauma of those who narrowly escaped death, including surviving members of families, and orphans.[26] There is a burgeoning literature on questions of how traumatized societies that have undergone experiences of war and oppression should deal with their losses. Dominick LaCapra is one scholar who is concerned for instance about the hazards of substituting mythological losses for real losses thus making proper mourning and working through those losses difficult or impossible.[27] In the post-genocide years some observers think, a metanarrative of a re-imagined Rwanda is being constructed in which the genocide is dangerously transfiguring into a myth. Such near mythical beginnings could "downgrade the significance of particular historical losses" and undermine the reality of the losses of the victims and the need for urgent redress of the historical trauma.[28] On that score, to legitimize the post-genocide government of Rwanda in the eyes of the world, Johan Pottier argues, interlocking narratives have been constructed:

> [That] rule by the pre- and early colonial royal court was benevolent until destroyed by the European colonial powers. The world today, it follows, has every reason to be confident that the return to power of the Rwandan Tutsi diaspora will herald a new era of righteousness and social justice. To spread the message successfully, Rwanda's post-genocide leaders have tried to persuade members of the international community that the history books need to be rewritten, that the numerically dominant ethnic Hutu, whose ethnicity was invented by outsiders, have nothing to fear unless guilty of genocide, and that victimhood bestows the right to dictate to the world how reality is to be understood.[29]

Because of the urge to turn a new leaf in Rwandan history, the pressure on the post-genocide regime to re-imagine a new Rwanda is such that national and intellectual projects exhibit symptoms of deeper structural trauma – the absence of a strong Rwandan political identity. Christopher C. Taylor warns that racist overtones such as Hamitism cannot be ignored. He is referring to the contested myth of origin that the Tutsi are descendants of a "Hamitic" people who are the Ethiopians. He writes: "In the case of Rwanda and Burundi, with its persisting potential for enormous human catastrophe, we achieve nothing by refusing to challenge those among the Rwandan and Burundian interlocutors who wittingly or unwittingly mistake the facts of their history. Discredited in academic circles though it may be, Hamitism is still capable of motivating the thoughts and actions of thousands of Rwandans and Burundians."[30] Others, such as Mamdani, argue for the decolonization of the mind, to transcend ethnic identity. Mamdani asserts that continued violence between Hutu and Tutsi "is connected with the failure of Rwandan nationalism to transcend the colonial construction of Hutu and Tutsi as native and alien. Indeed, if anything, the revolutionaries of 1959 confirmed the Tutsi minority as aliens and the Hutu majority as natives – in the well-known phrase, *Rwanda nyamwinshi* – finally and rightfully comes to power."[31] On the other hand, another observer points out the sense of frustration among the Rwandese concerning "the unnecessary reification of 'ethnicity'."[32] Even after the global acceptance of the genocide the ethnicity question lingers in this delicate period of reconstruction and the beginnings of reconciliation.

The last zone of the Kigali memorial is called "Aftermath." It has presumably changed its name from "reconciliation," according to Rory Carroll, after survivors asserted that peaceful coexistence should not be taken as forgiving and forgetting. The zone includes "exhibits about refugee camps, reunited families, the impact of HIV/Aids, self-help groups and the rounding up of thousands of alleged killers."[33] In the aftermath of the genocide there is rebuilding at every front including the psyche of individuals who have survived, relatives and orphans of the dead, even the perpetrators and their collaborators. The silence of victims and the denial of perpetrators and collaborators also extend to others in the international community implicated by their inaction.

Silence as Denial

Benjamin Sehene, a Rwandan writer, writes, "Rwanda lived for 35 years in a state of growing amnesia, dominated by the law of silence, of the unspoken, of memories collectively repressed. Silence inevitably gave rise to impunity making amnesia acceptable."[34] Sehene is referring to the years of colonial injustices, ethnic strife and mass violence that have continued without reckoning and justice. Ten years after Rwanda's last violent societal convulsion, Rwandans are dealing with the recent bitter past in ways that are reminiscent of postwar Germany. The precarious and urgent questions of justice, reconstruction, rewriting history, and reconciliation demand immediate answers.

If Rwandan history has been marked by a "law of silence" in the past, the complicated challenges of national reconciliation have generated new "silences." The denial by perpetrators and the amnesia of traumatized victims is one type of silence. There is also a "structural silence" one imposed by the state, like in Rwanda, and another by a community of states in the international arena. The post-genocide Rwandan state has been criticized for imposing certain "silences" on the reconciliation process by not bringing to justice alleged war criminals by a vengeful Rwandan Patriotic Army (RPA), the military wing of past rebels and today's rulers, among other heavy-handed measures.[35] The same kind of imposed silences are germane to the international community and the key power players in the Rwandan epic tragedy. There were silences during the genocide as there were more after the fact.

In every case of the bystanding powers, with the exception of France that never apologized for its involvement, the sins of omission came after an extended period of silence. Clinton's acknowledgement to wrongdoing, even though it was newsworthy, was not preceded by any government-led initiative or policy-relevant debate about a human rights calamity that involved the United States, even if only indirectly. There was hardly any public outcry and no congressional inquiries to do with genocide.[36] Even after revelations regarding U.S. government's calculated decision to avoid humanitarian intervention in order to prevent the genocide, especially after the release of condemning documents by the National Security Archives, this most scandalous American foreign policy decision of the Clinton administration hardly made a political wave. States are slow to react to genocide taking place in far way places and are removed from their normal legal practices.[37]

The Belgian apology came late as well, but in 1997 the Belgian Senate Committee of Inquiry aroused public interest by reporting to parliament that the Belgian government had information regarding the preparation of large scale massacre at least four months prior to the beginning of the genocide. The Belgian parliamentary commission exposed Belgians to their intimate historical link to the former colony and reminded them of Belgium's failure in Rwanda painfully dramatized by the murder of 10 Belgian UN soldiers when the genocide began. Belgian public awareness and sense of guilt were further jolted by the trial in a Belgian court of four Rwandans for taking part in the genocide.[38] The precedence of these domestic events explains the categorically remorseful apologies of Prime Minister Guy Verhofstadt in the years 2000 and 2004 respectively.

If states are gagged by habitual and conventional ideas and practices of maintaining security and peace and therefore falter to predict and prevent genocidal violence, those very institutions established to avert mass violence fail, as they did in Rwanda. In December 1999, a U.N. commissioned report accused the world body for being "timid, disorganized and misguided before the massacres and failing to intervene once the killing has started." In April 2000, the UN. Security Council admitted responsibility for the inaction.[39]

The initial bedeviling question as to why the UN failed to respond to the cry calls of the UN commander on the ground have now been answered following revealing reports, investigations, and public admissions to wrongdoing. When Kofi Annan, the then head of the peacekeeping department of the UN, received Dallaire's fax of warning it was reported that he dismissed it as an "old story."[40]

There is consensus now that the UN debacle came not from any lack of information but from lack of political will by the most powerful in the UN. It is instructive that a repentant Kofi Annan wants to promote an international political culture that will promote transparency and prevent bureaucratic silence. In a speech during the 10th anniversary of the genocide, Annan confessed, "I believed at the time that I was doing my best. But I realized after the genocide that there was more that I could have done to send the alarm and rally support."[41]

Guilt and Acknowledgement

The acknowledgement criterion of an apology process demands that all those implicated be prepared to accept the blame for their action or inaction that resulted in their failure to prevent the genocide. Aside from the intervention by the Tutsi dominated RPF and other political oppositions, who else tried to head off the impending violence? The parts played by the countries involved in the international quagmire and its catastrophic outcome are as varied as the contending national and group interests involved. First the crash of the plane that carried the Rwandan and Burundian presidents precipitated the retreat of the international presence in Rwanda. Then when ten Belgian soldiers and six civilians were killed, the Belgians evacuated their citizens. This was followed by the withdrawal of UNAMIR troops and the Belgian branch of Médicins Sans Frontières. The rapid withdrawal by Belgian troops had dramatic consequences when Rwandan refugees in a school were left unprotected and as a result were massacred by government and militia forces.[42]

The Belgian prime minister is the second international leader, following President Clinton, who formally acknowledged wrongdoing on behalf of Belgium for its inaction during the mass killings of minority Tutsis and moderate Hutus in the spring of 1994. On the occasion of the sixth anniversary of the genocide, Belgian Prime Minister Guy Verhofstadt told Rwandans in Kigali "I don't know if I will ever know if the terrible events of 1994 could have been avoided, but I am convinced that we could have done more, and we could have done better. A dramatic combination of negligence, incompetence and hesitation created the conditions for the tragedy."[43] In spite of the hindsight judgment on whether the genocide was preventable or not, that the Belgian authorities came forward to partially assume blame was considered a "quite significant gesture of solidarity and sympathy."[44]

About a year later in 2001, four Rwandans – two nuns, a professor and a businessman were tried in Belgium for taking part in the genocide. The highly publicized trial and a parliamentary commission that examined Belgium's responsibility and the events before and during the genocide, made the Belgian public most interested and supportive of humanitarian interventions. It seems as if the story of Belgium's failure in Rwanda in 1994 has created more guilt than 80 years of Belgian colonialism.[45] Rwandan leaders actually expressed the wish that France and other countries follow in Belgium's footsteps in asking forgiveness. France resisted similar acknowledgement of transgression.

France's defensive response to charges of inaction, even complicity with the perpetrators of the war crimes during the genocide, can only be explained within the context of its postcolonial dealings with Africa. Being a former Belgian colony and at least partially francophone in culture, Rwanda was of interest to the French who wanted to incorporate it into their sphere of influence. Thus the French government's alliance with the Rwandan regime had more to do with this strategic interest than affinity with pro-Hutu policies.[46] Hence the French government came to the aid of a Francophone Hutu regime in violation of a UN Security Council arms embargo, even during the time of the genocide. The French authorities defended their action of supplying arms to the embattled regime as legitimate, in spite of the secrecy of the operation and the use of indirect delivery through Zaire across the border. The official line by the French government and denial of any complicity is best expressed by its Chief of Staff Admiral Jacques Lanxade who declared, "We cannot be reproached for having armed the killers," and then added, "In any case, all those massacres were committed with sticks and machetes."[47] The French government refused to acknowledge the countervailing moral charges made against it and pleaded not guilty. In fact former government officials like Prime Minister Balladour claimed France was the only Western power that "intervened to limit the horror" referring to the French-led Opération Turquoise launched in June 1994.[48]

France's resistance to acknowledge guilt was shared at the outset by the United States, Belgium and other states. The resistant language by states is a habitual knee-jerk reaction of modern states that share the norm of mass violence without admitting to mass murder. Josias Semujanga's explanation is: "As the criminal is always the state, and as states are bound to coexist, at least within the UN, genocide is a disturbance, for it constitutes the only mistake that might lower the prestige of a political regime. Propaganda then comes to the rescue of the crime, and the term is negated."[49] French prevarication about arming the killers of Rwanda is consistent with the conscious separation of what statecraft dictates in strategic interest and power calculations from international ethics and morality. Not only was French policy pro-Hutu and pro-interim government, it also voted for reducing the presence of UNAMIR in the Security Council and was not in favor of humanitarian intervention.[50] Operation Turquoise, authorized by the UN Security Council on June 22, was a calculated decision by France to avert the Rwandan Patriotic Army (military wing of RPF) takeover (considered an Anglophone movement by France), to elevate its international image after its support for the Hutu interim government, to provide a safe haven for retreating Forces Armées Rwandaises (Rwandan Army) soldiers, to improve the French image among Francophone African countries and to strengthen French sphere of influence in the region.[51]

French prevarication can only be matched with American reticence when it comes to the Rwandan genocide. Because of a background of disinterest in the region in American foreign policy, and compassion fatigue toward the continent and its ailments by an American public, the first reports on the genocide were lost in cliché accounts of the violence - tribal warfare, civil war, failed states, and ancient hatreds. In hindsight, serious reporting and better political leadership could have persuaded the public to support action to prevent the genocide by making the public aware of the true nature of the violence. On the contrary, the Clinton administration consciously redirected public opinion to avoid possible intervention, calling the killings anything other than "genocide." So "over the next couple of months officials were instructed to replace the 'g' word with classic Clinton-speak: 'acts of genocide.'"[52] The real intention for not recognizing the reported violence as genocide was to avoid the obligation to act on the part of U.S.[53] Thus, the intentional ambiguity and reluctance to call the Rwandan genocide by its name came "from a desire to escape responsibility for sending reinforcements and from a feeling that intervention in internal affairs posed a difficult political issue."[54] At an interagency conference, Tony Marley, a former official of the U.S. Department of State, rose above these obfuscations and called for the truth: "Let's at least be honest among ourselves. Let's acknowledge what is real and then make the political decisions as to whether or not we can do something about it. But let's at least not pretend that genocide is not taking place. Let's not try to find some word to camouflage reality."[55] One or a few clear voices cannot make a difference when hushed by a compliant media and a government sanctioned effort to hide the truth.

The United States, represented by President Clinton, acknowledged the facts to do with inaction, but did not admit the calculated statecraft of malign neglect. In the now controversial speech at Kigali in 1998, Clinton admits that the international community, including African nations, "must bear its share of responsibility for this tragedy, as well. We did not act quickly enough after the killing began. We should not have allowed the refugee camps to become safe havens for the killers. We did not immediately call these crimes by their rightful name: genocide."[56] Clinton's words of contrition are disingenuous in that they gloss over the calculated decision to withdraw the UN military force in Rwanda rather than strengthen it, driven as it was by the policy of realpolitik, Presidential Decision Directive 25, put in place in reaction to American casualties in Somalia.

The acknowledgement of inaction by the Clinton Administration that came months after the genocide in a form of pseudo-apology is not an admission of guilt but a matter of redeeming the image of the state by telling a story of justification. It is clear now that the United States government considered not intervening in Rwanda for a number of reasons, the main one being the overextension of peacekeeping operations in Macedonia, Bosnia and Haiti. Above all the recent debacle in Somalia, where 18 American soldiers had been killed, was also on the minds of legislators on Capitol Hill. As a result they were in no mood to send American ground troops to Rwanda. The "Somalia syndrome" had in effect begun to shape American foreign policy in Africa.[57] This was a departure from the neo-Wilsonian rhetoric during the beginning of the Clinton Administration.

Before 1994 and the Rwandan crisis, the Clinton administration was more measured in its multilateralism. Presidential Decision Directive 25 spells out under what conditions the United States would support a U.N. peace operation, participate, and contribute combat troops. In order for the United States to participate, those conditions required that an operation had to be in clear response "to a threat to international peace and security, serve U.S. interests, and have an international consensus."[58] In other words, in order for the United States to be committed, a clear exit strategy and acceptable risk had to be ascertained. *Realpolitik* interests dictated the decisions made at the outset on the international crisis in spite of other justifications for nonintervention that were given. Not only did the administration make it clear that it would not be undertaking military action to arrest the violence, it also actively sought the removal of UNAMIR and later settled for a reduction in its size.[59]

Finally, how is the acknowledgement imperative met by UN authorities? A year after the end of the genocide the then Secretary-General of the United Nations, Boutros-Ghali, arrived in Kigali to address the Rwandan National Assembly. The Secretary-General bragged that he was "the first to use the word genocide in the international assemblies in order to secure and mobilize and sensitize international public opinion."[60] The gist of his address is that he had done more than others on behalf of Rwandans, and therefore he had nothing to apologize for. Yet when the present Secretary-General, Kofi Annan, addressed the same political body three years later, he began with an acknowledgement that the world had failed to act and claimed lack of foreknowledge to absolve the United Nations organization and key officials saying: "looking back now, we see the signs which then were not recognized. Now we know that what we did was not nearly enough -- not enough to save Rwanda from itself, not enough to honor the ideals for which the United Nations exists. We will not deny that, in their greatest hour of need the world failed the people of Rwanda."[61] We can note that several African states had been ready to perform peacekeeping operations. However, the OAU (Organization of African Union) relegated responsibility to the United Nations that had the infrastructure and the means to provide logistics along with the major powers. In both UNAMIR I and UNAMIR II, African soldiers made up the majority. African units also contributed to the French-led Operation Turquoise.[62]

In each of these apologies, Belgium excepted, a narrative of excuse is advanced whereby the implicated nation constructs the facts to service – an account, an excuse or a justification in one's defense and thereby acquiring vindication without paying for the transgression. The narratives of excuse are the apologia true to the meaning of the written or oral defense, in the classic Greek sense.

Accountability and Moral Responsibility

The acknowledgement of genocide is tied to a political discourse that is rooted in state-centric institutions and a morality that wittingly or unwittingly privileges state violence. Thus the occurrences of mass murder are not immediately acknowledged as human tragedy until a concert of nations define it to be so as Joshua Semujanga aptly points out:

> A quick review of twentieth-century genocides shows that the genocide is a particular narrative insofar as the victim is recognized only when the UN accepts the discourse on murder as true. For this reason, the narrative of genocide is a narrative of justification, since it comes after the massacre in order to sanction the commission of a crime.[63]

Semujanga writes "we saw terrible scenes in the media, like *Interahamwe* militiamen murdering a woman in the presence of Blue Berets. When a journalist asked them why they did not intervene, they answered that they did not have any mandate to do so."[64] No matter how shocking an image it conjures in our mind, this inaction reveals the gap between state-legal institutions and humanity present on the ground, and between insensitive international civil servants and the vulnerable victims of mass violence.

Even after the Bosnian and Rwandan debacles the massacres in Darfur of the Sudan have fallen victim to the same old politics of semantics, legality and national interest, fatally delaying robust humanitarian intervention. The Rwandan genocide would not be unique in generating apologies that turned out to be, for the most part, narratives of justification that came only *post facto*. President Clinton's apology to Rwandans fits this bill. His apologetic speech on March 25, 1998 in Kigali was the first formal acknowledgement of failure by the United States to avert the genocide when it was in its power to do so. His mea culpa, however, is hidden behind repentance on behalf of the international community rather than the state he represented:

> We did not immediately call these crimes by their rightful name: genocide. ... It may seem strange to you here, especially the many of you who lost members of your family, but all over the world there were people like me sitting in their offices, day after day after day, who did not fully appreciate the depth and the speed with which you were being engulfed by this unimaginable terror.[65]

That widely publicized speech by Clinton was an apology, in the classic sense, of telling a story. Clinton's account and explanation for the inaction on the part of the international community, and the United States under that international umbrella, released him of any accountability.[66] That officials in Washington and New York had information prior to and during the violence is now well-documented. There were early reports from humanitarian and other international organizations, as well as the CIA warning of the building storm of violence. Human Rights Watch's Allison Des Forges had reported that some senior Rwandan military men had communicated with the Clinton administration warning of impending violence. Then of course was that urgent message from the UN Commander on the ground ignored by UN authorities referred to earlier. These facts fly in the face of the claim by the Clinton administration that it did not have full knowledge that genocide was in progress in the spring of 1994. Although one could argue that predicting the turn of events was impossible, the evidence is now clear that by April of that year mass killing was taking place, although it was not labeled as genocide at the time.[67] According to some observers, even though the United States can share the blame with the United Nations, "the Clinton administration must accept a disproportionate share of the responsibility, for it had a disproportionate amount of political, economic, and military influence in the United Nations and the international community. Only the U.S. government could have overcome the numerous obstacles to more forceful engagement."[68]

Clinton's apology is an extension of the narrative of justification by states that are expected to assume state responsibility or state culpability. When state agents acknowledge wrongdoing and that they are accountable for it, their moral position can only be weighed against what they did and what they failed to do. Also, when leaders bear guilt on behalf of states they represent, they become part of a newer narrative of guilt that is constructed by a performative language.[69] As Charles L Briggs puts it: "Constructing an event as genocide places it in relationship to other acts and creates conduits for the circulation of accusations."[70] The Rwandan genocide discourse therefore includes excuses, regrets and accusations emanating from contending sources.

Among the many regretful hindsight criticisms, one that stands out is the position that claims the Rwandan genocide could have been prevented if only the Western powers and those with military means had intervened. One observer concludes that the war crime tribunal in Arusha, Tanzania, is testament to the failure of the U.S. and other Western countries that necessitated the experiment in international justice. Hence, no war crimes meant "no war crimes tribunal."[71]

The "could have been" and "if only" arguments of the narratives of regret can be measured against a standard of ideal speech situations that inform the apology process. Among the consensus reached by participants in this discourse, one condemning argument is that the international community should have begun by disarming and disbanding the Hutu militia in that fateful spring of 1994. What needed to be done fell victim to squabbles among the U.N. civil servants and the commanding general on the ground. While the U.N. Secretary-General estimated a large force was needed, a more modest number of troops, but with forceful rules of engagement, requested by UNAMIR Force Commander General Dallaire was rejected outright.[72]

Michael Barnett's condemnation of failure to be accountable, against the Clinton administration and the United Nations, is among the most compelling of the discourses of regret. Barnett accuses the U.S. of muzzling "the call for intervention" and later obstructing "those who wanted to intervene."[73] Then, he goes on to argue, in response to criticisms the U.S. kept changing its justification: at first American officials argued there was no peace to keep in a civil war, later Clinton declared he was unaware of what was really going on. An apology for inaction seems to lend itself to malleable justifications and lame excuses. One of those is best expressed by Barnett: "The United States was only behaving like other states: sure, it did not care enough to send troops, but no state did. American behavior was excusable because everyone behaved badly."[74] Furthermore, the same author lays the blame at the foot of the United Nations for its collective silence. In spite of the best funeral faces and passionate speeches, the U.N. lacked the political will to deliver the necessary troops to prevent the genocide.[75]

A speech act such as the apologetic excuse given by Clinton disguises the true nature of power relations and the role presidents and prime ministers assume as state agents. A state agent who acts as mouthpiece for a collectivity becomes its moral agent only when he or she truly represents the people and makes binding commitments and on the record. Short of that, it lacks, as Tavuchis argues, "the moral imprimatur of the group, [and] amounts to no apology at all."[76]

While the efficacy of an apology is difficult to assess as demonstrated here by Clinton's attempt and earlier by that of the Belgian prime minister, it is even more equivocal when the Secretary-General of the United Nations delivers it as the representative agent of the international community. The UN leader was rebuked by Rwandan leaders before and after his speech. Annan defended the peacekeepers "blaming the lack of political will by member states to intervene and saying Rwandans must also take some responsibility," which did not go down well with Rwandan officials.[77] The Rwandan leaders had hoped "for an apology for the United Nations' failure to prevent the 1994 slaughter, despite warnings it was coming."[78] As one Rwandan official reacted, "Mr. Secretary-General, your speech yesterday at parliament made us suffer."

Accountability differs from acknowledgement in the questions it poses. Irrespective of the affective dimensions of trauma such as guilt and culpability, the accountability imperative demands who is morally responsible for the genocide. Obviously those who perpetrated the crimes, the genocidaires, are ultimately responsible. If we limit the question to only those who had the power to prevent the genocide, once again, how can we determine who is responsible? Is moral responsibility contingent on causality and consequences? Does it depend on role and institutional responsibility? Revisiting the cases of apology discussed so far, the Belgian Prime Minister, the American President, and the U.N.

secretary-generals acted as mouthpiece for their respective collectivity. As such, they accepted culpability for the most part but were careful not to be the delegates of collective guilt. In this sense, accountability and moral responsibility come easier for these state agents because they can represent their communities without any authoritative commitment. Clinton, for example, did not account for the U.S. role in the failure by bringing the U.S. under the international umbrella in his apology, thereby "lumping together responsibility with global indifference."[79] By the same token, when Kofi Annan was asked why the U.N. had not intervened, he replied: "The question should not be addressed only to the United Nations, or even to its Member States. Each of us as an individual has to take his or her share of responsibility."[80] Michael Barnett points out appropriately: "The very individuals who had made the momentous decisions were now relocating responsibility by 'democratizing' blame."[81] Seen in this light, these apologies amount to obfuscation of personal responsibility, and in democratizing blame they lay the ground for further indifference excluding any hope of genuine remorse. This flaw in public apologies is directly related to the next imperative of telling the truth.

Truth-telling, Memories and Narrative

The process of reconstructing the event of the Rwandan genocide to come to terms with the past involved acknowledgement, accountability on the part of all those implicated, and exposing the truth. The truth about the genocide was first reported and investigated by fact-finding commissions, and finally was introduced to the forum of the United Nations to be officially acknowledged. Comparisons were made with other genocides, especially the Holocaust.

One comparison suggests, in its stages and extent of destruction, Rwanda is similar to the Holocaust considering the "registration of victims, organized indoctrination of killing squads, systematic use of media, mobilization of armed groups and escalation of violence."[82] The Holocaust-like efficiency and the ideological propaganda and ideology of hate is best demonstrated in the fine-tuned hate campaign by Hutu extremists:

> Prejudice in Rwanda was carefully nurtured by the memory of this earlier imbalance so that Tutsi's became the hated 'other,' considered 'cockroaches' to be exterminated. In March 1993 the Hutu newspaper *Kangura* published an article entitled, 'A Cockroach Cannot Give Birth to a Butterfly.' In graphic terms, Kangura underlined the insect like qualities it attributed to the enemy and underscored the ideology that a 'cockroach,' whatever one might think of him as an individual, is part of a group he can never leave.'[83]

If Rwanda's genocide has been compared with the European Holocaust, it did not solicit similar response from the rest of the world. While the political discourse of the 1990s and after may have established Rwanda among the most brutal genocides of the twentieth century, the debates on the true nature of the genocide and how to best bring about reconciliation are far from over. Even the legal steps taken to establish an international tribunal have been no substitute to genuine changes of heart and commitment by the international community to prevent other genocides in the new century. For one scholar, legalist words have been substitutes for political actions in Rwanda and Bosnia. As Judith Shklar implies, "The idea that all international problems will dissolve with the establishment of an international court with compulsory jurisdiction is an invitation to political indolence. It allows one to make no alterations in domestic political action and thought, to change no attitudes, to try no new approaches and yet appear to be working for peace."[84] This observation is similar to charges of burying the truth of the genocide under either bureaucracy or myth. The establishment and work of truth commissions have gained respect in their truth-telling and restorative powers.

In South Africa's Truth and Reconciliation Commission (TRC) radical experiment exposing the truth became paramount to its success. It sought to bring about in post-apartheid South Africa a restorative rather than a retributive justice. That democratic forum gave the possibility for victims and survivors to tell their stories of victimization as much as it allowed perpetrators to confess and repent. Driven by the Christian idea of penance and the African concept of *ubuntu*, meaning compassion or empathy, the commission's philosophy, as articulated by Archbishop Desmond Tutu, aimed at forgiveness. In Marina Warner's astute assessment:

> The TRC did not require apology as such from those who appeared before it. If the crime were committed for political ends, full disclosure was deemed sufficient. Above all, it did not follow up any crime, however heinous, with penalties if the perpetrator cooperated. By implication, the witnesses combined the two opposing discourses of apologia as vindication and apology as we know it. By explaining what and how they had done what they did, they were somehow divested of it; by fully acknowledging their guilty participation in evils, they contributed to the purification of the nation's memory.[85]

Criticisms regarding the shortcomings of the TRC abound, such as: the pursuit of truth for healing compromised evidence, relativized truth, and most seriously, led to the miscarriage or neglect of justice. Some pointed out the fact that national truth commissions could "turn perpetrators into social outcasts" and force them "to face victims," but that those sanctions were not proportional to the crimes committed.[86] Yet the South African model was not a legal tribunal as in Nuremberg. Truth-telling was meant to be therapeutic and healing not punishment. Such a public effort toward reconciliation was carried out at the expense of evading justice and would not bring about closure, others argued. One such critic is Nahla Valji who says:

The TRC was tasked with uncovering and recording instances of 'gross human rights violations' – defined narrowly as killings, torture, and severe mistreatment. This exclusive focus on individual crimes and the 'excesses' of the apartheid regime came at the cost of largely ignoring the institutional violence that characterised National Party rule for over four decades.[87]

Nigerian writer and human rights activist, Wole Soyinka, would agree with the above assessment considering reparations as the missing link between Truth and Reconciliation. In his characteristic honesty, Soyinka imagines Archbishop Desmond Tutu approaching his compatriots and saying to them: "White brothers and sisters in the Lord, you have sinned, but we are willing to forgive. The scriptures warn us that the wages of sin are death but, in your case, they seem to be wealth. If therefore you chose to shed a little of that sinful wealth as a step toward atonement … etc. etc."[88] What Soyinka is warning against is the indefinite postponement of harmonization founded on responsibility and justice because pragmatism requires making deals and concessions in the short run in societies in transformation.[89] It could also be a hint that the proved antidotes against bureaucratic silence or myth are historicity and art.

Just as the history of the genocide is debated and through that process we come to understand the fact of the genocide, artistic works will help to convey the truth in imaginative ways. Lamko's novel derives from a writers' project that was initiated in the late 90s by a Chadian writer, Nocky Djedanoum, who challenged other African writers to create a literary monument for Rwanda by breaking what he characterized as the silence of African intellectuals on the genocide. Ten African writers answered his call, went to Rwanda to speak to survivors and visit mass graves, and the majority of them wrote literary pieces. Lamko, the author of *The Moth of the Hills*, has remained in Rwanda to direct the national theater. The writers' aim is to write "because of the duty to remember, to write to counter oblivion, and to commemorate the dead."[90] These artists are reckoning with what happened. It is as if they were beckoned by the spirits of the dead to tell the truth about the genocide. It is a lofty task because not only are these Africans among all of "us" implicated but they have also the burden of witnessing, an awesome responsibility that can result in feelings of guilt.

When asked about his emotions while he was writing his novel *The Moth of the Hills*, Koulsy Lamko replied: "I had the choice between silence and speaking: an unbearable dilemma when one is neither deaf nor dumb. For the former, silence would reinforce the 'blackout' over Rwanda and would strengthen revisionist theories. The second exposed me to criticism but at least enabled me to talk about it."[91] Lamko writes trauma as a process, as a therapeutic project, to work through the trauma and give voice to the painful past.[92]

Lamko's Phalène des Collines complements the specificity of historiography with empathy in the representational voices of the Rwandan genocide - the

Rwandan queen ravaged and killed brutally in the genocide; Pelouse, a Rwandan-American journalist who is on assignment to discover the truth; Epiphany,
Pelouse's cousin and a survivor whose family was slaughtered in her presence;
Fred, an African exile obsessed by the genocide; a curious fat American priest
and a young African priest depicted as a European stooge. The queen's spirit in
the guise of a moth and which can also assume other bodies, can find peace only
when she is acknowledged and properly mourned with the traditional celebration
of her life and the rites of libation and offerings to the ancestors.

Among the poignant moments of the narrative is the apparition queen expressing her outrage at the attempt by tourists, curiosity seekers and the voyeurs
of the gruesome to measure the horror in statistics. She rages:

> How many did you say? 20,000 dead in this tiny church? Are you sure of what
> you are saying? ... It is more like 5,000 to be closer to the truth. The awful Ma-
> sungu with his arithmetic and his doubts. I started to boil when visitors spent
> time on numbers and with their eyes started counting one head, two heads,
> three skulls, one hundred fibulas, one thousand femora, 19,980 shoulder blades,
> so many trash bags full to the brim, as if our shiny bones were to be counted
> like matches in kindergarten."[93]

And she hovers, intervenes and plays mischievous tricks on those who ignore her ignoble murder, who misrepresent the truth of the genocide, and are
simply tourists of death. In the end it is the Rwandan-American, Pelouse, who
fulfills her wish by performing the proper rites that will release the queen from
this world enabling her to enter the City of Time. In order for wandering souls to
rest with finality, according to many traditional African religions, their living
kindred are obligated to appease them, to fulfill their wishes, to answer their
questions in order to avoid being haunted by them. For the African, settling outstanding issues with the dead takes precedence over memorializing. Then comes
commemoration - a task that was earnestly undertaken by the post-genocide
Rwandan government.

The remains of victims were retrieved from mass graves in order to be re-
buried. Individuals sought surviving relatives to reestablish a bond. On the one-
year anniversary of the outbreak of the genocide, commemorations and official
remembrances multiplied. Monuments were erected to remember the victims. In
some places skulls were piled up in public locations while the remaining were
put to rest in mass graves. In other areas the original sites of the killings such as
churches and school compounds were left as they were to memorialize the dead
and remind the living. More personal remembrances were the naming of the
newborn after dead family members, the planting of trees at mass graves, and
the keeping and guarding the personal belongings of the dead to honor the deceased.[94] Lessons seem to have been learned from the European Holocaust to
avoid a genocide metanarrative that would undermine the memories of victims
and the lives of survivors. African traditions in commemoration and healing are

active and alive at the grassroots to prevent "forgetting" and to encourage redress.

In the apologies made by the leaders charged with inaction, we have seen a variety of evasive excuses by those who are not prepared to take any responsibility for wrong-doing. With the exception of those cases where a truth commission is formed, as in South Africa, truth claims will continue to be made by historiography to reveal past misdeeds and wrongdoing. In addition the truth claims of fiction and art in dealing with a traumatic past are equally important as a weapon against the banalization of unimaginable crimes.

Public Remorse

Apology for inaction compounds the problem of accountability and remorse. The fact the implicated parties – namely, the U.S., Belgium and the UN are only guilty of not acting to prevent the Rwandan genocide has a bearing on what each is expected to be responsible and remorseful for. After all, even though each is implicated in varying degrees, none can be accused of being the perpetrators of the horrendous crime. One should keep this premise in mind when assessing the presence, lack or degree of remorse of these states. Let me first consider President Clinton's apology to Rwandan survivors.

Clinton's apology at Kigali Airport in 1998 is significant since it was the first to come from among the major power players of the Rwandan tragedy. Yet the apologetic remorse of that speech act is fraught with problems. To begin with, the particular choice of words used in the speech does not singularly identify the United States and the role it played in the final months and days before the 1994 genocidal killings began in Kigali. The acknowledgement of wrongdoing and responsibility by the United States is buried in a diffusion of guilt referring to America among others. The undifferentiated "we" does not underscore that fact that the Clinton Administration purposefully decided not to authorize forceful intervention by the United Nations to prevent that catastrophic violence. Thus not owning up to America's part of the consequences of its moral negligence undermines the weight of this public remorse by proxy.

Another aspect of the speech act also subtracts from the weight of the sincerity of the remorse for American inaction. Clinton in that speech justifies the inaction more than he apologizes for the consequences thereof. His statement about not being aware of the impending disaster, contrary to what was to be revealed later, is disingenuous, to say the least. The Kigali speech is devoid of any language of contrition either as an apology by proxy, on behalf of the American people, or in the personal sense. The most sympathetic of the words he used in his speech were not exactly repentant: "I have come today to pay the respects of my nation to all who suffered and all who perished in the Rwandan genocide."[95]

The absence of any trace of affect in the speech is rather remarkable for a president known for his Baptist pulpit style.

Furthermore the remorse imperative is not fulfilled in this case because it lacked the formality of an address before a legislative body or as a part of public record such as a treaty or an agreement. The brief interlude in Rwanda and his speech at the Kigali Airport, while the engines of the Air force One were running, gives the impression of an African safari stop rather than an official state visit with a solemn agenda. Moreover, if the apologetic speech act is representative of U.S. apology for inaction in Rwanda, it was not accompanied by similar sentiments in the U.S. Congress that could have legitimized that apology.

Ten years after the Rwandan genocide, Clinton's personal repentance and regrets have been actualized in his humanitarian missions and projects in Africa including Rwanda. The Clinton Foundation has contributed money to HIV/AIDS programs as well as towards the construction of the new genocide memorial. However, on April 7, 2004, the tenth anniversary of Rwanda's 1994 genocide, all Western leaders, President Clinton included, were conspicuously absent from the memorial ceremonies, with the exception of Belgian Prime Minister Guy Verhofstadt.

Guy Verhofstadt is the second international leader after President Clinton to assume publicly responsibility for Belgian inaction to avert the genocide. In his 2000 speech of apology to Rwandans, Verhofstadt was much clearer in pronouncing Belgium's share of blame for failure to act than Clinton was. The presence of the only Western leader for the 10th anniversary memorial observations and Belgium's contribution for the commemoration were seen as reconciliatory and remorseful. On the same day of the anniversary another memorial site was also officially opened, in the presence of the prime minister, for the ten Belgian UN peacekeeping soldiers who were slaughtered at the outset of the genocide ten years earlier.

Kofi Annan, the Secretary-General of the United Nations, whose "I and the whole international community share your pain" apology speech before the Rwandan parliament received a chilly reception in 1998, did not go to Kigali either in 2004. Annan had apologized again in 1999 after a UN-sponsored report rebuked the UN and its members for failing to heed the warning of genocidal plans and act on it. Annan's expression of "deep remorse" failed to satisfy Rwandans who expected a more formal public apology. A week before the occasion of the 10th anniversary Annan had accepted a more pronounced institutional and personal blame for not doing enough to prevent the Rwandan genocide by saying, "I realized after the genocide that there was more that I could and should have done to sound the alarm and rally support."[96] On the day of the anniversary, Kofi Annan was in Geneva addressing the UN Human Rights Commission: "We cannot afford to wait until the worst has happened, or is already happening, or end up with little more than futile hand-wringing or callous indifference."[97] He was referring to the Darfur crisis in the Sudan.

Most political leaders have come to agree on the lessons of Rwanda by the year 2004, a healthy departure from just a few years earlier when many were oblivious of what was taking place on the ground. When Secretary of State Madeleine Albright addressed the Organization of African Unity in Addis Ababa in December1998, she admitted that there is a consensus of opinion now that the international community "should have been more active in the early stages of the atrocities in Rwanda in 1994, and called them what they were – genocide."[98] Her words were regretful but not apologetic. Philip Gourevitch recounts, "On the morning of Albright's visit to Rwanda in December, Hutu Power terrorists, shouting 'kill the cockroaches,' had hacked, bludgeoned, and shot to death more than three hundred Tutsis at an encampment in the northwest, and in the days before Clinton's arrival in Kigali, as many as fifty Tutsis were killed in similar massacres."[99] The Rwandan genocide is perhaps setting a new precedent in that leaders cannot easily ignore crimes against humanity with bureaucratic indifference. This new reality heralds a moral community where international public opinion holds global leaders responsible.

Bill Clinton was in the presence of a few of the survivors of the Rwanda genocide when he gave his Kigali apology. Even so, staged and performative communication falls short of the power of apology by the wrongdoer in the presence of the victims. He was more forceful in his repentance but his words, as well as Albright's, diplomatically correct and soothing as they were, were not too reassuring nor were they related to the realities on the ground. The words of contrition by Albright, Clinton and the leaders of Belgium and the United Nations will finally gain their currency if the apologies are on public record and political actions are taken to honor those records. Did these leaders commit their governments in the reconstruction of Rwanda, for example?

The last imperative in the apology process, that of public remorse, is most complicated since we conceive remorse as an individual affective response to one's regrettable actions. Exchanges between collectivities and their deputies are few and far between by the very fact that remorse is delegated, which makes it lose its affective force. If we were to judge the success of the public remorse of Belgium, the United States and the United Nations then, we have to look not only into the languages of contrition by their deputies, but whether the victims are assured that the wrong will never happen again, and if the deputies contribute to the rebuilding, restoring and healing the society.[100]

Claims and Deeds

On the eve of the tenth anniversary of the Rwandan genocide a representative of Ibuka, one of Rwanda's genocide victims organizations, in a speech broadcast by Radio Rwanda, angrily calls for compensation and rehabilitation and an investigation of the big powers, notably, "USA, Great Britain, France, Belgium" and of "any person guilty of non-assistance to persons or group of persons in danger, anyone guilty of complicity by silence, anyone of ignoring facts."[101] This desperate voice is representative of the demands for reparation made by survivor individuals and groups. Rwandan government officials were more diplomatic. During a memorial conference in Canada, a few days before the tenth anniversary, Rwandan Foreign Affairs Minister Charles Murigande said, "his government had 'hoped for much better support' from the international community for rebuilding the country and compensating survivors." [102]

Whether the demands for reparations are private or public, the reactions by officials of the big powers, those who were accused of not intervening to prevent the genocide have remained the same. They say the international community can be blamed for institutional failure, as UN Secretary-General Kofi Annan likes to say, but massive reparations are out of question. It is as if responsibilities have been diluted by the democratization of blame. As Canadian Foreign Affairs Minster Bill Graham bluntly declared, "I don't believe the Canadian government would take the position that reparations would be an effective way to address the tragic consequences of the Rwandan genocide. Reparations assume that you have a process whereby you can clearly indicate who's responsible and how much they have to pay."[103]

In spite of opposition to reparations, multinational agencies and individual countries have provided aid for reconstruction purposes. Moral responsibility seems to be subsumed by individual nations and the international community through the UN, without pursuing restitutive justice. For example, in 2004, the Support of International Partnership against AIDS in Africa (SIPAA), a UK funded body, donated 47 billion Rwandan francs for fighting HIV/AIDS.[104] The United States has contributed over 700 million dollars in development and economic assistance since 1994 to support reconstruction and reconciliation. According to OECD statistics the top aid giving countries in 2002-2003 were the US, the UK, Netherlands, Belgium, Sweden, Germany, and France, in that order. These bilateral aids were also supplemented by the UN and other multilateral assisted programs. Yet, by 2004 several aid programs are barely meeting the needs of survivors who make nearly half of the country's population. The funding needs are many including reuniting families, education and medical care for children, micro-finance projects for women, and rebuilding the justice system.[105]

Rwanda's ability to pay for reconstruction and reconciliation is dependent on, at least viewed from top-down, on the nature of its economic development. The misleading characterization of economic stability and growth in Rwanda one sees in the headlines does not account for the fact that 40% of its national budget comes from international donors including grants and loans.[106] While the government's budget deficits are being made up by the relief funds, the more structural nature of Rwanda's economy reveals the weakness of the state in meeting the pressing reconstruction and reconciliation needs. Until the year 2000 Rwanda's external debt of US $1.2 billion was a drain on the economy obliging it to spend more on debt service than on health. Charging that debt is hampering reconstruction, the British House of Commons International Development Committee noted in a 1998 report that "The international Community failed to act when the genocide took place in Rwanda in 2004. It now has a responsibility to act to do everything possible to prevent such events recurring. Obviously debt relief is not the only condition necessary for recovery from genocide, but it is clear that debt relief can make a significant contribution." The second report from the same committee goes further in condemning the international financial institutions. The 1999 6th Report *Conflict Prevention and Post-Conflict Reconstruction* was highly critical of the IMF and World Bank:

> We requested memoranda from the IMF and the World Bank to find out their policies to Rwanda in the years leading up to the genocide of 1994 ... What is striking is the fact that the memoranda make no criticism of the Government's policy towards the Tutsi minority during this period. The end of the war is discussed as a prerequisite for the resumption of economic growth. Throughout the period, even when programmes were suspended, the IMF and the World Bank continued to talk with the Rwandan Government about conditions for the resumption of the programmes. [107]

This description of the vulnerability of Rwanda's polity and economy to external economic forces reveals a more permanent structural problem typical of postcolonial states in a capitalist global economy. There are those who see the events which led up to the genocide rooted in Rwanda's integration into the global economy during colonial times, monocropism, and eventual debt. The most acute of such criticisms is Peter Uvin's idea of "structural violence" applied to Rwanda's development or rather underdevelopment translated into poverty, inequality, exclusion, prejudice, humiliation feeding directly into the workings of genocide.[108]

A paradox of sorts has emerged in the reconstruction and reconciliation processes in Rwanda. On one hand, all the good intentions, programs and funding directed at rebuilding Rwanda are running against the inflexible ideas of neoliberal economic development, the overly privileged position of the Rwandan state to macro-manage the reconstruction, and Rwanda's geopolitical interests and conflict with its neighbors. On the other hand, a number of creative and positive steps are being taken to advance the reconciliation process. The release of 36,000 genocide suspects in July 2005 and the plan for their psychological rehabilitation and reintegration into society has raised hopes for the future. The released prisoners will pass four to six weeks in solidarity camps (*Ingando*) where they take part in group counseling, recreational activities and communal work, as well as instruction on justice and reconciliation.[109] The release of those prisoners is provisional with the stipulation that those who have confessed to genocide crimes will face *gaçaça* courts. Aside from relieving the congested jail houses, the gaçaça courts are designed to pave the way to national reconciliation. The focus of this traditional justice is on confession and apology. Those convicted receive usually short sentences or carry out public service, while those who confess and ask for forgiveness are freed. This system of justice has attracted wide international support because Rwandans are beginning to own the post-genocide reconstruction process. Among the creative projects and initiatives contributing toward the reconstruction of Rwanda I will include former American President Clinton's campaign to mobilize funds to combat HIV/AIDS and more importantly to broker a landmark deal whereby four companies in India and South Africa agreed to reduce the cost of drugs that can provide medications for millions of people in Africa and the Caribbean at less than a third of the cost of patented versions. [110]

The apologies made by President Clinton in Kigali in 1998 were uttered long before the apologetic deeds by groups, nations and international organizations manifested themselves in Rwanda. Clinton's repentant words rung hollow because they were hidden behind the hazy language that describes the international community and did not articulate the moral responsibilities of those in the august halls of the United Nations who actually made the crucial decisions of not intervening to prevent the genocide. It is only when the personal remorse is separated from the remorse by proxy that we can assign credibility to Clinton's depth of remorse. On July 23, 2005, when visiting the Treatment and Research AIDS Centre in Kigali, his sixth tour of the African continent, the former president expressed that the genocide was his "personal failure." Ironically, for a politician with rhetorical skills, his deeds have spoken louder than his words.

Notes

1.   Dominick LaCapra, *Writing History, Writing Trauma* (Baltimore: John Hopkins University Press, 2001), 19.

2.   Rory Carroll, "Arts: In memory of murder: Can art help ease Rwanda's pain?" *The Guardian (London),* March 24, 2004, feature pages, http:www.lexis-nexus.com/.

3.   The term genocide coined by Raphaël Lemkin in 1944 on the basis of its etymological roots to genos (race) and cide (kill) has been subject to many interpretations and debates. In 1945 the United Nations General Assembly approved a convention on genocide giving such crime a legal content. For a thoughtful discussion of genocide and the social discourse associated with it, see Josias Semujanga, *Origins of Rwandan Genocide* (New York: Humanity Book, 2003), 49-70. Semujanga asserts that using the word genocide is a moral act: "The performative dimension of the word is so important that the speaker uttering 'genocide' says also, and necessarily, 'I condemn murder'." see, 50.

4.   Journalist Fergal Keane lists this fact in his "A Chronicle of Genocide" section of his book, *Season of Blood: A Rwandan Journey* (New York: Viking, 1995), 195.

5.   In *Me Against My Brother*, Scott Peterson discusses French intervention in Rwanda in the context of colonial interest in Africa. The French, he concludes, went

beyond protecting their reputation in this part of Africa by maintaining that "the battle being waged was all-important and on a different plane: to preserve the gains of French culture and language against what were seen as threats from Anglo-Saxons." *Me Against My Brother: At War in Somalia, Sudan, and Rwanda* (New York: Routledge, 2000), 280.

6.   Arthur Jay Klinghoffer, *The International Dimension of Genocide in Rwanda* (Washington Square, NY: New York University Press, 1998), 30.

7.   Klinghoffer, 35-37.

8.   Klinghoffer. 35.

9.   Rory Carroll.

10.   Josias Semujanga, in *Origins of Rwandan Genocide,* describes CDR (Coalition for the Defense of the Republic) as the extremist Hutu party responsible for the ideology of the 1994 Tutsi genocide. The ideology is a "readaptation of the program of a strong popular party, the Party for Hutu Emancipation (PARMEHTU)." Parmehutu-Cederism is then "self-perceived as the sole defender of the republic and considering the other parties as "accomplices of the enemy." This ideology is referred to as "Hutu power" in other works, 46.

11.   Anthropologist Christopher C. Taylor's *Sacrifice as Terror* is most incisive in its insight as it employs Rwandan ritual and practices in order to explain much of the politics and the violence.   See Taylor, *Sacrifice as Terror: The Rwandan Genocide of 1994* (Oxford: New York: Berg, 1999), 131.
Taylor, *Sacrifice as Terror*, 131-132.

12.   Taylor, *Sacrifice as Terror*, 131-132

13.   Rory Carroll.

14.   I am borrowing LaCapra's intriguing notion of the need for "empathic unsettlement," discursively speaking, to undergo or act out traumatic events without avoiding and repressing memories. See Dominick LaCapra, *Writing History, Writing Trauma*, ix-42.

15.   Human Rights Watch Report, "Leave None to Tell the Story: Genocide in Rwanda," March 1999, 171-1, <http://www.hrw.org/reports/1999/rwanda/> (January 1, 2004).

16.   Human Rights Watch Report, "Leave None to Tell the Story."

17.   See Christopher C. Taylor, *Sacrifice as Terror*. Taylor concludes: "The Rwadan genocide of 1994 differs from earlier incidents of massive violence in the country's history in that women were targets of violence as much as, if not more than, men. This was especially the case where Tutsi women were concerned, but were not confined to them," 176.

18.   See Elizabeth Neuffer, *The Key to My Neighbor's House: Seeking Justice in Bosnia and Rwanda* (New York: Picador USA, 2001), 272.

19.   See Helmut Walser Smith (ed), *The Holocaust and Other Genocides* (Nashville: Vanderbilt University Press, 2002) for a valuable introduction and source. The collaborative work prepared as a curriculum is aimed for use by teachers and students.

20.   See Carol Rittner, John K. Roth, and Wendy Whitworth (eds), *Genocide in Rwanda: Complicity of the Churches?* (St. Paul, Minn.: Paragon House, 2004).

21.   Marie Césarie Mukarwego, "The Church and the Rwandan Tragedy of 1994," in *Genocide in Rwanda: Complicity of the Churches* (St. Paul: Minn., Paragon House, 2005), 122-123.

22.   Rory Carroll.

23.   Smith, 201.

24. For a good analysis of the process of the decision not to act on the part of the United States consult Robert C. DiPrizio, *Armed Humanitarians: U.S. Interventions from Northern Iraq to Kosovo* (Baltimore: The Johns Hopkins University Press, 2002), 77-83.

25. DiPrizio, 79. See also United Nations Report: U.N. Department of Peacekeeping Operations, "Comprehensive Report of Lessons Learned from the United Nations Assistance Mission for Rwanda (UNAMIR), October 1993-April 1996," available at www.un.org/Depts/dpko/lessons/rwanda.htm and Daalder in William Durch (ed) *UN Peacekeeping, American Policy, and the Uncivil Wars of the 1990s.*

26. A descendant of the Armenian Genocide, Peter Balakian, attaches importance to Robert Lifton's notion of numbing as a process by which "[the] self distances itself from traumatic experience." Of the pragmatic silence of his grandmother, Balakian writes: "In the case of my grandmother, Nafina, I'll never know of her inner life in the years following the Genocide. Perhaps no one did. After the Genocide, she was silent for more than two decades until the dam broke and she had a breakdown in the wake of the Japanese attack on Pearl Harbor in 1941. The U.S. entry into World War II triggered genocide flashbacks. But after the electroshock treatment worked, she returned to silence… If my grandmother did not often go to that inner place of the deep wound, it may have been in good part because she lived in a state of numbness," Peter Balakian, *Black Dog of Fate: An American Son Uncovers His Armenian Past* (New York: Broadway Books, 1998), 286-289.

27. LaCapra, *Writing History, Writing Trauma*, 76-81.

28. LaCapra, 50-51.

29. See Johan Pottier, *Re-imagining Rwanda: Conflict, Survival and Disinformation in the Late Twentieth Century* (Cambridge, UK: Cambridge University Press, 2002), 47.

30. Taylor, *Sacrifice as Terror*, 93.

31. Mahmood Mamdani, *When Victims Become Killers: Colonialism, Nativism, and the Genocide in Rwanda* (Princeton, NJ: Princeton University Press, 2001), 34.

32. Nigel Eltringham, *Accounting for Horror: Post-Genocide Debates in Rwanda* (London: Pluto Press, 2004), 33.

33. Rory Carroll.

34. Benjamin Sehene, "Rwanda's collective amnesia," *UNESCO Courier* (December 1999), 33.

35. For an excellent treatment of the reconciliation challenges of the post-genocide regime see Eugenia Zorbas "Reconciliation in Post-Genocide Rwanda." *African Journal of Legal Studies*, 1, 1 (2004), 29-52.

36. It is interesting to note, according to Samantha Power, a few years after 1994, Clinton displayed outrage and surprise when he read Philip Gourevitch's stories in the New Yorker that gave details of the horrors of the genocide. Samantha Power, "Bystanders to Genocide: Why the United States Let the Rwandan Tragedy Happen." *The Atlantic*, September 2001.

37. The National Security Archive is a nonprofit organization that uses the Freedom of Information Act to secure the release of classified U.S. government documents. The documents released in 2001 reveal that the U.S. government had information to act on and avert the Rwandan genocide. See "The US and the Genocide in Rwanda 1994." *The National Security Archive*. Ed. William Ferroggiaro, August 20, 2001. <www.nsarchive.org>

38. Colette Braeckman, "Rwanda Trial Opens Belgians' Eyes." *BBC News*,

June 7, 2001.

39. Grant McCool, "At Rwanda Memorial Panel, Annan Admits UN Blame." *Reuters*, March 26, 2004.

40. Farhan Haq, "Annan's Qualified Apology for Inaction in Rwanda." *Inter Press Service*, May 2, 1998, <http://www.oneworld.org>

41. "Annan Accepts Blame For Rwandan Genocide." *U.N. Wire*, March 29, 2004. <http://www.unwire.org/UNWire/20040329/449_22259.asp>

42. Klinghoffer, 89.

43. "Belgium apologizes for inaction during genocide," *The Gazette* (Montreal, Quebec), April 8, 2000.

44. "Belgium apologizes."

45. "Rwanda trial opens Belgians' eyes," BBC News online, June 7, 2001, < http://news.bbc.co.uk/2/hi/europe/1375603.stm> (February 22, 2003).

46. Klinghoffer, 87-88.

47. Peterson, 281-282.

48. "Ex-French officials deny France aided Rwandan genocide," CNN, April 21, 1998. <http://www.cnn.com?WORLD/africa/> 9804/21/rwanda.inquiry/ (October 22, 2003).

49. Josias Semujanga's *Origins of Rwandan Genocide*," 53-54.

50. In the months leading to the fateful spring of 1994 the French foreign ministry was receiving in Paris Rwandan interim-government officials and leaders of the Hutu extremist CDR party, Klinghoffer, 80-81.

51. Klinghoffer, 81.

52. DiPrizio, 81.

53. Klinghoffer, 99.

54. Smith, 206.

55. Tony Marley interview, *Frontline*: The Triumph of Evil, January 26, 1999, electronic files, Public Broadcasting System, <www.pbs.org/wgbh/pages/frontline/shows/Evil> (November 2001).

56. USIS Washington File, *Transcript*: "Clinton Meets with Rwanda Genocide Survivors," March 25, 1998. <www.usia.gov/regional/af/prestrip/w980325a.htm> (February 9, 2000)

57. Klinghoffer, 95.

58. Derision, 73.

59. Derision, 71-73.

60. Michael Barnett, *Eyewitness to A Genocide: The United Nations and Rwanda* (Ithaca and London: Cornell University Press, 2002), 153.

61. UN Secretary-General, "Secretary-General pledges support of UN for Rwanda's search for peace and progress," UN Press Release SG/SM/6552, AFR/SG, May 6, 1998, <http://www.reliefweb.int> (May 19, 2004).

62. Klinghoffer, 79.

63. Semujanga, 55.

64. Semujanga, *Origins of Rwandan Genocide*, 245. Avoiding other methods of analyzing genocide, Semujanga claims various forms of discourse and textual analysis can illuminate the nature and causes of genocide.

65. " Clinton Addresses Rwandan Genocide Survivors, U.S. Information Service," Transcript, Washington File, March 25, 1998, <www.usinfo.state.gov/regional/af/prestrip/w980325d.html> (October 2003).

66. In *Mea Culpa: A Sociology of Apology and Reconciliation*, 15, Nicholas Ta-vuchis notes the semantic divergence between its Greek root (*apologos*, a story; *apologia*, speech in defense) and its modern meaning. In the older meaning, apology meant "telling a story," an account, or offering an excuse for an offense. In its modern connotation an apology begins where the old self-serving form of "telling a story" leaves off.

67. DiPrizio, 84-86.

68. DiPrizio, 86.

69. Dominick LaCapra, *Representing the Holocaust: History, Theory, Trauma* (Ithaca: Cornell University Press, 1994), 205-223.

70. Charles L. Briggs, "Specificities: Introduction, The Power of Discourse in (Re) creating Genocide, *Social Identities*, Volume 3, no. 3, 1997, 408.

71. Gary Jonathan Bass. *Stay the Hand of Vengeance: The Politics of War Crimes Tribunals.* Princeton and Oxford: Princeton University Press, 2000, 283.

72. Michael E. Brown and Richard N. Rosecrance, *The Cost of Conflict: Prevention and Cure in the Global Arena.* (Landham, New York, Oxford: Rowman & Littlefield Publishers, Inc., 1999). 70-71.

73. Michael Barnett, *Eyewitness to A Genocide*, 2.

74. Barnett.

75. Referring to the question of lack of political will, Barnett concludes, "sometimes this platitude is the code used to single out particular, powerful states. In this instance, however, practically the entire council can be credited for 'failing Rwanda'. Barnett, 2-3.

76. Tavuchis, 100-101.

77. "Rwanda demands apology from UN," *Guelph Mercury*, Ontario, Canada, December 18, 1999, C8.

78. Karen Davies, "Rwandans take Annan, U.N. to task for genocide," *seattletimes.com*, May 8, 1998. <http://seattletimes.com/news/nation-world/html98/altrwan_050898.html> (February 5, 2000).

79. Girma Negash, "Apologia Politica: An Examination of the Politics and Ethics of Public remorse in International Affairs," *International Journal of Politics and Ethics*, vol. 2 number 2, 132.

80. Barnett, 154.

81. Barnett.

82. Smith, 201.

83. Smith, 203.

84. As quoted in Gary Jonathan Bass. *Stay the Hand of Vengeance: The Politics of War Crimes Tribunals* (Princeton and Oxford: Princeton University Press, 2000), 282.

85. Marina Warner, "Scene Four: Red Dust by Gillian Slovo," *OpenDemocracy*, March 11, 2002 <http://www.opendemocracy.net/articles/ViewPopUpArticle.jsp?id=3&articleId=649> (7 Jul. 2003).

86. Mariam J. Aukerman, "Extraordinary Evil, Ordinary Crime," *Harvard Human Rights Journal*, 15 (Spring 2002), 39-44.

87. Nahla Valji, "South Africa: no justice without reparation," *Open Democracy*, February 7, 2003. <http://www.opendemocracy.net/articles/ViewPopUpArticle.jsp?id3&articleId=1326> (7 July 2003).

88. Wole Soyinka, *The Burden of Memory: The Muse of Forgiveness* (New York: Oxford University Press, 1999), 25-26.

89. Soyinka, *The Burden of Memory*, 26-27.

90. Koulsy Lamko, "Rwanda, mémoire d'un génocide, La Parole des Fantômes," *L'Interdit*, Lille, novembre, 2000. <www.interdits.net/2000nov/rwanda6.htm>

91. Koulsy Lamko, Rwanda, mémoire d'un génocide

92. For LaCapra writing trauma is a process of "acting out, working over, and to some extent working through in analyzing and 'giving voice' to the past – processes of coming to terms with traumatic 'experiences,' limit events, and their symptomatic effect that achieve articulation in different combinations and hybridized forms." He emphasizes, however, that writing trauma is a metaphor and that "there is no such thing as writing trauma itself if only because trauma, while at times related to particular events, cannot be localized in terms of discrete, dated experience," *Writing History, Writing Trauma*, 186.

93. Koulsy Lamko, *La Phalène des collines*, Paris : Les Serpent à Plumes, 2002, 22-27.

94. For a useful documentation on how building a memory of the dead began, see John M. Janzen & Reinhild Kauenhoven Janzen, *Do I still have a life?: Voices from the Aftermath of War in Rwanda and Burundi*. Publications in Anthropology, 20 (Lawrence: University of Kansas, 2000) 209-210.

95. "Clinton Meets the Rwandan Genocide Survivors, U.S. Information Service."

96. "UN Chief's Rwanda Genocide Regret." *BBC News*. March 3, 2004.

97. "Western Leaders Absent as Rwanda Mourns, 10 Years After the Genocide. *The Independent (London)*. April 8, 2004.

98. Philip Gourevitch, *We Wish to Inform You that Tomorrow We Will Be Killed with Our Families: Stories From Rwanda* (New York: Farrar Straus and Giroux, 1998), 350.

99. Gourevitch, 351.

100. With lessons from the Rwandan catastrophe and in order to reassure victims that genocide will never happen again, a Canadian initiative had advanced the idea of "responsibility to protect,' meaning the international community has responsibility to protect civilians where governments are unable or unwilling to do so. The United Nations world summit on reforms approved the principle of "responsibility to protect" in September 2005, but not to the satisfaction of the Rwandan foreign minister who alleged that the anti-genocide statement must be backed with action.

101. "Genocide Victims Body's Official for Investigation of 'Big Powers'," *Financial Times*, April 6, 2005.

102. Steven Edwards, "Canada opposes massive reparation payouts to Rwanda." *The Gazette (Montreal: Quebec)*, March 27, 2004.

103. Edwards.

104. "Rwanda: UK-Funded Body Donates 47bn Rwandan Francs for Fight against AIDS." *BBC Monitoring International Reports*, March 23, 2004. See also United States Department of State, "United States Leads Support for Rwandan Reconstruction and Reconciliation." *AllAfrica*, April 1, 2004.

105. Beatriz Pavon, Rwanda, Ten Year Later: Genocide Survivors Still Face an Uncertain Future." *UN Chronicle*, 2004, Issue 4. <http://www.un.org/Pubs/chronicle/2004/ issue4/0404p63.html>

106. "Rwanda sees 'fast growth' in 2005." *BBC News*, December 5, 2004. <http://news.bbc.co.uk/2/hi/business/4070577.stm>

107. "Rwanda says debt hampers reconstruction." *Jubilee 2000: News*.

<http://www.jubilee2000uk.org/jubilee2000/news/rwanda0909.html>

108. Peter Uvin, Aiding Violence: The Development Enterprise in Rwanda. West Hartford, CT: Kumarian Press, 1998. See also Eugenia Zorbas, "Reconciliation in Post-Genocide Rwanda." African Journal of Legal Studies, (2004), 1, no. 1, 29-52.

109. "The Role of Re-Integration and Reconciliation of Ex-Prisoners." *New York Times*, August 12, 2005.

110. "Clinton Brokers Landmark Aids Deal." BBC News Online, October 10, 2003.

Chapter 5

Diplomacy and Crocodile Tears:
U.S. Apologies to China

This chapter focuses on the problematic of agency and responsibility as they relate to "inter-national" conflicts. These are markedly different from those we have so far associated with public apologies that addressed mass atrocities of colonial violence, wars, and genocides. It concentrates on those situations of wrongdoing by states that have caused diplomatic crises and where public apologies have turned out to be desired diplomatic assets or unwelcome liabilities. Such is the case of the two highly publicized American apologies to China involving the U.S. bombing of the Chinese Embassy under NATO auspices on May 7, 1999, and the collision of an EP-3 spy plane with a Chinese F-8 fighter plane off the China coast on April 1, 2001. These types of state apologies, even when they are made on behalf of national collectivities and are delivered by state agents such as national congresses, heads of state, and governments, pose different questions of representation, agency and moral identity.

The two cases of apologies by the U.S. to China provide us with the opportunity to examine apology in the diplomatic context. To this end, this chapter will first describe the high stake negotiations that took place between the two countries over the content of the apology elaborating upon the dictates of *realpolitik*, legal conventions and cultural-linguistic negotiations involved in those cases. Second, it will assess the successes and limitations in resolving the specific conflicts according to the criteria of acknowledgement, accountability, truth-telling and public remorse. Finally, it will draw conclusions and generalizations on state apologies as diplomatic tools.

These apologies to China, putting Rwanda aside, differ from the German/Israeli/Jewish and the Japanese/Neighbors cases in at least two critical ways. First, each apology to China was confined to a single incident, and the outcome, negotiations, and resolutions lasted only for weeks or a few months. The two historical cases, on the other hand, entailed multiple parties and numerous layers of grievances that involved prolonged conflicts and drawn out negotiations. Second, the contemporary cases were about resolving conflict and restoring diplomatic relations, while the historical cases pertain to reconciling peoples and collectivities alienated from each other and bringing them into a new moral community and a more lasting peace. In the historical cases, apology was considered to be part of the healing process; in the contemporary ones, it was taken as an exploitable diplomatic measure.

Apology as a ritualistic act in the service of diplomacy is characteristically different from the reconciliatory gesture and action represented in the apologetic cases earlier. Apology as a power asset, so to speak, is distinctive in the following ways. First, it is instrumental in facilitating conflict resolution; as such, it is employed as a means to a diplomatic end. Second, the affective dimensions of the apology processes inherent in the historical cases are subordinate or secondary to the imperatives of rational decision-making in state-centric international politics. Third, the distance between victim and perpetrator is at its widest in this case as states and governments are the only agents of the apology process without even pretending to act as proxies, as in the historical cases. Finally, the claims to universalism in the earlier cases are continuously challenged here by the particularism of each of the contending cultures involved.

The use of apology as part of a negotiation process in interpersonal, intergroup or international conflict situations varies according to the goals of the parties. An apology could be an end in itself or be part of the redress sought by the injured party. An apology could also be part of a strategy aimed at reducing uncertainty and anxiety in a hostile environment.[1] The value of the apology asset is particularly on the rise, one might argue, in this age of apology.[2] This is the case in Japan and the neighboring countries where the politics of memory will be present as long as Japan remains officially unrepentant for war crimes associated with World War II.

The concept of apology as understood in this power-related context is stripped of its redemptive and moral meaning. Instead, a verbal or written apology implies simple admission of wrong-doing with all the implications of legal liability. As long as international law remains based on state-centric considerations, states and their representatives are understandably reluctant to admit to offences and to apologize. Such behavior is in keeping with the underlying rules of international politics and the central assumptions upon which they are predicated. All states are presumed equal in spite of their asymmetrical power relations and jealously guard their individual sovereignties. Thus their leaders are customarily expected to assert those presumptions of equality and sovereignty with Machiavellian "righteousness." If morality is in the balance, it is state morality that is at stake with the primacy of survival and other instrumental considerations of the nation-state. In a near-Hobbesian environment, dispassionate state interests prevail over affective considerations and a sense of justice.

In the diplomatic use of apology, the distance between victims of serious wrong-doing and the leaders of the perpetrator-state who seek to address the grievances is extremely far or virtually removed. In this modality, the state agents or governments are at the forefront claiming to speak for the victims or to address them from the perpetrators' end. When governments are struggling for legal or righteous redress, the actual victims and perpetrators tend to be outside the arena of action unless their demands are employed for propagandist ends. In diplomatic crises precipitated by state violence the main diplomatic actors, the governments, are engaged in a bargaining process with each other, with their respective domestic audiences, and perhaps a global audience. But least of all with the victims of the violence. A juridical apology becomes part of the conflict settlement, a restoration of diplomatic normality, and a renewal of an alliance perhaps, but is not intended to address those who are victimized and those who empathize with them.

Diplomatic negotiations primarily anchored in the universalized beliefs of liberal internationalism - including state equality, popular sovereignty, and human rights – fail to take into account other considerations such as asymmetrical relations of power, ideological differences, nationalisms, and perceptions and misperceptions that may reside in cultural and linguistic differences and nuances. Even when used in response to new international expectations and norms, the efficacy of apology is influenced by the particularities of cultural and historical circumstances. In spite of the expanding consensus of international norms and regimes, diplomats are best served in recognizing the particular histories and political cultures of others. Consider Michael Walzer's dualist metaphor parade for the ends of justice and truth. We may empathize with people's parade or protest in defense of those values in far away places, but at the same time have our own parade at home. That dualist metaphor captures the moral realities of our times. As Walzer suggests:

> Societies are necessarily particular because they have members and memories, members *with* memories not only of their own but also of their common life. Humanity by contrast, has members but no memory, and so it has no history and no culture, no customary practices, no familiar life-ways, no festivals, no shared understanding of social goods.[3]

Walzer's rather broad distinction between "thick" morality that is represented by particular cultures, and the "thin" morality that goes into the making of global and universal norms is relevant to the tensions we perceive between the cosmopolitan norms that can accommodate the waves of collective apologies and the particular cases in which apologetic efforts are resisted by particularistic and maximalist moral realities that are slow to change.

In all matters of bringing about or maintaining a desirable order, including reconciliation and peace, we can recognize the maximization of morality at both the local and the international level although we cannot agree on the density of these values. Such is the case of face-negotiation – "the projected image of one's self (or one's national identity or image) in a public negotiation situation."[4] Face or face-saving seems to be universally desired in conflict situations, but can be situationally and culturally determined. Hence it is important to consider both the cultural-universal and cultural-specific dimensions of face.

The literature on face-saving in negotiations tends to be more negative and self-oriented than positive and other-concerned. Ting-Toomey and Cole believe that "while the face-saving or face-threatening model is reflective of a high self-face concern and a low other-face concern perspective, the face-honoring process is reflective of a mutual-face concern attitude."[5] Apology made during negotiations, even on demand, would be considered part of the face –honoring process.

Two Diplomatic Faux pas and Acknowledgement

In each diplomatic crisis involving China, the nature of acknowledgement of charges of wrongdoing by the United States government was severely limited in scope by the dictates of *realpolitik*, so much so that apology could only be conditional. In the two demands for apology by China following the Chinese embassy bombing in 1999 and the spy-plane collision in 2001, transparency or acknowledgement of the facts of what had happened fell victim to expediency and self-serving national interest goals. In a crisis like this involving global competitors and set in a politically sensitive environment, national leaders are not expected to be objective. For example, after the 1999 bombing of the Chinese embassy in Belgrade that killed three Chinese citizens and wounded 26 others, Chinese officials angrily accused the U.S. of a deliberate attack. The insistence by American officials that the bombing was a case of mistaken identification of a target was rejected outright by the Chinese side. The facts of the incident were equally contested in the 2001 spy plane case. Chinese authorities immediately claimed that the spy plane flew inside the territorial waters of China, whereas the U.S. side maintained that the plane was flying in international airspace. Although most sources reported that the American spy plane was well beyond the 12-mile legal limit of territorial waters, the Chinese interpretation of the same fact translated into territorial violation, especially if territoriality extended to its economic zone and old Chinese territorial claims. On the other hand, if the plane was flying 50 to 60 miles off the coast as it was reported, it was indeed well beyond the 12-mile territorial limit and international airspace. Nevertheless, "China claimed that the United States demonstrated insufficient respect for its rights as a coastal State when it performed what China characterized as a provocative military surveillance mission in China's EEZ." [6] Thus acknowledgement of the facts of the incident was subject to the perceptions of the leaders of the two competing powers, their interpretations of the facts, and legal justifications of their respective positions.

If full acknowledgement of the facts of the international incidents suffered at the high stakes of diplomacy, acknowledgement of wrongdoing by the offending party met a worse fate. In the first case, the bombing of the Chinese Embassy, the explanations by NATO spokesmen of what had occurred were confused and varied initially. Then the military spokesmen settled on one story that ascribed the accident to an outdated map that failed to show the site of the Chinese Embassy.[7] In spite of accusations and counter-accusations and lack of full accounting of what exactly went wrong, most in the international community assumed that it was an accident because there was no understandable motive for the U.S. to bomb the embassy considering the diplomatic cost involved. Yet American and Chinese officials proceeded to resolve the conflict from an opposing perspective.

Ever conscious of the legal liability of admitting wrongdoing, U.S. officials started with an explanation that was to be followed by apologies and compensation. Chinese officials, on the other hand, immediately demanded "an official apology, a complete and thorough investigation, a detailed public announcement of the results and severe punishment for those responsible."[8] The U.S. acted promptly. President Bill Clinton made a half-hour telephone call to Chinese President Jiang Zemin to offer personal apologies for the NATO bombing. He also sent a private letter to the president expressing condolences to the families of the three Chinese killed in the air strike. These actions were supplemented further with public statements of regret from U.S. officials.[9] Secretary of State Madeleine Albright walked to the Chinese Embassy to personally deliver a letter of apology after Foreign Minister Tang Jiaxuan had refused to talk to her on the telephone.

The Chinese reaction was equally calculated and meant to express outrage and demand swift justice. Prompted by the government, tens of thousands of protesters took to the streets in 20 cities for three days, besieging and throwing rocks at the American Embassy.[10] The depiction of the bombing by Chinese officials as deliberate, and the accusatory reports in state-media were adequate enough to provoke the anger of the populace. The Chinese leadership went further in its media manipulation by failing to report the apologies from Clinton and the NATO Secretary-General in its state-run media for three days. When the apologies were finally reported, Chinese officials announced in essence that apologies alone were insufficient unless their other demands were met.[11] From the Chinese point of view the crisis would not be over until admission of guilt or until acknowledgement of wrongdoing came from the U.S. government. During diplomatic negotiations, U.S. officials took steps to repair the damages to Chinese-U.S. relations, while the Chinese sought to win concessions beyond the immediate demands for apology, investigations, and compensations. Stanley O.

Roth, then Assistant Secretary for East Asian and Pacific Affairs, testifying before a subcommittee of the Senate Committee on Foreign Relations, conjec-
tured:

> I understand that the Chinese word for 'crisis' is a combination of the charac-
> ters for 'danger' and 'opportunity.' There are those who undoubtedly speculate
> both in China and the United States, that perhaps the crisis of the last few
> weeks, this trough in the U.S.-China relationship, represents an opportunity for
> China to press for concessions from the U.S. on issues such as the terms for
> China's WTO accession, human rights, Tibet, and non-proliferation. These
> speculators are dangerously mistaken.[12]

Although Roth's interpretation of Chinese etymology might be questioned
by native Chinese speakers, his assertion about the timing of Chinese officials to
press for certain advantages might have been correct. The word for time *ji* is
what the characters for crisis, *wei ji* and for opportunity *ji hui* have in common.[13]
The ritualistic dance by the U.S. around acknowledging culpability and by
China ignoring American attempts to put things right were repeated again in the
2001 spy plane crisis.

In the April 1 incident in which a U.S. Navy EP-3 spy aircraft collided with
a Chinese fighter plane, sorting out the facts was more complicated than determining intentions. Who was responsible for the mishap? The immediate Chinese
accusation was that the American plane had penetrated Chinese airspace and
intentionally collided with one of the two fighter planes that had tried to inter-
cept it. Acknowledgement by U.S. officials of such an act would amount to
provocation. In the intense negotiations that followed the incident, the truth
about the facts became more contentious as they were being shaped and re-
shaped by hardening positions on both sides of the conflict, even after new facts
had been revealed.

Contradicting the Chinese assertion is the statement by the American mission commander and pilot that the Chinese fighter plane had crashed into the
wing of the reconnaissance plane sending it into a 7,000-foot dive. There were
indications that after some of these facts were revealed Chinese public opinion
tempered somewhat, even though it seemed that Chinese officials could not back
down from the official version of events. At the time, David Shambaugh, an
expert on the Chinese military said, "The posture that both sides have taken and
their lack of leeway, for domestic political reasons, suggests that it will be hard
to accomplish much" in a few meetings.[14] After the Chinese Ambassador in
Washington Yang Jiechi met with Deputy Secretary Richard Armitage for the
fifth time, the Chinese government increased the pressure by sending a letter to
Secretary of State Colin Powell urging that the "U.S. side should take up its responsibilities for the incident" and apologize. The letter from Chinese Vice-
Premier Qian Qichen continued: " It is essential for the U.S. to face up to the
facts squarely, adopt a positive and practical approach and apologize to the Chi-

nese people." [15] Only then, according to the Chinese, could they move on to other points of contention. In other words, the Chinese were seeking some kind of acknowledgement of culpability that the increasingly frustrated Americans were not ready to make. Colin Powell's initial response – "there's nothing to apologize for" - resulted in a diplomatic stalemate. According to *Time* reporter Tony Karon, to end the standoff Beijing and Washington "may require some particularly creative diplomacy that allows each side to give a little without appearing – at least to their own public – to be giving anything. The kind of formula that in some parts of the U.S. might be called 'lawyering'." [16]

Propaganda and Truth-telling

In general, public diplomacy and confrontations on national security grounds lend themselves more to propaganda than truth-telling. In the instance we have been examining, government posturing and virulent diplomatic language on both sides hampered the investigations and led to shifts in attention and priority. After the Chinese Embassy bombing in 1999, journalists attempted to get to the truth amid the charges and denials of the two governments. Two European newspapers implied the bombing had been deliberate while *The New York Times* reached a conclusion to the contrary after interviewing more than thirty sources in Europe and the U.S. That report and the assessment by Pentagon officials spread the blame for the incident by attributing it to systemic failure. [17] On the other hand, the American apologies and explanations were not made accessible to the Chinese public for several days. In the spy plane case, the Chinese held the United States responsible for the death of the pilot of their fighter plane and the violation of Chinese sovereignty and unleashed a scathing propaganda through the government-controlled press accusing the U.S., among other things, of "being locked in a Cold War mentality intent on subduing China." [18] The Chinese pilot Wang Wei was elevated to a hero and "martyr" figure and his wife and parents were prominently displayed in the state media. In a letter addressed to President Bush, Ruan Guoquin, the pilot's wife tauntingly wrote, "you are too cowardly to voice an 'apology.' Can this be the human rights and humanism that you have been talking about every day?" [19] In both cases, just as the prospects for acknowledgement of the facts of the incident and wrongdoing fade, truth-telling suffers in the hands of *realpolitik*. Thus the facts of the truth are buried under the organized denials serving the imperatives of the state in which only partial truths surface from time to time from the bureaucracies that serve the "traditional lie." We are reminded here of the distinction between the "traditional" and "organized" lie Hannah Arendt makes in her essay, "Truth and Politics," separating the cold-blooded lies states engage in in defense against enemies from the lies and self-deception that create an image-reality cancerous to civil society. [20]

Truth-telling as part of apologetic discourse was far removed from or external to the public space in the diplomatic crises between China and the U.S., more so than the earlier cases of mass violence and apology involving Germany, Japan and Rwanda. In those societies recovering from civil wars, violent dictatorships, and crimes against humanity, revealing the truth about the crimes perpetrated has been an essential part of seeking justice. Truth-telling was the basis for compensation to victims, and became the essential ingredient to help victims, survivors and perpetrators to recover and promote reconciliation in such divided societies. These were the aims of the South African Truth and Reconciliation Commission. Truth commissions, however, have drawn criticism for undermining the administration of justice as well as compromising the very value of truth-telling. By necessity truth commissions can only deliver partial truth. In Andrew Rigby's cogent assessment:

> The very process of uncovering a part of the truth and granting it the status of official, public and authoritative record can serve to cover up other aspects of the past. ... From the perspective of those that survived this meant that the perpetrators continued to enjoy impunity and justice was forfeited, leading some critics to portray truth commissions as a relatively cost-free way to meet popular demands for an accounting, creating the impression that the past has been dealt with, so that people would be prepared to move on and face the future together – a future based on victims and survivors becoming *reconciled* to their loss.[21]

Thus, while the truth is compromised for the pragmatic reasons of restoring order and reconciliation, there are hardly any pretensions to truth-seeking when it comes to conflict resolutions between competing states in the international arena. The establishment of truth commissions in transnational societies is the result of struggles on the part of victims, survivors, and/or their advocates. In diplomatic crises, however, the agency of those who suffered most is overshadowed by the demands of states and their agents. For example, in the Belgrade bombing and in the 2001 collision in the air, the lives of those killed and injured were secondary to the perceived danger of escalating tensions between the two powers and the potential harm to their overall relations. The apologies demanded by the Chinese government, and whatever regrets and sorrow expressed by U.S. officials to the families of the deceased were only incidental and, at best, pro forma. A Western correspondent wrote on the spy plane incident: "The wife and parents of the missing pilot have been paraded by the state media. But the campaign has more to do with politics than a family's suffering ... The same weekend, Amanda de Jesus, whose son was one of the detained crew, confessed that it was hard to stand by America's refusal to apologise. 'The mommy in me says, say anything'."[22]

If the politics of apology in both the Belgrade and spy plane cases was mostly the affairs of state, what role did public pressures and opinion play in both countries? In the spy-plane standoff, Chinese President Jiang Zemin might have been under pressure to harden his stance in response to the strong criticism he took "for letting the U.S. off the hook too easily over the Belgrade embassy bombing two years ago, and he's clearly under pressure from the hawks in Beijing to hang tough."[23] Added to domestic public pressures, the very public nature of the diplomatic crisis tended to compel both sides to hold firmly to their official version of the events, leaving room only "to agree diplomatically to disagree."[24]

Reckoning and Accounting for Injuries

Accountability or taking responsibility for those actions that the aggrieved party calls attention to has been an essential part of apologies we have looked at so far. In the cases of genocide and war crimes, accountability is one of the imperatives that has to be satisfied in seeking reconciliation with those alienated by mass violence. By contrast, the contemporary diplomatic crises we have examined underscore responsibility with all its legal and political implications in negotiating a peaceful resolution. Any performative apology, oral or written, becomes part of a settlement along with other means of compensating the wronged state. If we substitute apology for forgiveness in this context, Jacques Derrida's judgment becomes relevant, that "all sorts of unacknowledgeable 'politics', all sorts of strategic ruses can hide themselves abusively behind a 'rhetoric' or a 'comedy' of forgiveness, in order to avoid the step of the law."[25] Accountability on the part of the United States in the bombing of the Chinese embassy was demonstrated not only in the formal apologies by American officials beginning with President Clinton, but also in fulfilling most of the demands made by the Chinese. Eleven months after the bombing, the Central Intelligence Agency dismissed a mid-level officer who was blamed for the targeting error. In addition, it carried out administrative punishments to six of its other employees.[26]

By spreading blame among many individuals the agency characterized the "tragic accident" as a systemic error, while George J. Tenet "properly assigned accountability within his agency." [27] China immediately rejected the official explanation of the bombing and demanded once again a "thorough and comprehensive" investigation but the American response to the renewed demand was that the matter was closed.[28] When it came to compensation for damages to the Chinese Embassy and associated buildings, the initial readiness by the U.S. to pay for the damages was opposed in Congress as retaliation for damages to the U.S. Embassy in Beijing incurred by angry Chinese protesters.[29]

In December 1999 the United States government agreed to pay China $28 million in compensation for damages to the Chinese Embassy in Belgrade. China, in turn, agreed to pay the U.S. $2.87 million for damage to the American Embassy and other diplomatic buildings in China during the weeks of demonstration following the bombing.[30] Chinese hostility toward the U.S. eased after President Clinton met with President Jiang Zemin in New Zealand in September of the following year and when the administration agreed on the terms for Chi-

nese entrance to the World Trade Organization in November. So the U.S. decision to pay the compensation cleared the final obstacle to the resumption of
high-level military contacts with the United States after China had suspended
the contracts following the Embassy bombing.[31] More than a year later after the
NATO bombing, during a visit by Secretary of State Madeleine Albright, the
Chinese Foreign Ministry spokesman was able to say that "relations between
China and the United States had 'greatly improved' because of efforts on both
sides."[32] Nevertheless, acceptance of full accountability on the part of the United
States did not come even on the day (January 20, 2001) the latter received the
$28 million in compensation. China was still demanding "a full investigation
and punishment for those responsible."[33]

In the spy-plane incident, being responsible and accountable implied admitting guilt and giving a formal apology to the "state victim." Since there were no
other outstanding matters to settle, with the exception of compensation for the
family of the deceased Chinese pilot, the apologetic wording became central
with regard to accountability. As a result, the secret negotiations between Chinese and American officials focused on the phrasing of an apology. The "very
sorry" epithets for the loss of the Chinese pilot and entering China's airspace
satisfied the demand for accountability as far as both states were concerned despite their hawkish detractors. The Communist Party and the state media played
up the apology extracted from the United States as a major victory and concession.[34] There was also the marginal question of compensation. China sent the
U.S. a $1 million bill for expenses incurred while holding the spy plane; the U.S.
threatened to bill the Chinese for damages to the EP-3. In terms of material settlement, nothing came out of such posturing.

The Split-Personality of the "Regretful" State

The apologies by the United States to China - oral, written, or as part of public
record – as other apologies between states - include expressions of regret and
remorse, among other things. When words of regret, sorrow, and remorse are
expressed in this mode of apology *who* is speaking and in what capacity? Do
those words emanate from an individual representing the state, a speech-writer,
or an anonymous bureaucrat? In apologies arising from a diplomatic crisis, the
words of apology are carefully constructed just as in legal documents and treaties, but human sensibilities are injected into the discourse. In this case the state,
as Trouillot has suggested, mimics the confessing individual.[35]

The language of regret, in the U.S. apologies to China was undoubtedly
shaped by the cultural, linguistic, and legal conventions of the West as well as
the dictates of *realpolitik*. For example, the words used by President Clinton on
television, after the NATO bombing of the Chinese embassy, were explicit: "I
want to say to the Chinese people and to the leaders of China, I apologize; I regret this."[36] He also wrote a private letter of regret to Chinese President Jiang

Zemin in which he voiced regrets for the tragedy and personal expression of condolences to the families of the three Chinese killed in the air strike.[37] He had earlier expressed the same words of apology in a half-hour telephone call to the Chinese President. The Chinese Foreign Ministry noted later that during the telephone conversation with Clinton, Jiang Zemin had told him that "he had received his recent letter and information about his talks with Li Zhaoxing, the Chinese ambassador to the U.S., earlier [that day] and said that he had noticed the apology President Clinton had made again." And Jiang Zemin had said, "The Chinese government has solemnly expressed its stance and made its demands clear in its statement and relevant representations."[38] The reported remark by the Chinese President reflects his acknowledgement of an apology qualified by his reaffirmation of China's demand for a thorough investigation and public report of its results. The U.S. Secretary of State, Madeleine Albright, did not do as well at first. Chinese Foreign Minister Tang Jiaxuan, who was in Washington D.C. at the time, refused to talk to her on the telephone.[39] She had to personally deliver a letter of apology to the minister, in which she wrote: "I wanted to express personally to you my sincere sorrow for the loss of life, injuries and damage. On behalf of my government and as a member of NATO, I extend sincere apologies and condolences."[40] Note the schizophrenic co-existence between the personal ("my sincere sorrow") and the juridical ("on behalf of") apologia. The response by Foreign Minister Tang to Albright's overture in the press was not so subtle and conciliatory. He declared that Albright's pledge to negotiate for compensation and apologies were not enough and that "the United States must make a full and comprehensive investigation of the incident and (it) must punish those who are responsible."[41] The apology by the U.S. Secretary of State failed to repair the damages done, and as the diplomatic standoff continued the apology was detached from the other issues of contention.

Such direct and indirect diplomatic exchanges become impersonal and bureaucratic. They are far removed from a moral-temporal communion that brings together victims, perpetrators and all those implicated, and in which genuine remorse would have its place. Even though one is tempted to believe that the efficacy of apology is at its lowest in the hostile environment of diplomatic and military rivalry, Donald Shriver's argument that remorse even under such circumstances is possible and useful is a welcome relief. Shriver suggests that genuine remorse on the part of a political leader can produce results. It can lend credibility to the apology. It can also invite the domestic constituency to an imitation of remorse.[42]

The efficacy of apology in the diplomatic setting can also be measured against the conduct, both historical and contemporary, of statesmen acting remorsefully when apology is sought to bring about reconciliation or diplomatic breakthroughs. While plenty of thought has gone into the problem of "dirty hands" regarding the moral choices individual statesmen have to make in the name of preserving national interest, we have not reflected yet on the somewhat opposite gesture of "washing hands"- of cleansing oneself of guilt and blame. Political leaders can of course engage in apologetic discourse in the course of diplomatic negotiations, even secretly. However, when leaders apologize as political agents of their state or nation, their moral identities need defining. Since remorse is the expression of sorrow for a wrongdoing, is public remorse really public in the sense that it is collectively felt? If this is not the case, is public remorse simply a ritualistic act on behalf of a collectivity? Is it possible to conceive expressed sorrow by an individual leader about a collective wrongdoing? On rare occasions, such as the remorse displayed by Chancellor Willy Brandt, individual performative remorse has its intended impact.

Public remorse is also inhibited in diplomatic apology because the incentive to be remorseful in order to be forgiven or redeemed is absent. In fact, the possibility of being held responsible or guilty does not encourage sincere apologies. In the compressed time of negotiations to resolve an international crisis there is no room for sincerity. In public diplomacy "saying sorry" means taking full responsibility and meeting certain legal obligations. In such considerations of either avoiding liabilities or compensating for them there is little room for moral considerations. The moral identity of those political agents who engage in remorseless apologies on behalf of collectivities is shallow and thin for at least two reasons. First, there is typically no actual offended party to whom appropriate remorse can be expressed. For example, the apologies from Clinton and Albright were to Chinese leaders and not to the families of those who died in the embassy bombing. It was the same situation during the spy plane crisis with the exception of a letter sent by pilot Wei's wife to President George W. Bush castigating his presidency. Second, the individual and emotional attributes of remorse can not be attributed to a collective one. The instrumental use of apologies deforms the original nature of apology. Imagine Chinese President Jiang Zemin departing, as he did, on an official state tour to Latin America after laying down the strategy for his aids on how to win the diplomatic game of apology with the United States. When apology is brought down to the level of a diplomatic ploy the affective response is conspicuously absent.

Context and Influences on Apology

Before considering the place of public remorse in the diplomatic context, it is worth examining other elements that affect apologies between nation-states. In the apologies to China, geopolitical considerations, collective memory, language and cultural differences, as well as nationalism figured significantly. For example, the spy-plane standoff came down to negotiating the wording of the apology. Those who prepared the apologetic diplomatic note in that incident took pains to come up with nuanced language. They specifically chose linguistic ambiguity - a double-edged diplomatic scheme that can also create unforeseen problems. Decisions also had to be made by negotiators to address questions in both languages related to conveying meanings to their multiple leaders. Apparently the Chinese translation of the American letter of apology was different from the embassy version. The apologetic words regarding the unauthorized entry into Chinese airspace conveyed different meanings. Thus according to Perry Link, an expert in Chinese language and literature, "the use of the syllable 'qian' in that part of the embassy's translation 'does imply that the speaker acknowledges wrongdoing.' That syllable, however, appears more frequently in the Chinese translation than in the embassy's ... enabling a Chinese reader of the Chinese translation to infer that the admission of wrongdoing extends to larger issues."[43]

Although form and substance of apologies are subject to cultural influences, I would not want to unduly emphasize the cultural differences impacting on behavior. Yet cultural interpretations of such ideas as apology and forgiveness are worth examining even when one avoids the pitfalls of cultural essentialism. For example, it has been suggested that the insistent demand for apology in China is linked to Confucianism. Certain Chinese characters like *li* (courtesy) *yi* (ceremony) and *rang* (yield), which are associated with the Confucian principles of hierarchy and harmony, enhance the value of restoring order by way of apologetic rituals.[44] On the other hand, some scholars argue that Confucianism has less to do with apologizing than with self criticism and confession in so far as magistrates used to extract confessions in exchange for lesser punishments in imperial times. That practice was reintroduced by the Communists, especially during the Cultural Revolution.[45]

The Diplomatic Context

The Chinese demands for apology and the official responses by the United States raise serious conceptual questions about the nature of state apologies. Especially those called for, given, and received by states and their agents in international affairs. The demands by China for apologies from the U.S. have raised once again a basic question of whether states should apologize.[46] Apologies are misplaced in a diplomatic communication driven by national self-interest. In a realist moral economy, such a position holds; an aggrieved state such as China merits compensation for damages and restitution. An apology therefore is of value in so far as it offers advantages such as restoring national prestige and promoting the national interest.

In the two cases of apology to China, Presidents Clinton and Bush were respectively under the pressures of expediency, so as not to jeopardize delicate relations in the first instance, and to protect the lives of American servicemen in the second incident, and therefore they had to apologize. Second, their apologies were not intended to do what was right and just, but to mend endangered relationships in which apologies served as bargaining chips with China.

After the 1999 bombing incident the Chinese learned that they could have been in better control of negotiations and could have benefited more if only they had avoided arousing too much sentiment at home that reflected badly on their national face. Thus they did not want to repeat the same mistakes in the 2001 confrontation with the U.S. Consequently a fascinating tale of diplomatic cunning takes place behind the scenes in Beijing's corridors of power. Willy Wo-Lap Lam reports that Chinese President Jiang Zemin took charge of the diplomacy of apology by first of all instructing government officials to prevent unruly anti-U.S. demonstrations. According to Wo-Lap Lam, Jiang Zemin wanted to teach a lesson to George W. Bush, a novice American president, "who had infuriated Beijing by his statements on Taiwan and on deploying anti-missile systems." The Chinese president also specifically instructed his aides that negotiations over the spy plane should not be prolonged and that "Beijing should take a flexible line in finding a face-saving formula for both sides." The negotiated apology turned out to be the outcome of a calculated act of diplomacy with a "flexible approach under the veneer of toughness." The performative act on a world stage is part of a public diplomacy that is aimed to enhance national face and to be used for public consumption at the domestic front. Jiang Zemin asked Vice President Hu "to start a nation-wide patriotic campaign whose theme would be to celebrate Beijing's new-found strength on the world stage."[47] The skill with which President Jiang Zemin used apology underscores the difference between the performative acts of diplomacy and a quiet diplomacy that can prevent the parties from assuming rigid positions. A number of experts on China think that the spy plane crisis could have been headed off if only the U.S. government had contacted China to strengthen mutual trust and had a discussion on how to resolve it before making it public conflict.[48]

The parts played by statesmen like Presidents Clinton, Bush, and Jiang Zemin performing in the apologetic rituals of normal diplomacy once again remind us of the problems statesmen face in acting morally in an often immoral international environment. Lying and deceit have been accepted as diplomatic necessities by realists and others who care for the moral dimensions of statecraft, but they are often defended on the grounds that statesmen use them when grave national security matters are at stake. Yet an apology that is purely self-serving, worse still, one based on a dishonest premise, undermines trust and confidence. Yet, under the right circumstances apologies can serve to reinforce existing international norms. As Andrew Nathan argues, "apologies are particularly powerful norm-setting devices (let's say, compared to international conventions that countries sign) because of the degree of psychological commitment they carry."[49]

Historical Influences

A country's history especially as it relates to the one with which it is in conflict, can affect apology diplomacy. As Richard Tomkins wrote at the height of tensions between China and the United States in the wake of the spy plane crisis:

> In China's case, its fundamental loss of face was being carved up into trade concessions, or cantonments, by European powers during the twilight years of the Manchu Dynasty in the late 19th century. The upstart European business people and other colonizers, ruled the roost in their concessions – primarily trading port cities – even to the point of placing "No Dogs or Chinese Allowed" signs on the gates to public gardens within their controlled areas. It rankled. Rightfully so. Time, however, has not diminished the insult to a people or dimmed a collective memory of the humiliation.[50]

The collective memory of colonial domination was reinforced even more when the very same power that helped the colonizing powers put down the Boxer Rebellion against the foreigners, namely the United States, showed its presence in the South China Sea and supplied arms to Taiwan, the entity they consider a province of China.[51] John W. Dower, a historian of Japan and World War II, believes that the Chinese need for apology has less to do with culture than its being part of the new age of apology that morally valorizes victimization. Referring to the spy plane incident, Dower says "For the Chinese, this little plane became a metaphor for 150 years of imperialist victimizing of China."[52] In a similar vein Peter Gries refers to the "fourth-generation" nationalists, those who were in their formative youth during the Beijing Spring 1989 and the 1980s of romantic and pro-Western idealism. Calling themselves "pragmatic" conservatives they "returned to the pre-'Liberation' narrative of a 'Century of Humiliation' during which Chinese were victimized by the West, and the new 'victimization.' Narrative now coexists with the earlier 'heroic' version."[53] A more conventional interpretation of the new Chinese nationalism by Yongnian Zheng focuses on China's desperate longing for international respect and hence its nationalism arises "when other great powers ignore China's national dignity in their dealings with it."[54] Scholars like Yongnian Zheng and Peter Gries redefine Chinese nationalism by letting us see what the Chinese say it is, rather than our accepting the Western interpretations that have distorted our perceptions of China, its policies and reactions.

Gries argues that the new consensus in understanding China then is not to dwell on whether or not Chinese nationalism is growing in a malevolent direction, but to recognize the stake in its outcome and to avoid inconsistency in policy toward China. He maintains, "If Chinese popular opinion perceives China's leaders to be successfully maintaining China's "national face" on the world stage, however, I believe that most Chinese will seek to further integrate China into the existing world order."[55] Our understanding of Chinese nationalism and the nature of apology in a diplomatic context stands to gain from a more comprehensive examination of 'face.' The spy plane incident illustrates best the importance of a well-placed apology when, aside from fulfilling legal liabilities, a restoration of national esteem and dignity is at stake. Apology in the service of saving face therefore is best understood by looking into the meanings of face and in what ways face is maintained or enhanced as it is relevant to nations and states.[56]

"Face" and Apology

Implicit in our discussion of these two incidents involving China and the U.S. is the importance of the concept of "face" in Chinese culture. There are two words in Chinese that are equivalent to face but have different meanings and applications - *mien-tzŭ* and *lien*. The first term mien-tzŭ (or *mianzi*) is a social and an interactive concept, while the second refers to individual action and moral behavior. Hsien Chin Hu explains:

> *mien-tzŭ* stands for … a reputation achieved through getting on in life, through success and ostentation. This is prestige that is accumulated by means of personal effort or clever maneuvering. For this kind of recognition ego is dependent at all times on his external environment. The other kind of "face," *lien*, … is the respect of the group for a man with good moral reputation: the man who will fulfill his obligations regardless of the hardships involved, who under all circumstances shows himself a decent human being.[57]

Peter Gries employs the idea of *mien-tzu* in the Chinese context in reference to China's relations to others. This particular interpretation of "face" figures importantly especially in the public arena and diplomacy. As Gries sees it, "Chinese discussions of *face* use theatrical allusions, suggesting performances before audiences of popular opinion, whether these are individuals or groups. A person or group may 'give' *face* to another through public praise or deference, or it may 'leave' another *face* by not publicly exposing a *faux pas*. Conversely, public criticism prevents one from 'getting off the stage' – stuck in the spotlight of public scrutiny." In the context of public diplomacy in which nations seek to maintain power and prestige, the "face-game" can become "a battle over the zero-sum resource of social status" making *face* a fundamentally political concept.[58] Building upon this political interpretation of *face* Gries advances a new conceptualization of Chinese nationalism based on the Chinese "mianzi" or *mien-tzu* culture that he calls face nationalism.

As an alternative to the prevailing debate on Chinese nationalism between the pessimists who see a threat from a rising power and optimists who minimize

Chinese militarism, Gries proposes a culturally specific understanding of Chinese "face" nationalism that captures both the emotional and instrumental motivations of China's nationalists.[59] By extending the general understanding of "face" as "the figurative self shown to others" to that "face nationalism" to mean "a commitment to a collective vision of the 'national face' and its proper international status as presented to other nations," Gries assigns nations personal attributes creating a useful conceptualization that takes into account both the affective and instrumental dimensions of nationalism:

> People become emotionally attached to the self-image they present to the world. If a person's face is assaulted, their feelings are often hurt. But face is also an issue of authority. One who 'loses face' loses status and the 'social credit' necessary to pursue instrumental interests … The commitment to "national face" - the national self presented to other nations - is no different: emotions and interests are intertwined.[60]

Thus the Chinese "mianzi" has two sides: one that brings psychological satisfaction, and the other, social credit. Applied to nationalism in the Chinese context, a public apology can be used to maintain national dignity as well as social credit. Related to the self-image China needs to present to the world, an apology to China comes at the expense of its adversary in conflict and earns legitimacy for the regime in the eyes of its people. Apology then becomes a diplomatic asset and not a moral act to either restore dignity or harmonious relations. Such an understanding of state apology, including one served by face saving and face enhancing, undermines normative considerations that transcend nationalism and self-interest. A revisiting of the concept of "face" to address this insecurity can be useful.

Returning to the distinction made by Hsien Chin Hu between *mien-tzu* and *lien,* we find *lien,* the concept that is related to individual obligation and moral reputation, to be a useful building block in constructing an ethical mode in which an apology toward reconciliation can find its place. In one of the requisites of *lien* proximity matters. Hsien maintains that *lien* operates within the community as a means of insuring the social-economic security of the individual and for maintaining his self-respect. In order for the community to judge his moral character, an individual necessarily has to live continually in the same locality."[61] In other words, by changing locality the person can be out of range and create a "loss of *lien*." Hsien claims that in the business world and in the cities an individual seeking employment would have to produce a written statement affirming good reputation in one's own original neighborhood. This limitation poses a problem as well as an opportunity to elevate the "*lien*" concept of its spacio-temporality to a more universal moral category. If Gries's "*face* nationalism" is a projection of the personal to the national, *lien* can represent the consciousness of individuals within wider moral boundaries.

In both cases of diplomatic crises the Chinese went beyond protestation to demand full responsibility and apology for the mishaps. In the 1999 bombing, questions of acknowledgement and accountability withstanding, apology was immediately given. After the spy plane incident, the fact that official apology was not immediately forthcoming from the U.S. side raised the stake of apology for the Chinese and the pressing demand for it. In the earlier case the gravity of the incident in terms of human casualty in a war atmosphere and the angry response by Chinese at home and overseas was such that the Chinese severed military and other relations with the United States. In the more recent crisis, however, the Chinese were willing to jeopardize vital interests in terms of its relations with the U.S., such as trade and investment, in order to avoid their authority being "openly defied in front of the world, posing an irreparable loss of face and power."[62]

Face saving as understood across cultures is aimed at preserving self-esteem and honor. As such when face and apology come together, they work best in a non-confrontational setting, which is not always the attribute of diplomacy. In diplomatic communicative terms, face-negotiation involves face-honoring and face-threatening processes as part of maintaining face. Both American apologies to China turned out to maintain national face; although the apology was hardly acknowledged by China in the first instance, and became a negotiated speech act on public record in the second. If one accepts the emerging normative consensus, apology becomes a viable diplomatic asset in itself, not only in the service of restoring national dignity, maintaining face or as a moral imperative, but as instrumentally valid as a restitution and legal settlement.

The impossibility of an effective apologetic discourse in a hostile climate applies to *realpolitik* and diplomacy as aptly articulated by Tavuchis:

> … apology cannot come about and do its work under conditions where the primary function of speech is defensive or purely instrumental and where legalities take precedence over moral imperatives. Once apology is defined as merely a pawn or gambit in a power game, it becomes part of another moral economy in which individuals or nations find little to be gained by apologizing for their transgressions as opposed to remaining silent, counterattacking, or trying to cut their losses to a minimum.[63]

Another moral economy indeed. What the two American apologies have in common is that they both were not given "to make things right," but to restore diplomatic relations by means of negotiating face-saving formulas to reach a pre-conflict equilibrium. They were by no means employed to improve standing relationships. From the Chinese point of view, the importance of saving national face was not only influenced by culture but by historical circumstances in a new international environment conducive to valorizing the voice of the victimized. This view is supported by those who argue that the politics of historical memory is in ascendance, the currency of which is salient particularly in Asia. As Gerrit

Gong asserts, "In East Asia, Europe, and other places where history extends further into the past than in the United States, memory, history, and strategic alignment are inextricably linked."[64] The demand for apology by China in the two cases discussed here are as much about saving face as they are part of addressing historic grievances concerning China's victimization in the hands of Western powers in the past, and a continuation of perceived "bullying" by the hegemonic U.S.

Diplomatic Crises and the Apology Process

This last chapter encompassing the two American apologies to China is markedly different as a mode of apology because it questions the imperatives of an apology towards reconciliation as they were applied so far. In the first instance, acknowledgement of wrongdoing is coupled with collective guilt or some kind of culpability in those cases of mass violence by states or groups. In the apologies to China and similar cases that occur in a diplomatic setting, apologies could be of symbolic value to a few, but often they are undermined by the ever-present necessities of political and legal expediency. However tragic they are in their consequences, these diplomatic incidents are often overtaken and driven by state and government bureaucracies whose principal goals are to attain competitive advantages. Thus states prefer a no-fault insurance against such international liabilities.

The diplomatic language of apology reserves for itself the most self-serving and instrumental aspects of a speech act that is paradoxically both ambiguous and clear in its usage. As in the case of all diplomatic language, it is open to different interpretations and sometimes linguistic nuances that allow flexibility and face-saving that prove useful during diplomatic standoffs. Such was the case of the text of apology sent to the Chinese leadership after the spy plane collision incident. Its vague wording left room for varying interpretations on both sides. At the same time, diplomatic apology maintains the two primary aims for apology to acknowledge and confess and at the same time seek expiation and freedom from guilt and liability. If we employ the classic distinction J.L. Austin makes in his *How to Do Things with Words*, we recognize the difference between the constative utterance of "sorrow" or "regret," which represents expression of guilt or admission of wrongdoing (which can be judged as true or false) and the performative utterance of "I apologize" that is aimed to produce effects. Applying Austin's mode of analysis to confessional speech, Peter Brooks writes, "When one says 'Bless me Father, for I have sinned,' the constative meaning is: I have committed sins, while the performative meaning is: absolve me of my sin." [65] Similarly, the two American apologies to China are parallel speech acts that reproduce the meaning and initiative of a diplomatic apology.

After the bombing of the Chinese Embassy in 1999 President Clinton and his Secretary of State Madeleine Albright let their regret be known concerning

the "accident," and a subsequent formal apology promised proper investigations
and compensations. In the spy-plane incident of 2001 the apologetic performative utterance took the form of a legal document or treaty rather than a statement
that conveyed an apologetic initiative. An apology performative is supposed to
convey certain emotions, in this case, remorse. Thus "since our emotions or
wishes are not readily detectable by others," Austin says, "it is common to wish
to inform others that we have them."[66] This performative formula suits well the
diplomatic "lie." Austin points out:

> Understandably, though for slightly different and perhaps less estimable rea-
> sons in different cases, it becomes *de rigueur* to 'express' these feelings if we
> have them, and further even to express them when they are felt fitting, regard-
> less of whether we really feel anything at all which we are reporting.[67]

The apology mode in a diplomatic context has no room for true confessions.
When it comes to acknowledging all the facts underlying a diplomatic crisis,
both perpetrators and victims assume intransigent positions that only third-party
mediation may ameliorate. The Hobbesian impulse of the state for survival does
not permit voluntary transparence of wrongdoing. The 1999 Belgrade incident is
illustrative of this. The U.S. officials' explanation and excuse that the bombing
of the Chinese Belgrade Embassy was an error of targeting based on an outdated
map, was questioned by two European newspaper sources. Although a New
York Times investigative report later exonerated the NATO bombing of intentional targeting, another suggestion – that Chinese intelligence was eavesdrop-
ping for the enemy, namely Milosevic and the Serbians, and that therefore the
intelligence wing had to be targeted - is a tantalizing proposition. Assuming the
latter were the case, it is unlikely U.S. officials would admit wrongdoing even
under the fog of war. Ironically the Chinese side was unprepared to accept that
the bombing was an accident, but would not, as it turned out, have been able to
explain to the world why the bombing was intentional. Under such circumstances the mutual distrust between the two sides is so high that the competition
to stay on a high moral ground on the world stage comes at any expense including the truth. In societies in transition, most attempts to reconcile after mass violence are meant to bring out and air past atrocities as in the case of the truth
commissions. In those cases truth can be compromised for the sake of partial
justice and quicker restoration. In the apologies to China any consideration to
bring out the truth would have been contrary to a diplomatic settlement. In fact
any modicum of truth-telling is part of a carefully constructed narrative agreed
upon by both parties for the consumption of both the domestic and the international publics.

The US apologies to China also illustrate the rather ambiguous and shifting
identities that makeup the contingencies between perpetrators and victims in the
diplomatic setting. An interpretation of Sino-Chinese relations will concentrate
more on the shared ways of seeing the world and the discursive practices be-

tween the two. Just as the two powers through their government agents were able to construct and redefine what was at stake in their relationship during the 1999 crisis, the two sides were also able to construct an apologetic language to save-face on both sides. Such a constructivist perspective recognizes the importance of the self-identity of states that comes into being through domestic and international practices that in turn establish norms. The apologetic practice between the US and China succeeds and fails both to establish norms relevant to their future relationship.

Certain interpretations of the apology diplomacy between the two countries undermine its reconciliatory power. The neorealist approach is one that emphasizes the utilities of apology in the service of power politics.[68] Such a perspective has a bias toward accepting the order of things leaving little room for justice or peace to prevail. A redemptive ethic of apology would reverse the neorealist order and focus on power serving apology and not the other way around. Similarly, a social psychological take of apologies serving to save face emphasizes the restoration of self-respect for the individual as well as the nation. Such an approach attends well to the dignity of the victim, but puts less weight on the *restoration* of the relationship or community.

Compared to the German/Jewish, Rwandan/international community, Japan/neighbors cases discussed earlier, the American apologies to China represent particular responses to diplomatic contingencies rather than episodes in the evolving norms of international reconciliation. These three historical cases of apologies in response to mass violence were aimed at transcending the alienation between victims and perpetrators in order to heal and overcome that alienation. In Germany's case, dealing with the past necessitated the creation of a moral-temporal community. This implies that, "continuous selves are the foundation of holding individuals and political communities to account for their past; and they also lay out a claim of duty toward the future continuation of this same self." [69] Such moral communities can be imagined in the Rwandan and the Japanese cases by extending their construction from the national to the international level.

In Rwanda's case, the apologies of the international community to Rwandans as represented by individual apologies from the American President and the Belgian Prime Minister, among others, were far removed from the community of perpetrators and victims, and it is a stretch in logic to say that they contributed to the construction of a moral community regarding the genocide. However "thin" the morality is in the outer sides of the concentric circles of guilt, there exists an international moral community that is advancing a consensus on how to deal with mass violence such as genocide. The case of the Japanese and their neighbors differs from the Rwandan case. There is a larger moral community made up of surviving victims, families, NGOs, Japanese and the leaders of some of the neighboring countries. At the same time there are the occasional moral communities that bring together perpetrators and victims or at least their direct representatives. Compared to such moral communities shaped through shared memories and extraordinary and brave initiatives of reconciliation, the American apologies to China, offered or taken under diplomatic suasion and coercion, fall short of the true measures of an apologetic speech act that aims to heal and reconcile.

If the meaning of apology has been perverted by the dictates of *realpolitik* why should we refer to it as an apology? The two apologies given to the Chinese fail in acknowledging wrongdoing to its fullest extent, stay far from truth-telling, and are certainly lacking in remorse. It is as if the new international validation of victimization and apologies has not yet deepened in a world in which states still do not quite apologize to each other.[70] The two apologies, however, lived up to the expectations of accountability and responsibility of the offending power. The expressions of remorse, if we can call them truly sorrowful, became part of public record. Affected by the constraints of *realpolitik* put upon them, the apologies and their responses were subject to mistrust. The apologies and their responses were affected by the constraints put upon them. Thus they were subject to mistrust and cynicism as to their authenticy. Power politics creates a split personality in the diplomatic persona between the leader who could shed tears (albeit crocodile tears) and the deputy who is expected to be conspicuously detached. The apologia, in the diplomatic context, is meant to avoid diplomatic retaliation by explaining that the incidents were accidental and therefore should be excusable. They are more self-justifying rather than regretful and apologetic. For the most part the apologies to China are impersonal, bureaucratic, and far removed from the moral-temporal communities in which genuine remorse is rendered and received.

Notes

1.   See William B. Gudykunst, "Diplomacy: A Special Case of Intergroup Communication," in Felipe Korzenny and Stella Ting-Toomey eds. *Communicating for Peace: Diplomacy and Negotiation* (Sage Publications, 1990), 9-39. Apologies in conflict resolution scenarios are believed to reduce tensions and help to maintain and repair relationships. See Stephen Goldberg, Eric Green, and Frank Sadler, "Saying You're Sorry," in *Negotiation Theory and Practice*, ed. J. William Breslin and Jeffrey Rubin (Cambridge, MA: Program on Negotiation Books, 1991), 141-146.

2.   Roy L. Brooks, "The Age of Apology," in *When Sorry Isn't Enough: The Controversy over Apologies and Reparations for Human Injustice,*
ed. Roy L. Brooks (New York: New York University Press, 1999), 3-11.

3.   See Michael Walzer, *Thick and Thin: Moral Argument at Home and Abroad.* (Notre Dame: University of Notre Dame Press, 1994), 8.

4.   Stella Ting-Toomey and Mark Cole, "Intergroup Diplomatic Communication: A Face-Negotiation Perspective," in *Communicating for Peace: Diplomacy and Negotiation*, ed. (Newbury Park, Cal: Sage Publications, 1990), 78-79.

5.   Ting-Toomey and Cole, 81.

6.   China based this claim on the LOS Convention's reciprocal "due regard" formulation. See W. Allan Edmiston, III, "Showdown in the South China Sea: an international incidents analysis of the so-called spy plane crisis." *Emory International Law Review*, 16 no. 2, (Fall 2002), 639-88.

7.   Mobo C. F.Gao, "Sino-U.S. Love and Hate Relations," *Journal of Contemporary Asia*, 30, 4, 547.

8.   "Clinton apologises for embassy bombing" BBC News Online, May 10, 1999, <http://news.bbc.co.uk/1hi/world/340280.stm> (July 8, 2004).

9.   "Clinton calls Chinese president with apology." *CNN News*, May 14, 1999, <http://www.cnn.com/WORLD/europe/9905/14/kosovo.china> (July 8, 2004).

10.   "China demands fuller NATO apology." *Star Tribune (Minneapolis, MN)*, May 11, 1999.

11.   "Washington: Firing not likely over bombing of Chinese embassy." *CNN.com*, May 11, 1999, <http://www.cnn.com/US/9905/11/us.china> (July 19, 2004).

12.   Stanley O. Roth, "The Effects on U.S.-China Relations of the Accidental Bombing of the Chinese Embassy in Belgrade." Testimony before the Senate Committee on Foreign Relations, Subcommittee on East Asian and Pacific Affairs, Washington, DC, May 27, 1999, State Department, <http://usinfo.org/USIA/usinfo.state.gov/regional/ea/uschina/roth527.htm>

13.   I am indebted to Yanrong Chang, a communications scholar and native Chinese speaker, for this linguistic insight.

14.   Elizabeth Rosenthal, "Knotty Task of Beijing Talks on Plane: Reconciling Reality With Posturing," *The New York Times*, April 18, 2001, Section A.

15.   "China official echoes demand for apology," *United Press International*, April 7, 2001

16.   Tony Karon, "Wanted: Some Diplomatic Choreography to End China Standoff." *Time*, April 04, 2001, <http://www.time.com/time/world/printout/0,8816,105006,00.html> (July 8, 2004).

17.   Steven Lee Myers, "Chinese Embassy Bombing: A Wide Net of Blame." *The New York Times*, April 17, 2000.

18.   "Chinese press steps up anti-American rhetoric," *Agence France Presse*, April 5, 2001.

19.   David Rennie, "Pilot is forgotten in anger at crime against the state." *The Daily Telegraph* , April 9, 2001.

20.   See Hannah Arendt, "Truth and Politics," in *Between Past and Future*, 1968, 250-259. For a good discussion of the relevance of truth-telling to democratic politics, see Antonia Grunenberg's "Totalitarian lies and post-totalitarian guilt: The question of ethics in democratic politics." *Social Research* 69, i2 (Summer 2002), 374.

21.   Andrew Rigby, "Three contrasting approaches for 'Dealing with the Past': collective amnesia, retributive justice and prioritising truth." Committee for Conflict Transformation Support. Newsletter 18. <http://www.c-r.org/ccts/ccts18/3apprch.htm> (July 8, 2004)

22.   Rennie, "Pilot is forgotten in anger at crime against the state."

23. Tony Karon, "Wanted: Some Diplomatic Choreography to End China Stand-off," *Time*, April 4, 2001,
<http://www.time.com/time/world/printout/0,8816,105006,00.html> (July 8, 2004).

24. Elizabeth Rosenthal, "Knotty Task of Beijing Talks on Plane: Reconciling Reality with Posturing."

25. Jacques Derrida, *On Cosmopolitanism and Forgiveness* (London: Routledge, 2001), 50-51.

26. Steven Lee Myers, "C.I.A. Fires Officer Blamed in Bombing of China Embassy." *The New York Times*, April 9, 2000, http://web.lexis-nexis.com/.

27. "Blame in the Chinese Embassy Bombing." *The New York Times*, April 11, 2000.

28. Steven Lee Myers, "China Rejects U.S. Actions On Bombing of Embassy," *The New York Times*, April 11, 2000. http://web.lexis-nexis.com/.

29. House Concurrent Resolution 157, 106th Congress, 1st session, July 16, 1999.

30. Elisabeth Rosenthal, "U.S. Agrees to Pay China $28 Million for Bombing." *The New York Times*, December 16, 1999.

31. Steven Lee Myers, "Chinese Military to Resume Contacts With Pentagon." *The New York Times*, January 6, 2000.

32. Jane Perlez, "With Relations Warming, Albright Presses China on Taiwan." *The New York Times*, June 23, 2000.

33. "A Payment to China for U.S. Bomb Error." *The New York Times*, January 21, 2001.

34. Frank Langfitt, "China launches battle for public opinion." *The Baltimore Sun*, April 13, 2001.

35. See Michel-Rolph Trouillot, "Abortive Rituals: Historical Apologies in the Global Era," *Interventions*, 2 (2), 171-186.

36. President Clinton, "Excerpt from Remarks at White House Strategy Meeting on Children, Violence, and Responsibility," State Department briefing, May 10, 1999, <http://www.state.gov/www/policy_remarks/1999/990510_clinton_kosovo.html> (10/27/00).

37. "Clinton calls Chinese president with apology." *CNN.com,* May 14, 1999, < http://www.cnn.com/WORLD/europe/9905/14/kosovo.china/ > (July 8, 2004).

38. Ministry of Foreign Affairs of PRC, "Chinese and U.S. Presidents Held Phone Conference." May 14, 1999, <http://www.fmprc.gov.cn/eng/wjdt/2649/t15797.htm> (August 15, 2004).

39. Henry Chu and Maggie Farley, "China Seeks to Restrain Public Anger Over Embassy Bombing." *Los Angeles Times*, May 11, 1999,
<http://www-tech.mit.edu/V119/N26/china_26.26w.html> (August 15, 2004).

40. Secretary of State Madeleine K. Albright. "Letter to Minister of Foreign Affairs of the People's Republic of China." Office of the Spokesman, U.S. Department of State. May 8, 1999.
<http://secretary.state.gov/www/statements/1999/990508.html> (10/27/00).

41. Albright, "Letter to Minister of Foreign Affairs of the People's Republic of China."

42. Personal communication, February 20, 2000.

43. Steven R. Weisman, "The Art and Artifice of Apologizing to China," *The New York Times*, April 13, 200, http://web.lexis-nexis.com/.

44. Yanrong Chang, Personal Communication.

45. Steven R. Wesman, *The New York Times*, April 13, 2001. Lexis-Nexis. See also Pei-Yi Wu, "Self-Examination and Confession of Sins in Traditional China. *Harvard Journal of Asian Studies*, 39, 1 (June 1979), 5-38.

46. In a roundtable discussion sponsored by the Carnegie Council on Ethics and International Affairs, following the U.S.-China standoff of 2001, Council staff accompanied by China scholar Andrew Nathan debated the question of whether a nation should "apologize to another nation for what is perceived by the latter as unacceptable behavior." Andrew Nathan asserted that the confrontation is part of *realpolitik*. As such "in demanding an apology, China merely wanted to protect its national sovereignty." Tony Lang concluded that "both China and the United States acted as states normally do – more concerned with their status and their reputation as states than with the need for an honest relationship." Finally, Lili Cole pointed out that "understanding a people's history – especially the political uses of history and historical memory -- are very much relevant, even crucial, to the debate about what China had in mind when demanding an apology from the United States." See "Should States Apologize?" Roundtable Discussion, Carnegie Council on Ethics and International Affairs, April 2001.
<http://www.cceia.org/lib_pov_apology.html> (May 21, 2001).

47. Willy Wo-Lap Lam, "Analysis: Behind the scenes in Beijing's corridors of power." *CNNcom.*, April 11, 2001, <http://www.cnn.com/2001/WORLD/asiapcf/east/04/11/china.plane.wlam/> (June 8, 2004).

48. Dru Sefton, "Chinese Concept of 'Saving Face' Contributes to Spy Plane Stalemate," *Newhouse News Services*, <http://www.newhouse.com/archive/story1c040501.html>

49. Andrew Nathan, "Should States Apologize?"

50. Richard Tomkins, "Commentary: It's all about 'Face'," *United Press International*, April 5, 2001, <http://web3.infotrac.galegroup.com/itw/infomark/926/309/43173000w3/purl=rc1_EAIM_0_A7279> (November 21, 2001).

51. Tomkins, "Commentary."

52. Steven R. Weisman, "The Art and Artifice of Apologizing to China." *New York Times*, April 13, 2001, http://web.lexis-nexis.com/.

53. Gries, *China's New Nationalism: Pride, Politics, and Diplomacy* (Berkeley: University of California Press), 52.

54. Yongnian Zheng, *Discovering Chinese Nationalism in China.* (Cambridge, U.K.: Cambridge: Univeristy Press, 1999), 138.

55. Peter Hays Gries, "A 'China Threat'?" *World Affairs* 162, i2 (Fall 1999), 63.

56. The idea of saving face is universal enough for all of us to associate it with maintaining one's dignity and self-respect in our interaction with others. Among those specialists who are in a position to shed light on the concept of "face" would be social psychologists who focus on issues of self-esteem in human development and interactions. Anthropologists would dwell on questions of its universality or culturally-specific meanings. The face concept should also be seen from other perspectives including ethics and moral theory because of its relevance to right or wrong behavior, societal norms, and/or more transcendental considerations of justice, peace, and other redemptive ends.

57. Hsien, Chin Hu, "The Chinese Concepts of 'Face'." *American Anthropology*, 1944 (46): 45-64.

58. Gries, *China's New Nationalism*, 26.

59. Gries, "A 'China Threat'?"

60. Gries, "A 'China Threat'?"

61. Hsien, Chin Hu, "The Chinese Concepts of 'face'," 62.

62. Richard Tomkins, "Commentary"

63. Nicholas Tavuchis, *Mea Culpa: A Sociology of Apology and Reconciliation* (Stanford, Cal.: Stanford University Press, 1991), 62.

64. Gerrit W. Gong, "The Beginning of History: Remembering and Forgetting as Strategic Issues." *The Washington Quarterly* 24, i2 (Spring 2001), 48.

65. Peter Brooks, *Troubling Confessions: Speaking Guilt in Law and Literature.* Chicago: The University of Chicago Press, 2000, 21.

66. John .L. Austin, *How to Do Things with Words.* The William James lectures delivered at Harvard University in 1955. Cambridge, Mass.: Harvard University Press, 1975, 78.

67. Austin, 78-79.

68. Such are the views of Peter Hays Gries who argues that apologies between states are about power relations. Apologies like vengeance, he says, "are another means of restoring threatened social hierarchies." Apart from that, Gries insists: "a public offense causes the injured party to lose face and is, therefore, far more offensive than one made in private. Vengeance and apologies not only help reestablish power relations, they also restore self-esteem." Gries, *China's New Nationalism*, 89.

69. W. James Booth, "Communities of Memory: On Identity, Memory, and Debt." *American Political Science Review*, 93, 2 (June 1999), 252.

70. Elazar Barkan has argued that the legitimacy of apology is growing as "the international validation of apologies transforms the ideological norm from nationalist righteousness – 'my history right or wrong' – to an attitude of reconciliation." See Elazar Barkan, *The Guilt of Nations: Restitution and Negotiating Historical Injustices* (New York: W. W. Norton & Co, 2000), 323.

Chapter 6

The Limits and Potential of Political Apologies

Apologies by national leaders for grievous or small infractions have drawn a variety of criticisms, even derision, for their lack of sincerity, for their manipulative ways, and eventually their banality. Most of such criticisms are justified while others come from common misperceptions.

The apologetic frenzy that has manifested itself especially since the end of the Cold War, and rendered so easily with fiat declarations and iterations, has contributed to the deflation of the weight and meaning of true apology. Because they have become somewhat customary, the sincerity of public apologies has been generally in question. The perception that apologies can be manipulative is especially true of apologies between states. These observations are compounded by the habit of apologizers who either expect too much or too little out of apologies. On one hand, there is the tendency of undermining or even avoiding the power of apologies because apologizers calculate the benefits of apologizing are not worth the legal or moral liabilities to be incurred by apologizing. On the other hand, apologizers could expect too much from their apologies. They immediately want something concrete in return thereby affecting adversely the moral weight of their act. They also have exaggerated expectations. They want forgiveness and expiation at the minimum, and in their impatience to move on, apologizers expect more than closure. From the outset, they impose on the apology process the unrealistic goal of starting with a clean slate. It is such common misperceptions and prejudices and the uncritical reactions to the apology phenomenon that cloud our understanding of the essence of public apology and of its prescriptive application in reconciliation. The focus of our inquiry here has been to examine apology in all its forms, to sort out the apologetic grains from the chaff so to speak, and propose an evaluative measure that distinguishes apologies that fail from those that succeed in bringing about reconciliation.

The Two Levels of Apology

If we are to prescribe a method or approach on how to employ this gesture/act to resolve a conflict and restore peaceful relations, we need in the first place to know what its goals are. I suggest that there are two levels of apology; one that aims at *mending* relations, while the second intends to fully restore or at least endeavor to *heal*.

Mending amounts to returning the two alienated parties to their original relationship, which means an apology can temporarily fix what is broken and make it functional again. As we have seen, the minimum requirements for mending relations are, first, admission of wrongdoing or meeting the acknowledgement requisite; and second, accepting responsibility. The reckoning of what took place, the facts and beyond that the admission of guilt, are the first gestures expected from the victim. Yet this acknowledgement is not enough if it is not followed by full accountability. A demonstration by the perpetrator to accept full responsibility for wrongdoing is the second requisite of an apology. The Japanese-North Korean abduction incident and the diplomacy of apology between the two Asian neighbors is an illustration of apology that fails to meet these basic requisites in spite of the rhetoric of mending strained relations.

When North Korean leader Kim Jong-il made the dramatic confession and apologized for the abduction of 13 Japanese citizens to visiting Prime Minister Junichiro Koizumi in 2002, the act was considered a step forward in resolving one of the deep-seated and emotive issues between the two countries, aside from "comfort women," colonial abuses and war crimes. Kim Jong-il's apology and promise to get to the bottom of the crime and Koizumi's routine apologies for Japan's past crimes and a second visit to Pyongyang by the Japanese Prime Minister did not lead to improved relations. Instead, that initiative on the part of North Korea backfired when the Japanese discovered that the returned remains of Yokota, a Japanese woman abducted in 1977, turned out to be somebody else after a DNA test. The resulting public uproar in Japan pushed the Japanese government to the point of considering economic sanctions against North Korea, which the North Koreans characterized as "an act of war." In spite of a promising beginning, the North Korean initiative to reckon with the wrongdoing soon floundered in the intentional or unintentional delivery of the false remains of the deceased turning the expected accountability for the crime by the North Korean state into a sham. The elements of full accountability that could include compensations and the showing of good faith were plainly missing in this case. The apologies failed to fulfill the minimum requisites of an apology to mend relations. This failure may also be related to the unresolved legacies of Japan's imperial past and World War II that require the second level of apology, which is to heal.

Apology to heal aims at reconciling societies and as such involves more parties and requires more requisites to be fulfilled for a successful outcome.

While apology to mend is partial and fulfills only the first two requisites (acknowledgement and accountability), apology to heal aims at full reconciliation demanding the last two requisites (truth-telling and public remorse) as well.

In this second level of apology, the commitment to acknowledge wrongdoing, to be fully accountable for it, even beyond that, to come clean about the past and to be prepared for unconditional remorse carries weight when it is legitimized by domestic public support. In other words, public support should be solicited through public knowledge and debate, a task actualized by moral leadership. The critical role played by leaders to apologize instead of choosing the politically expedient silence is also relevant to this level apology. There are evident political risks that are taken by leaders who declare wrongdoing and in doing so commit society to live up to the associated responsibility. Thus the ability of leaders to mobilize the domestic public in the completion of the apology process is important. As much as in other treaty obligations, apology between states benefits from legislative approval and legitimate support from the people on whose behalf the apology is rendered.

Categorical/Non-categorical Apologies

Questions have been raised about the demands for apologies by individuals, groups and nations holding states accountable for crimes and misdeeds more than ever before. And of these, more grievances have come from the inaction of states to intervene and to prevent human rights violations that in turn precipitate voluntary apologies by states for all kinds of inaction.[1] Among the cases examined in the last chapters, the Rwandan genocide prompted public apologies for inaction by the international community, especially from those countries with the means to prevent the genocide.

I am making a distinction between two apologetic speech acts one made for inaction to prevent harm, and the other for direct action in the wrongdoing. I am calling apologies given for the latter, for direct perpetration of the crime, *categorical*. In categorical apologies such as those made by German and Japanese leaders for World War II atrocities there is little ambiguity about the nature of the crimes involved even when the apologies are partial or incomplete. They are also difficult to render – to accept culpability, to assume responsibility, and express remorse. This is not the case of *non-categorical* apologies, apologies that are given for inaction to prevent a crime. The extent of implication in the crime in question could always be contested as in the roles played by the U.S. and Belgium in the Rwandan tragedy. In all non-categorical apologies where the excuses for not having taken action could be endless, apologies come easily. Let us reflect further on this non-categorical apology.

The excuses for not having acted for a crime are so many that all non-categorical apologies could draw ridicule. Recall the classic apologia of "if we only knew," "if we had the means," and "are we the only ones expected to act?"

From there one might come to the conclusion that apologies for inaction are either insincere or partial most often? I argue on the contrary that in fact sincere and remorseful apologies can be given for failing to act. Clinton's Kigali speech was a pseudo-apology because his carefully crafted words of regret, among other things, pleaded ignorance of the impending genocide in Rwanda, spread blames among other parties, and failed as contrition. What weakened the moral weight of his stated apology was his failure to assume full responsibility for the part played by the U.S. in the inaction of the United Nations to prevent the genocide - with no excuses. He could have begun by saying, "I will not make any excuses for the failure, but fail we did." What changes a potentially meaningful apology into a partial or pseudo-apology is the justification clauses politicians and diplomats are adept at attaching to what seem to be candid words of regret. Politicians who often do not want to take the risk or pay the price are more likely to hedge the truth, to offer a justification, and spread the blame to escape any liability. An apology made in good faith, an apology that is remorseful should be unconditional and absolute and *extra-ordinary*. Non-categorical apologies can be remorseful and forthcoming. They are also driven by certain moral obligations and duties.

Non-categorical apology is related to a moral responsibility akin to an international human rights regime that has been in the shaping in fits and starts since the Nuremberg Trials. This new moral regime is increasingly putting demands on powerful and influential countries that are being held accountable for action and inaction to prevent mass human rights violations from happening. By choosing not to act under such circumstances such countries are considered to be morally negligent. Moral negligence as I apply it here is neglecting to prevent harm advertently as opposed to unwittingly allowing harm, which is a legal concept. The major powers in the Security Council in one form or another knew of the impending catastrophe that awaited Rwandans in the spring of 1994. Yet they passed a resolution that would limit the necessary number of peacemaking forces to avoid the genocide. Considering the consequential neglect of the big powers, their inaction calls for full apologies in lieu of the partial apologies rendered by their leaders. But I am not making a moral equivalence between the Rwandan *genocidaires* who perpetrated the horrendous crimes and those who could have but failed to prevent it. Those big powers who had the means to prevent the atrocities to happen are morally accountable only in as much as they have pledged in the international covenants to which they are party of.

Voluntary or Demanded Apologies

Apology is normally given voluntarily not because one is coerced to do so. An apology given under coercion, like confession given in the same way, loses its affectivity and power of remorse. In apologies both voluntary and demanded there is an implication that it is expected to be given. There is an assumption that there is a moral order within which an apology is expected following a transgression. Apologies on demand however lend themselves to the pursuit of all kinds of political agenda. They could originate from people and groups with both legitimate and illegitimate grievances.

Remorse by Proxy

In state apologies, apologies are normally given through deputies and representatives, and that poses certain problems of representation, agency and legitimacy.

Under normal circumstances the apologizer is expected to represent the perpetrators whether the crime is attributed to a small group or the collectivity. He/she represents the people at large. The apologizer and the recipient are merely deputies of the specific or larger group implicated in the perpetration or the victimization of the crime. Thus the lack of proximity between the prime actors raises issues of affectivity and moral agency. There are marked differences between the apologizer facing survivors of mass atrocities, addressing a parliament in delivering an apology, and letting lower echelon bureaucrats hammer out a negotiated apology to be made public.

The presence or lack of voice on the part of both the primary apologizers and victims is problematic in political apologies. Consider the long drawn activism by Japanese NGOs and groups who sought Japanese apologies for war crimes and campaigned for years inside and out of the Japanese political process. The same is true of their counterparts – victims, survivors and sometimes the organizations representing them - in neighboring Koreas, Taiwan and the Philippines. While apology demanding groups and individuals in Japan struggled to put public pressures on the political parties in the Diet and Japanese courts, their counterparts in neighboring countries pushed for their cause in conjunction with and sometimes against their own respective governments. Apologies initiated by individuals do not gain immediate political currency if their cause goes against majority public opinion or the dominant ideology. How much is known of individual and group American apologies that were rendered for the Abu Ghraib prison tortures?[2] Very little. On the receiving end also, the victims and their families may not know of the apologies directed to them while their governments might. The strengths and weaknesses of agency are related to the support and the legitimacy for the apology in the apologizing country.

Legitimizing Apology

A state apology, which is by definition an apology by proxy, most often suffers from democratic legitimation. As they are in charge of foreign policy, it is the executive offices of nation-states that normally engage in state apologies. Also those demanding apologies routinely address governments to seek recognition

and eventually legal redress. These conventions therefore undercut more legitimate ways of mobilizing support and authorizing lasting reconciliation efforts.
They might even discourage the initiation of apology altogether. Left to the
affairs of state, apologies could become politicians' tools to appease, to normal-
ize, and to maintain the status-quo, but not to reconcile societies.

Apologies are successful when they are legitimized by a bottom-up popular
support first and then put on public record, as a legislative act for example. Public debate in Belgium on the country's role in the Rwandan genocide led to a
parliamentary investigative commission and eventually an endorsement of the
Prime Minister's repeated remorseful apologies to Rwanda. Somewhat similar is
the German Bundestag's apology directly to the people of Guernica, Spain, following the example of their president for the 1937 German bombing. In Japan
the failure of the Japanese Diet to pass a resolution of a comprehensive apology
for World War II crimes during the 50th anniversary of the war's end was a
missed opportunity of reconciliation that could have complemented and given
weight to the remarkable apologies made by Prime Minster Murayama in 2001.
Such a legislatively endorsed apology would give legal weight in the eyes of
victims.

When politicians use apology as political currency for ends other than reconciliation they are not only unaccountable to the public but in some cases they
usurp the sentiments of victims for reasons of state. The Japan-North Korea
political dance over the abduction issue is illustrative of this phenomenon. That
the Japanese government rode over Japanese public sentiment in order to get
political concessions (i.e. normalization, nuclear nonproliferation) was only
matched by the unprecedented apology made by the North Korean supreme
leader presumably to soften Japan for economic aid. Once again, short-term political expediency takes precedence over healing mutual historical wounds that
remain under the surface of political normalcy.

Assessing Success in Apologies

So far I have been alluding to successful and unsuccessful apologies without
explicit criteria of assessment. I will discuss here in ample detail the utilities and
goals of public apologies, the processes required to reach those goals, and finally
the overall measures of what would be considered a successful apology. To begin with, one would appraise success only if the goals of an apology are all met.
Based on the taxonomy of apologies outlined earlier, the distinction between "an
apology to mend" and "an apology to heal" become apparent at close examination.

The Measure of Apology to Mend

Apology is commonly used in diplomatic practice as a catalyst in crisis management. State officials pronounce apology not simply out of diplomatic courtesy, but they often use them and accept them from their counterparts as a matter of strategy. Malaysia in March 2005 was willing to accept Indonesia's apology via its ambassador following a protest and the burning of the Malaysian flag by Indonesians against the awarding of oil and gas concession to a multinational oil giant in a territorially contested maritime block. Malaysian officials were quick to accept the apology although it did not originate from the foreign ministry. Patching up relations between the two states was in the interest of the Malaysians. The Malaysian foreign minister declared, "They apologized ... we should not be arrogant and reject it because it came from its ambassador. I believe that he had his government's mandate (to apologize)." Referring to the Indonesian ambassador's apology rendered during a meeting with a youth group at the Indonesian embassy, the Malaysian foreign minister adds, "He said it in public... it is a public apology. I think it is good enough. We appreciate that he recognized that there had been some over-reaction ... there had been action that is unbecoming. It speaks well for both Malaysia and Indonesia's relationship." [3] In the context of diplomacy and international politics the use of public apology is instrumental.

When U.S. forces bombed the Chinese Embassy in Belgrade in 1998, Chinese-American relations slowly deteriorated in spite of immediate remedial actions taken by the Clinton Administration. The aim of the U.S. government was to rapidly repair damage of an already tenuous relationship with China on the Taiwan and other outstanding issues in a war environment. The swift acknowledgement of wrongdoing by the United States and decisions to compensate for the damages was adequate for the Chinese to reverse the initial angry diplomatic responses, including the severing of military relations. Months after the initial apologies by US officials to China and a decision by the US government to pay for damages to the Chinese Embassy the diplomatic chill between the two countries had thawed. More than a year after the bombing incident followed by US agreement on the terms of the Chinese admittance into the World Trade Organization, diplomatic relations between China and the US had normalized including the resumption of high-level military contacts between the two.

Apology to mend is typically in state apologies in which the acknowledgement and accountability imperatives of our apology mode feature importantly. In those cases where a state will be held responsible for violence or damages incurred, governments are often quick to acknowledge culpability and prepare to pay compensations if the relations with the other party are friendly to begin with. They fear their relations will be in jeopardy if they do not exercise the expected public contrition and prepare to be accountable for the damages. There are, however, those circumstances where the apologetic act is no longer instrumental but an end in itself. Such was the case of the American spy plane incident in 2002 in which the Chinese put a high stake on receiving an official apology from the United States government. In this particular conflict wherein the international legality of sovereignty and reciprocity were in question, power politics and "national face" made the apology itself a desirable but a highly contested end. Ultimately, the negotiated apology satisfied the Chinese to save face, and enabled the Americans to rescue the detained navy pilots without worsening the diplomatic stand-off. When apology to mend is rendered in purely utilitarian fashion as part of repairing damages, along with material compensation (if applicable), the apologetic language is often measured. Regrets may be expressed, compensations may be given, but it does not go beyond that. The American apology, *yihan*, is not the same as a remorseful apology, *daoquin*, which is considered a full apologetic expression. Consider the following fine lines between these varying understandings of what an apology constitutes in the rather bizarre Cambodian apology given to Thailand after a week-long anti-Thai riots that involved the burning of the Thai embassy and prominent businesses in Phnom Penh. Cambodian anger was sparked by unconfirmed reports that a Thai actress had said that Cambodia's famous Angkor Wat temple complex belonged to Thailand. In retaliation, Thailand unilaterally downgraded its diplomatic relations with Cambodia, severed its economic aid and sealed off the border.

The apologetic response by Cambodia, the interactions by the monarchs and government officials of the respective countries are instructive of the substantive and symbolic dimensions of public apologies. The Cambodians who would economically lose from deteriorating relations acted quickly, leading to some confusion about the depth of the apology. At first Cambodia's prime minister Hor Nam Hong personally delivered a letter from Cambodia's King Norodom Sihanouk to Thailand's King Bhumibol Adulyadej. The fact that the Thai King gave audience to the Cambodian prime minister was considered by the press as a reconciliatory gesture. In the meantime Cambodia's ambassador in the United States sent a letter of apology to his Thai counterpart in saying he had called "as many Thai friends as possible to convey my sincere apologies and profound regret for the harm that has been done to the noble Thai people." He goes on, "Although I do not have all the elements to explain what sparked these events to such a dimension, I also cannot hide how shameful I feel before such uncivilized behavior demonstrated by the rioters."[4] Protocol aside, that expression of contrition was seen as excessive even treasonous by the Cambodian King. The Thai prime minister, however, was not bothered by the angry reactions of the Cambodian king, saying that the diplomatic fuss was more about protocol and not substance. The Cambodian foreign minister criticized and corrected the ambassador's apology in a letter to him: "First, the government's position is to express our regret but not apology. Secondly, your Excellency had used the words, 'uncivilized' which seems to insult our nation."[5] The Cambodian government was prepared to fully acknowledge wrongdoing, and to be accountable by pledging to compensate for damages to the embassy and other Thai properties. Yet both the Cambodian government and the monarch were not prepared to offer the Thai side remorseful apologies. Bruised national pride aside regrets along with compensation were adequate for the normalization of relations.

To re-cap the essential measure of a successful public apology aimed at normalizing relations between states rests on whether the damaged relations are restored in short order with hardly any cost to the larger societies involved. In diplomacy what matters is figuring out the acceptable cost one incurs from an apology. Malaysians readily recognized Indonesia's apology in spite of the fact that it was delivered in less than full protocol (from Indonesia's ambassador who took it upon himself to do it), and that the two countries have a standing territorial dispute. The acknowledgement of wrongdoing (the burning of the Malaysian flag and property damages) accounting for the misdeed of the Indonesian protestors is an apology by proxy successfully delivered. The two apologies made by the U.S. government to China were successful after all is said and done. In the 1999 incident full diplomatic relations were restored even though the Chinese were protesting to the very end that the American side was not fully forthcoming as to whether the NATO bombing was intentional or not. The smell of "dirty politics" is written all over the case with suspicions whether the Chinese embassy in Belgrade was used to transmit information to the Serbs and NATO's bombing was aimed to terminate that intelligence link. Pragmatic politics prevailed, eventually ending hostilities with necessary apologies and compensation. In the 2001 Hainan spy plane incident, apology served the end of politics, at little cost once again, in spite of weeks of high diplomatic tension. According to one scholar American and Chinese leaders reached a compromise through semantic ambiguity and language flexibility in order to protect their bilateral relations and to address the criticisms of their respective domestic hardliners.[6] Taken as a whole, the acknowledgement and accountability mandates are adequate in restoring national pride, rendering justice, and mending relations for the long haul. The truth-telling and remorse mandates of our apology model play a far more important role in the deeper traumatic conflicts involving large segments of society over a longer period such as wars and genocides than in the brief crises between nations wherein government secrecy and cold rational calculations prevail.

The Measure of Apology to Heal

If assessing the degree of success of an apology to mend is difficult, plotting the routes to healing and knowing that healing has come to pass seems even more untenable. Two obstacles get in the way of aiming at healing. One has to do with the ambiguities in the meaning of healing as it applies to societies. Even if we manage to discover an operational understanding of healing, the difficulty remains as to when or if ever true healing can take place.

An apology to heal is directed to reconcile two alienated societies. The assumption here is that one society or group is wounded as a result of mass violence. This analogy of a wound that needs healing should be distinguished from a plague or some pathological illness in order to underscore that which needs healing, is damage caused by the victimizing party. The wounds of the victims can heal by the regeneration of the body cells, so to speak, or repair themselves, leaving a scar nevertheless. But unattended deep societal wounds fester and eventually kill. Consideration of both the physical and socio-psychological dimensions of victimization is important when we think of ways of helping individuals and groups to heal. Then follow the more difficult questions of comprehending the healing process and recognizing whether or not it has succeeded. Since my apology mode here has more to do with the apologizer than the victims who are the object of the healing process, talking about healing remains conjectural even when I suggest the following two elements indispensable to an apology that heals.

An apology to heal and to restore a community from damages arising from the wrongdoing of an individual, a group or state should seek as part of the restoration a cleansing of the past deeds. The goals of exposing the truths of wrong deeds of the past are reached in a variety of ways. For governments and victims who seek retributive justice, the courts and criminal tribunals have been the avenues through which the truths about the wrongdoing are exposed and punishments rendered. While the results of such dispensations may gratify victims and survivors, the complexity of determining guilt and consideration for a future-oriented reconciliation have compelled post-conflict societies to gravitate toward restorative justice. Among the advantages of restorative justice one that stands out is the opportunity it provides to perpetrators of past crimes to speak up. The most recent innovation in this area is of course the increasingly frequent use of truth commissions in exchange of amnesty or by way of conditional amnesty. In most of these cases it is the state that plays the central role in initiating and mediating the testimony and witnessing of past wrongdoing. In the aftermath of mass violence the successor state establishes a truth commission to cleanse "itself" of the crimes of the previous perpetrator state. Or the successor state may initiate alternative avenues of justice like the *gaçaças* in Rwanda where the state's capacity to administer justice falls short. The United Nations has increasingly acknowledged and supported the importance of truth commissions as part of transnational justice by creating those institutions to bring out the truth of the past in countries like East Timor and Liberia. However, when states are the representatives of either the perpetrators or the victims, the focus of our study here, there is a characteristic resistance to truth-telling by perpetrator states.

One of the difficulties a successor state faces (after a civil war, repression) is overcoming the inherent and structural tendencies of the state apparatus to cling to government secrets. In societies in transition how flexible and open will the status apparatus be to accommodate hearings and testimonies by making crucial documents and files available? This leads us to the next question. To what extent should the leadership and the institutions of the perpetrator regime be purged of individual perpetrators and collaborators in order to set up independent commissions to cleanse the state of its wrongful past? These obstacles to truth and justice require bold initiatives by leaders of the post-criminal state unless a third party, such as the United Nations, is invited in to carry out this difficult task. There is less thought put into initiatives to reconcile societies represented by states without an international mediation.

The second measure of an apology to heal asks whether a perpetrator group or society can collectively express sorrow and remorse to collectivities like we do to individuals, for the benefit of the victims of the crimes committed. While we have varying views on the question of whether we can attribute remorse to collectivities like we can to individuals, I will answer that question by suggesting four tasks that need to be accomplished in order to restore alienated communities. First, we look at the record of those individual leaders who have come forward, of their own accord, to apologize for the perpetrator states they represent. Does the leader's apology pass the tests of acknowledgement, accountability, truth-telling and remorse? Second, to ensure the efficacy of the leader's apologetic act, her or his mandate needs to be made clear by the formality, setting and publicity of the apology rendered. A well-publicized public support for the apology legitimizes the act. Third, a step further of such public apology is that it be established by legal and institutional means. While having the apology on record is important, the apology will be more permanent by virtue of what it does to restore, such as a standing fund for reparation, a memorial with public education as its goal, and the construction of an organizational relationship between the concentric circles of perpetrators and victims. Finally, the emotive aspect of the apology should be conveyed in a ritual that is commensurate with the repentance and sorrow that the apologizer is ready to convey sincerely. There is a tendency to undermine the value of such a ritualistic approach to collective remorse. The remorseful act or ceremony can be delivered by an individual leader, by a group representing the class of the perpetrator state, or by a legislative body that can carefully craft a language that will embody all the essential elements of complete apology.

So far I have been outlining all that needs to be done to make an apology to heal succeed. Even though the steps I proposed above fulfill the litmus test for the success of any apology it would seem that it will hopefully induce the primary and associated victims to forgive. Tavuchis found the power of apology to overcome resentment and induce forgiveness from the victim extraordinary, even mysterious. Grover and Verwoerd explain this mystery as a combination of acknowledgements by the perpetrator of wrongdoing, the moral status of victims, and the legitimacy of feelings of anger and resentment by the victims.[7] This is an elegant reasoning for explaining the potential of an effective apology for a shift of moral attitude on the part of the victim. In the ethic of apology advanced in the present study, however, the moral power of the apology derives from the fact that an apology is given unconditionally.

To expect forgiveness at the end of an apology process reduces the weight of remorse and repentance. A perpetrator-centered apology even with the telos of restoring community cannot presume that forgiveness is forthcoming. After all, remorse implies only regret and sorrow on the part of the perpetrator while repentance is the affirmation to oneself (as well as the public) that the crime will not be repeated. One can easily argue that these crucial initiatives of an apology could wear away the resentment or may even contribute to the moral shift in the victim that leads to forgiveness. But if forgiveness is not to be expected what else can take its place to bring closure and healing among alienated communities?

An apology aimed at healing should be considered successful if it accomplishes the following. First, victims should be able to recognize that all avenues have been pursued to bring into the public's eyes the truths of the crimes committed. Second, it is important as well that perpetrators come to learn and appreciate the depth of suffering borne by victims, survivors, and the outer circles of the primary victims. Third, material compensations ought to be paid to the satisfaction of victims. And finally, when both moral and material reparations are completed, partners of peace should work on consolidating those gains. Societal healing ushers when signs of the restoration of a new moral community manifest themselves as victims and perpetrators identify with each other and together look into the future and plan for it.

The plateau that needs to be reached then is where past enemies identify with each other. This can be assured by peace-building efforts including building institutions to reconstruct the post-conflict society, as well as dealing with the traumatic effects of violence on individuals and social groups. Along this line Malvern Lumsden's proposal that is most applicable to post-civil war societies can also deal with inter-state reconciliation goals. Lumsden's idea refers to:

> integrating survivors and even perpetrators into a postwar society; to providing a space for creative problem-solving and conflict resolution; to the need of catharsis and emotional expression in a secure 'holding environment'; to the need for reintegrating shattered selves; and for reintegrating individual, community and nation.[8]

While states take the most active role in societal reconciliation as in post-civil war situations, in those cases where states either represent or take the lead roles in inter-state reconciliation (i.e. Germany and Israel, Japan and Koreas) the state-centric demands for preserving sovereignty, the "dirty-hand" rationale of national leaders, the realities of an immoral society to use Niebuhr's words, confound those who want to act morally. How could states and their leaders overcome these real or imagined fetters of realist absolutism?

For an apology to heal on the part of a state, it entails accepting the risk of legal liabilities, reprisal, or national humiliation perhaps. Unlike most diplomatic deals that are reached most often surreptitiously, the public nature of apology to heal that openly acknowledges guilt is more likely to be resisted for fear of compromising national interests. This brings us to the second realist hesitation, and that is, leaders have to do what they have to do, learn how not to be good as Machiavelli advises, even dirty their hands to serve a higher good. This rationale of dirty-hands is so readily accepted that unscrupulous justifications are routinely made to act immorally. Finally, the presumption of a dangerous world and the mistrust of others especially those culturally distant from one's own are restraints to taking risks and acting boldly.

In the context of the ethic of apology that I proposed at the outset, an apology that would lead to permanent reconciliation between societies has to be an extraordinary act and this would require taking certain risks, even on the part of a political leader. The risk taken here is based on our understanding of state sovereignty that relies on coercive power, but when approached from the *telos* of an apology we are relying on the notion of moral power that resists realist hesitations for more permanent solutions to conflict. Therefore, such risk taking and visionary thinking can come only from either bold statesmanship or democratic deliberation in order to be able to overcome conventional fears and short-sighted interests.

The German/Israeli case demonstrates that the reconciliation process does not have to follow any logic or linear steps. It was rather the convergence of actions and initiatives that brought together a historic reconciliation between the two peoples and states. The initiatives of individuals like Israeli Prime Minister David Ben-Gurion who challenged the Israeli state to disassociate from the Nazi regime, the founders of Peace with Israel Movement who made the apologetic call, and Chancellor Adenauer who launched the political process for material restitution, were the critical actions that unraveled rigidity, intransigence and prejudice. Just as in the apology mode to mend, apology to heal would require that the imperatives of acknowledgement and accountability be satisfied at the minimum. However, since this mode involves the reconciliation of societies, the fulfillment of the other two requirements, that of truth-telling and public remorse becomes all the more important.

In Germany, knowledge and facts about Nazi crimes were extensively disclosed through the Nuremberg trials, fiction, memoirs, films and popular culture. There were also occasional historiological tempests when for example the publication of Daniel Goldhagen's *Hitler's Willing Executioners* exhumed old ideas of collective guilt. Truth-telling was also advanced by the debates on reparation in Germany and Israel and by the intense public discourse on how best to remember the holocaust. One of the most influential outcomes of the debate on the memorialization of the Holocaust is the eventual consensus to avoid aesthecization in the building of a national memorial. Inaugurated in May 2005, the Memorial to the Murdered Jews of Europe was approved by the Bundestag in 1999 following intense debates about its location and design. The memorial, designed by American architect Peter Eiseman, is situated in the heart of Berlin and features a field of stelae representing the dead complemented by historic memorial sites and an underground information center. The anti-monument movement prevailed in the debates about this architectural representation in making this memorial at once commemorative and educational. One of the outcomes of that postmodernist critique of representation is perhaps the influence it had on other memorials like the Kigali Genocide Memorial in Rwanda for instance.

Public remorse was late in coming in West Germany and even later in East Germany, but the memorable images of Chancellor Willy Brandt on his knees in 1970 in Poland and of German Chancellor Schroeder and Israeli Prime Minister Barak at the Sachsenhausen death camp in 1998 are etched in public memory.[9] So was the emotional apology for the Holocaust by President Johannes Rau in 2000 in the first address to the Israeli parliament by a German leader. Public remorse as part of a process in motion toward reconciliation becomes an important facilitator to bring alienated *peoples* together as those symbolic public images of remorse are reproduced in popular culture across generations.

The limits and potential of political apologies have been illustrated in the four cases examined so far from which certain lessons can be learned.

Gleaning Lessons: Germany/Israel

The first lesson of the German/Israeli case is that it proved the four requisites for a successful of apology can come in any order. The German and Israeli case presents a complex and unusual unfolding of events that eventually brought together two deadly enemies in a rather short order. Much credit has been given to the presence and structural arrangements dictated by the victors of World War II for a stable and peaceful democratic West Germany to emerge and hence a political culture that permitted free debates and deliberations in how to deal with its Nazi past. The issue of dealing with Jewish survivors and a new Jewish state could have been resolved differently in hindsight considering the ideologically heated debates in the renewed democracy of postwar Germany, but the vision and pragmatism of the Christian Democrats prevailed with Chancellor Adenauer at the helm. Thus accountability led the way when in fact all of the reckoning with the facts of Nazi crimes was not in, when silences and denials still prevailed, and long before public remorse was ever expressed for the Holocaust.

The key player and contributor to the historic reconciliation between Germany and Israel is undoubtedly Chancellor Konrad Adenauer, who, after a cursory acknowledgement of the crimes committed by the Nazi regime, in a famous speech to the Bundestag launched a solution of material indemnity, and a restitution plan that made Israel the major beneficiary of Jewish restitution. Successive German leaders pretty much followed the pragmatic but less repentant tone set by Adenauer that emphasized the accountability of the German state for the consequences of Nazi crimes and the need for atonement through restitution. Adenauer's singular contribution was to take that one bold step of material atonement that was to become the backbone of the rest of the reconciliation process including dealing with public guilt and memory. When Germans inaugurated the new Memorial to Murdered Jews of Europe in Berlin in May 2005 they completed an epic reconciliation project that has already been a model for other human tragedies like the 1994 Rwandan genocide.

Gleaning Lessons: Rwanda

The German lesson was not lost on Rwandan leaders and their international supporters who built and opened a national memorial for the 1994 genocide only 10 years after the last genocide of the twentieth century. The memorial benefited from the debates on memorials and monuments in the 80s in Germany with an anti-monument bias and a focus on remembering and learning at the same time. The Rwandan genocide itself and the debate it generated about the prevention of crime against humanity and global responsibility will perhaps make it as defining a historical event as the Nuremberg trials were in the 1940s for the following reasons. In hindsight, the failures of the United Nations in Rwanda reminds us of the failures of the League of Nations in the 1930s that fell victim to selfish national interests and political expediency except that a host of other supportive institutions and movements existed in the 1990s. There is a maturing human rights regime supported by ceaseless efforts of professionals and volunteers. The international community has decades of peacekeeping experience behind it. Sovereignty has been redefined to accommodate humanitarian interventions accompanied by the establishment of the International Criminal Court. Regional organizations have also assumed more responsibility for their international securities. Nevertheless these movements and forces for peace failed to prevail over power politics once again. The Rwandan genocide has posed a challenge for the United Nations to redefine itself in order to prevent the next genocide from taking place.

The challenge to members of the international community is a more pronounced global accountability for genocide and other preventable mass violence of violations of human rights. A human rights regime buttressed by the institutions and movements mentioned above is strengthening a moral community that will hold nations responsible for their actions as well as their inaction. Just as British and French leadership were stigmatized for their appeasement of Nazi Germany, all the powers who had the means to prevent the Rwandan genocide can be blamed for negligence in this new moral community. The apologies given for that negligence by the parties involved could have given weight to that moral community.

Gleaning Lessons - Japan

The case of Japan and its neighbors has always been about overcoming the alienation between neighboring nations caused by the legacies of war and colonialism. On the surface these countries including, Japan, China, Taiwan, the Koreas and the Philippines are good neighbors for the most part, with robust economic ties and cultural relations. Yet occasional bursts of anger and defensiveness are exchanged between these countries and Japan, manifesting long-held grievances from the years of World War and the Japanese imperial periods earlier. The grievances and campaigns by war slaves, comfort women and others who seek apologies and redress have continuously put pressure on the Japanese state and caused blame in the international community for Japan's intransigence against those grievances. Japan paradoxically has also the reputation for giving economic aid to its neighbors, for meeting its treaty obligations, for its pacifist constitution. Regardless, its pursuit to maintain normal relations with its neighbors thanks to its economic clout has not allowed Japan to shed its war legacies. Japan actually made gains in its efforts to come to terms with its past through paying reparations and increasingly more remorseful speech acts of apologies by its prime ministers, and goodwill state visit exchanges. Yet the Japanese governing elite has lacked the political will so far to go that extra mile in making historical breakthroughs in dramatic gestures of public remorse. What would be the cost of such a gesture to the last of the aging "comfort women"? Can the Japanese Diet attempt to pass a resolution of apology for war crimes like the one it attempted to pass for the 50th anniversary of the end of World War II? A combination of renewed nationalism, conservative incrementalism and status-quo politics is holding back Japan from taking those bold steps toward reconciliation with its neighbors.

Gleaning Lessons – China

The apologies associated with Germany, Rwanda, and Japan are about remedies and redress involving large-scale historical injustice and violence. The apologies regarding China constitute a simpler contemporary type of brief infraction causing a diplomatic crisis. I have tied together thus both the contemporary and the historical in order to generate generalizable observations about political apologies regardless of the extent of injustice or violence. The inclusion of the American apologies to China with the other cases has enabled us to explain how the extent of transgression affects an apology process. From such cases of diplomatic crises and the intervention of apology we could all the more appreciate the apologies that play a role in resolving minor infractions that can precipitate larger conflicts are by no means modest, although I may have painted such apologies negatively for their moral limitations. Maintaining good open channels of communications, normalizing relations that are severed or weakened by unsettled deep historical injuries in order to avert potential violence is no small feat. For these very reasons we should suspend doubts about them in order to learn more about their dynamics and prescribe norms.

What the two American apologies to China revealed to us is that apologies under a diplomatic context pose different problems and opportunities compared to the historical apologies. In each of the apologies to China, the apology process is part of a crisis decision-making characteristically made under little time, political pressures and a threatening international environment. These cases brought up as we noted different sets of questions concerning apology and conflict resolution.

Among the observations we made about apologies in diplomacy a few stand out. In the first place apologies pass as diplomatic currencies affected seemingly by some sort of market system of apologies where they are in high demand in some circumstances and almost devalued in others. They are offered at little cost in certain situations while they are highly prized in others. This brings us to another observation, and that is, in the two American apologies to China the apologies were subject to intense diplomacy and negotiations influenced by the unsettled historical grievances in the region. As a result of these historic sensitivities, face-saving played importantly in the negotiated apologies. In the final analysis, the apologies aimed at mending and normalizing relations (i.e. the apologies to China) are *sui generis* different from the historical ones (i.e. apologies regarding German, Japan and Rwanda) where apologies are not simply political currencies but have intrinsic moral values in themselves. Nevertheless, I contend the two types are in fact related as the vicious circle of violence, historical grievances, contentious relations, and the return of violence have revealed.

Policy Prescriptions

The cases discussed in this study are representative, but by no means exhaustive of the types of political apologies that have been made in recent years as part of conflict resolution and peace-building efforts. The lessons gleaned from them might inform policy-makers and peace practitioners. I draw here a number of condensed guidelines for practical and ethical considerations in making public apologies. I have separated the prescriptions for apologies to mend from apologies to heal.

Prescriptions for Apologies to Mend Relations

Here are specific recommendations to those who have discovered that apologies can be a catalyst in resolving an international conflict when one state has clearly incurred injuries to persons and properties of another.

1. **Expediency.** Although there is no statute of limitations on apologies, an apology given expeditiously proves to be effective. In state apologies this is simply a matter of rational decision making. A state stands to benefit in the long-run by admitting immediately to wrongdoing for which it is legally responsible. Under the gaze of international media, delayed admission can prove to be diplomatically costly.

2. **Formality and Legality.** These two go together. Is important that the apologetic speech act itself be of official nature, delivered in a public space with a fitting décor and ritual. This setting should also provide an opportunity to display remorse publicly. Closely associated with such formality is to put the apology on public record to make the commitment legally relevant.

3. **Proximity between Apologizer and Recipient of Apology**. In order for an apology to be effective and to satisfy the representatives of the victimized side, it is vital that the apologizing state and its agents make sure that the primary victims or those closest to them are addressed and that they know of the gesture even if this is done by proxy.

4. **Legitimacy and Support**. The deputies of the state or society doing the apologizing have automatically the diplomatic recognition to apologize on behalf of the state they represent but not the mandate and legitimacy to do so. Also the apologizer will have a stronger position to mend damaged relations through an apology if the action has popular support at home.

Prescriptions for Apology toward Societal Healing

In severely wounded societies apology by proxy falls short and obviously calls for a qualitatively different apology that is deep and more comprehensive. Here are a few broad guidelines to provide direction for those committed to starting a process of reconstruction of societies totally alienated from one other and wherein the violence and trauma have been extensive.

1. **Social Reconstruction.** While thought is put into post-civil war and post-genocide reconstructions, the building of communities that are set

apart by competing state loyalties is uncharted ground in peace build-ing. State policymakers can learn from the successes of NGOs that successfully engage with each other to reconcile alienated groups across national borders.

2. **Democratic Accountability**. In order for apologies to have legal and moral weight it is best that they have the approval of the people on whose behalf the public apology is being made. Thus a bottom-up le-gitimation should garner the support of public opinion and then be leg-islated. That will put the apology on public record permanently.

3. **Restoration of Moral Identity**. Restoring community being the goal of an apology toward healing, guilt and responsibility for wrongdoing by implication extend beyond the proximate parties of perpetrators and victims. The moral thread that ties these parties facilitates the apology process to the point of not necessarily forgiveness but the identification of victims with their perpetrators when they recognize that their suffer-ing has been acknowledged.

4. **An Extraordinary Act**. Bold statesmanship or popular will as ex-pressed in a legislative body is required sometimes to jump start a stalled process and toward bringing together two alienated societies for the benefit of the future. Here the role of a dramatic move by a leader or leaders to make a breakthrough cannot be underestimated. Such moves demand taking calculated risk and good timing. This is the other half of democratic accountability, where the people's agency is com-plemented with governmental power.

Apologies by Proxy

Although much is made of the plethora of public apologies given by political and religious leaders in recent years, in diplomacy, in peace initiatives and in politics at large, the importance of state apologies has yet to be acknowledged at its true value.

The reasons for cynicism toward state apologies are many. For one, there are too many of them. The numerous apologies made by Pope John Paul VI and President Clinton added to apologies by other leaders and corporate groups, has prompted media analysts to declare that apologies are in vogue or are part of the new age of political correctness. One can argue that the increasing frequency in the utterances of apology has made the meaning of the speech act banal and cheap. In reality it is the quality of apology, its content and delivery that have given it a bad name.[10] Another reason why apology is taken less seriously than it should be has to do with the simplistic ideological apposition made between realists and liberals in their view of morality and its place in global politics. Those who bring in the practice of apology and forgiveness in statecentric politics are accused of moralizing, although realists in the extreme can do the same. As Sissela Bok so aptly puts it, "Singling out one's opponents as moralizers and stressing the realism of one's own views can therefore in itself be far too simplistic."[11]

It is important to note that the apology process in itself cannot carry the load of conflict resolution or reconciliation. It is by no means a panacea when one considers the advancements made in diplomatic creativity, peacemaking, legal developments, new organizations, or the reintroduction of old ones. The introduction of apology and forgiveness to diplomatic and peace practice wherever they are needed stems from the new innovative norms that have produced positive results in recent years. Think how far we have come in peacekeeping practices, demobilization of previous enemy forces and the reconstruction of civil institutions in post-civil war societies. As we have pointed out above, among the most innovative catalysts in reconciling groups alienated by violence is the introduction of truth commissions - the South African Truth and Reconciliation Commission being the most noted - that were established to present official accounting of past violence in some 20 countries since 1973 with varying degrees of success in reconciliation. In some cases, the new peace initiatives involve reintroducing traditional practices such as the *gaçaça* courts in Rwanda and the attempt to introduce a traditional system of reconciliation in Uganda.

Taking political apology seriously calls for its strategic application in diplomatic crises and postwar reconstructions. Thus diplomats, policymakers, peace practitioners and NGO workers require some criteria or standards to follow to enhance the efficacy of apology in a given context and can benefit from a better understanding of the concept of apology, its utilitarian and moral dimensions, and its limitations in peacemaking.

Among the traits of failed or botched apologies, to use psychologist Aaron Lazare's terms, it is in the acknowledgement stage that perpetrators or their representative state (in the case of state apologies) reject, ignore, or express further insult to injuries. Many apologies are rejected outright for not being timely and forthright. As seen above, timing is of utmost importance. Delay and hesitancy in accepting wrongdoing take away from the seriousness of the act. When the IRA apologized to the widow of a police officer killed in 1996, the widow rejected it on the grounds that the apology was "self-serving, dishonest and nine years too late."[12] Political apologies have failed also because officeholders and leaders utter them carelessly and not in a formal setting. Not following the correct protocol undermined the Malaysian apology to Indonesia, as was President Clinton's famous apologetic speech delivered in transit at the Kigali Airport. Apologies have been rejected also for lack of specificity in the admission of wrongdoing. State apologies are most often in vague diplomatic language to reduce the chances of liabilities. Spokesmen also tend not to have the victims in mind when making the apologetic speech acts; once again this exhibits the weaknesses of an apology by proxy.

Apologies – individual, corporate or state – can fail when legal liabilities are at stake and the offender is reluctant to take full responsibility for wrongs committed. This perhaps explains why offenders hold their cards close to the chest, particularly self-interested states, to avoid unlimited liabilities. There may also be fear of opening a Pandora box of guilt in associated crimes. While accountability entails bringing around the offender to admit and take responsibility for wrongdoing, there is often a lack of clarity as to who should be party to the apology. A government can come forth to take some responsibility on behalf of the actual offenders, but in reality, several entities are involved on both sides of the apology dyad. Ultimately, the apology by the offending party would fall short of full accountability if it is not aimed at doing justice proportionate to the wrongs. The material compensation can be considered insufficient for instance. The moral weight of the apology is also measured by the atonement (non-material) of the offending party demanded by victims but rarely delivered. Different types of accountability mechanisms have been introduced in recent years to address the claims of restorative justice and reconciliation.

Victims of mass violence seem to seek the disclosure of the truth just as much as they demand justice. Corporate and state apologies fail too often to fully disclose what they are apologizing for. As discussed previously this behavior is to be expected in a competitive and state-centric system where government secrets prevail. On the other hand, individuals and groups victimized by state or group violence want their stories to be told. The customary denials and the obfuscations of atrocities by states have been successfully countered by victims and their advocates to expose the truth in many places. Memoirs, testimonies, witnesses, and truth commissions have followed in this tradition. Where criminal courts and tribunals have failed the introduction of amnesty in truth commissions, for example, have succeeded in the telling of the truth, even if at the expense of justice.

Finally, apologies have failed or have been declared only partial because the moral dimension of the apology is lacking. In most public apologies the spokesmen may express regret for the hurt they have caused but not necessarily repent their deeds. On the part of the potential forgiver or victim a simple sorry, regret, or "too bad this had to happen," is not reassuring as much as deeply felt sorrow or remorse. A simple regret does not save face or restore the dignity of the victim or victims. That is why apologies by proxy, the way state agents deliver them, are most of the time bereft of the emotions that are always associated with personal remorse. In apologies by proxy the distance between the offender and the victim is far and is bureaucratic. Such apologies lend themselves to the legal and material parts of the apology but are most often inconsequential in their moral impact.

An apology toward reconciliation will demand taking risks as well as suspending the victim syndrome that would actually enable the leaders on both sides to address historic grievances. The politically convenient stance for the consumption of both domestic and international audiences is to say "you first," but there is the alternative for both to act at the same time, to start a process of an open-ended apology to come to terms with their common past. That extraordinary mutual apology between the Czech and the Germans is a case in point. Granted such initiatives can take place in more open and democratically active civil societies, this model, in which each side takes the historical grievance of the other seriously enough to act, is often overlooked. Behind such neglect lies an entrenched and widely spread convention that emphasizes political expedience over moral justice and material compensation over the other immeasurably important question of dignity. This last notion is continuously undermined by the demands for security, justice, even rights. Over and above these demands, a full apology involves the recognition of the Other even to the point of vulnerability. When leaders take into account or are prompted by the humane impulses of their citizens, their apologies are more likely to restore human dignity, which is the key to a successful apology.

Notes

1.   I am indebted to Michael Barnett and David Rudrum for raising questi-ons about the proliferation of apologies for *inaction* and the special problems this type of apology poses. Rudrum suggests that a tentative distinction can be made between "positive" and "negative" apologies. I have extrapolated on his idea to come up with the categorical/non-categorical apology distinction. Personal communications, November 2004.

2.   "Faith Group Broadcasts Apology for Abu Ghraib Abuse." *National Catholic Reporter.* July 7, 2004.

3.   "Malaysia Willing to Accept Indonesia's Apology," *Financial Times*, March 18, 2005.

4.   "Cambodian King Calls Ambassador's Apology for Anti-Thai Riots Treason," *Agence France Presse*, February 13, 2003.

5.   "Cambodian King Calls Ambassador's Apology for Anti-Thai Riots Treason."

6.   Albert S. Yee, "Semantic Ambiguity and Joint Deflections in the Hainan Negotiations." *China: an International Journal* 2.1 (2004) 53-82.

7.   Trudy Grover and Wilhelm Verwoed, "The Promise and Pitfalls of Apology," *Journal of Social Philosophy* 33, no. 1 (Spring 2002), 68-70.

8.   Mavern Lumsden, "Breaking the Cycle of Violence," *Journal of Peace Research* 34, no. 4 (November 1997).

9.   Donald Shriver reinforced my position on the importance of the affect- ive dimension of public remorse, in regard to Brandt's gesture, by raising the rhetorical question: "Why is that incident so often referred to by us who write about this subject if it

does not somehow gather into one gesture the complexities of historical recollection, official responsibility, and the emotional and ethical elements in remorse?" Personal communication, 22 October 2004.

10. Aaron Lazare offers eight ways offenders fail to adequately acknowledge offences, by: "1) offering a vague and incomplete acknowledgement; 2) using the passive voice; 3) making the offense conditional; 4) questioning whether the victim was damaged; 5) minimizing the offense; 6) using the empathic "I'm sorry"; 7) apologizing to the wrong party; and 8) apologizing for the wrong offense." See Aaron Lazare, *On Apology* (Oxford University Press, 2004), 86-88.

11. Sissela Bok identifies four kinds of morlizers: the hypocrites who arrogantly recite "moral standards that they are the first to break," individuals "who are high-handed in the face of complexity" and thus "distort reality," those who are "excessively strict and uncompromising," and finally, the most dangerous, those who are "so obsessed by the desire to combat what he or she takes to be some particular evil as to ride roughshod over other moral principles." Sissela Bok, *A Strategy for Peace: Human Values and the Threat of War* (Vintage Books, 1990), 119-121.

12. Shawn Pogatchnik, "Widow Rejects IRA Men's Apology for Killing Irish Detective." *The Associated Press*, March 14, 2005.

Bibliography

Adelman, Howard, and Astri Suhrke, eds. *The Path of a Genocide: The Rwanda Crisis from Uganda to Zaire*. New Brunswick: N.J.: Transaction Publishers, 1999.

Agence France Presse, "After German Apology, Namibia's Hereros want a 'Marshall Plan'," August 19, 2004.

____, "Chinese Press Step up Anti-American Rhetoric," April 5, 2001.

____, "Cambodian King Calls Ambassador's Apology for Anti-Thai Treason," February 13, 2003.

Agger, Inger, and Buus Jensen, Soren, *Trauma and Healing Under State Terrorism*. London: Zed Books, 1996.

Agreement on the Settlement Problems Concerning Property and Claims and on Economic Cooperation, June 22, 1965, Japan-Korea, 583 U.N.T.S.

Albright, Madeleine. "Letter to Minister of Foreign Affairs of the People's Republic of China." Office of the Spokesman, U.S. Department of State. May 8, 1999. <http://secretary.state.gov/www/statements/1999/990508.html> (10/27/00).

Ang, Audra. "Chinese, Japanese leaders fail to reach settlement in dispute over Tokyo's wartime past." *The Associated Press*, April 24, 2005.

Arendt, Hannah H. *The Human Condition*. Chicago: University of Chicago Press, 1958.

____, *Between Past and Future: Eight Exercises in Political Theory*. New York: Viking Press, 1961.

Asahi News Service, "No-War Resolution can Help Japan Chart Future Course," March 6, 1995.

Associated Press, "Germany's President Conveys Grief to Survivors of Guernica Attack," April 27, 1997.

Aukerman, Miriam J. "Extraordinary Evil, Ordinary Crime: A Framework for Understanding Transnational Justice." *Harvard Human Rights Journal* 15 (Spring 2002): 39-97.

Austin John L. *How To Do Things With Words*, Cambridge, Mass.: Harvard University Press, 1975.

Babington, Charles. "Clinton: Support for Guatemala Was Wrong." *Washington-Post.com*, March 11, 1999.

Balabkins, Nicholas. *West German Reparations to Israel*. New Brunswick, N.J.: Rutgers University Press, 1971.

Balakian, Peter. *Black Dog of Fate: A Memoir*. New York: Broadway Books, 1998.

Barkan, Elazar. *The Guilt of Nations: Restitution and Negotiating Historical Injustices.* New York: W. W. Norton, 2000.

Barnett, Michael. *Eyewitness to A Genocide: The United Nations and Rwanda.* Ithaca: Cornell University Press, 2002.

Bartov, Omer. *Mirrors of Destruction: War, Genocide, and Modern Identity.* Oxford, N.Y.: Oxford University Press, 2000.

Bass, Gary Jonathan. *Stay the Hand of Vengeance: The Politics of War Crimes Tribunals.* Princeton, N.J.: Princeton University Press, 2000.

BBC Monitoring International Reports. "Rwanda : UK-Funded Body Donates 47bn Rwandan Francs for Fight against AIDS," March 23, 2004.

BBC News Online, "Clinton Apologises for Embassy Bombing," May 10, 1999.

____, "Clinton Brokers Landmark Aids Deal." October, 10, 2003.

____, "Germany Apologises for Spanish Civil War Bombing of Guernica," April 24, 1998.

____, "Rwanda sees 'fast growth' in 2005." December 5, 2004. <http://news.bbc.co.uk/2/hi/americas/3209741.stm> (October 3, 2005).

____, "Rwanda trial opens Belgian's eyes," June 7, 2001.

____, "UN Chief's Rwanda Genocide Regret." March 3, 2004.

Ben-Natan, Asher. "Bridges Over Many Chasms," in *Thirty Years of Diplomatic Relations between the Federal Republic of Germany and Israel*, edited by Otto R. Romberg and Heiner Lichtenstein Publishers, 33-49. Frankfurt: Tribüne-Books, 1995.

Benoit, William L. *Accounts, Excuses, and Apologies: A Theory of Image Restoration Strategies.* New York: State University of New York Press, 1995.

Berger, Allan L., and Naomi Berger, eds. *Second Generation Voices: Reflections by Children of Holocaust Survivors and Perpetrators.* Syracuse, N.Y.: Syracuse University Press, 2001.

Bernstein, Richard. "In Berlin, A Nation Bares Its Shame." *The New York Times*, May 11, 2005.

____. "Berlin Holocaust Memorial Opens." May 12, 20005.

Berry, John A., and Carol Pott Berry, eds. *Genocide in Rwanda: A Collective Memory* Washington, D. C.: Howard University Press, 1999.

Bielefeldt, Heiner. "'Western' versus 'Islamic' Human Rights Conceptions?: A Critique of Cultural Essentialism in the Discussion on Human Rights." *Political Theory* 28, no. 1 (February 2000), 90-121.

Bok, Sissela. *A Strategy for Peace: Human Values and the Threat of War.* New York: Vintage Books, 1990.

Booth, James W. "Communities of Memory: On Identity, Memory, and Debt." *American Political Science Review* 93, no. 2 (1999): 249-263.

Botman, Russel H. and Robin M. Petersen, eds. *To Remember and to Heal.* Capetown: Human and Rousseau, 1996.

Boyes, Roger. "Germany Finally Admits the Holocaust to Its Dark Heart." *The Times (London)*, May 11, 2005.

Brandt, Willy. *Friechens Politik in Europa. English. A Peace Policy for Europe.* New York: Holt Rinehart and Winston, 1969.

Braeckman, Colette. "Rwanda Trial Opens Belgians' Eyes." *BBC News*, June 7, 2001.

Briggs Charles L. "Specificities: Introduction: The Power of Discourse in (Re) creating Genocide." *Social Identities* 3, no. 3 (1997): 407-413.

Brooks, Peter. *Troubling Confessions: Speaking Guilt in Law and Literature.* Chicago University of Chicago Press, 2000.

Brooks, Roy L., ed. *When Sorry Isn't Enough: The Controversy over Apologies and Reparations for Human Injustice.* New York: New York University Press, 1999.

_____. *Atonement and Forgiveness: A New Model for Black Reparations.* Berkley: University of California Press, 2004.

Brown, Michael E., and Richard N. Rosecrance, eds. *The Costs of Conflict: Prevention and Cure in the Global Arena.* Lanham, Md.: Rowman & Littlefield Publishers, 1999.

Buruma, Ian. *The Wages of Guilt: Memories of War in Germany and Japan.* New York: Farrar Straus Giroux, 1994.

_____, "For Germany and Japan, An Agenda Beyond Apologies." *New York Times,* December 30, 1998.

Calgary Herald (Alberta, Canada), "Blair admits British Blame in Ireland's Potato Famine," June 3, 1997.

Carnegie Council on Ethics and International Affairs, Roundtable Discussion. "Should States Apologize?" April 2001. <http://www.cceia.org/lib_pov_apology.html>

Caroll, Rory. "Catholic Unease at the Pope's Apology for Church Sins." *Observer,* March 12, 2000.

_____. "Arts: In Memory of Murder: Can Art Help Ease Rwanda's Pain?" *Guardian* (London), March 24, 2004.

Carr, Rosamond H. and Ann Howard Halsey *Land of A Thousand Hills: My Life in Rwanda.* New York, N.Y.: Viking, 1999.

Cavalier, Robert J., ed. *Ethics in the History of Western Philosophy.* New York: St. Martin's Press, 1989.

Channel News Asia (Singapore), "WW II Comfort Women Face Upward Battle in U.S. Courts," June 27, 2001.

Chorbajian, Levon and George Shirinian, eds. *Studies in Comparative Genocide.* New York: St. Martin's Press, 1999.

Chu, Henry, and Maggie Farley. "China Seeks to Restrain Public Anger over Embassy Bombing." *Los Angeles Times,* May 11, 1999.

CNN.com, "Ex-French Officials Deny France aided Rwandan Genocide," April 21, 1998.

_____, "Polish Apology for Jewish Massacre," July 10, 2001.

_____, "Clinton Calls Chinese President with Apology," May 14, 1999.

_____, "Washington: Firing not likely over Bombing of Chinese Embassy," May 11, 1999. <http://www.cnn.com/WORLD/europe/9905/14/kosovo.china>

Cobban, Helena. "The Legacies of Collective Violence: The Rwandan genocide and the limits of law." *Boston Review,* April/May 2002. <http://www.bostonreview.net/BR27.2/cobban.html>

Cole, Debra. "Anti-Semitism Charges Spark New Struggle over German Identity." *Agence France Presse,* May 30, 2002.

Colletta, Nat J., and Michelle L. Cullen, eds. *Violent Conflict and the Transformation of Social Capital: Lessons from Cambodia, Rwanda, Guatemala, and Somalia.* Washington, D.C.: The World Bank, 2000.

Congressional Record, 106th Congress, 1st Session. Cong. Rec. H3529, 145, no. 76, May 25, 1999.

_____, 106th Congress, H. Con Rec. 157, July 16, 1999.

Corey, Charles W. "*Transcript: Clinton addresses Rwanda Genocide Survivors.*" *U.S.I.S.* (Washington File), March 25, 1998.

Crawford, Neta C. "Postmodern Ethical Conditions and A Critical Response," *Ethics and International Affairs,* 12 (1998): 121-140.

Crouch, Gregory. "Norway Tries to Resolve A Lasting Nazi Legacy." *New York Times*, December 16, 2002.

Cunningham, Michael. "Saying Sorry: The Politics of Apology." *Political Quarterly*, 70, 3 (1999): 285-293.

Davies, Karin. "Rwandans take Annan, U.N. to task for genocide." *seattletimes.com*, May 8, 1998. <http://seattletimes.com/news/nation-world/htm198/altrwan_050898.html> (February 5, 2000).

Davis, Douglas. "France remembers Dreyfus and Zola." *Canada Jewish News*, June 15, 1998.

Derrida, Jacques. *On Cosmopolitanism and Forgiveness*. Translated by Mark Doley and Michael Hughes. London & New York: Routledge, 2001.

Desmond, Edward W. "Finally, A Real Apology." *Time*, 146, 47, August 28, 1995.

Destexhe, Alain. *Rwanda and Genocide in the Twentieth Century*. Washington Square, N.Y.: New York University Press, 1995.

Deutsche Presse Agentur, "Norwegian Parliament Backs Compensation for Wartime Victims," March 18, 2005.

____, "Roundup: Israel and Germany Create Fund to Improve Relations," May 30, 2005.

____, "German Ministers in Emotional Apology to Namibia's Herero," August 15, 2004.

De Waal, Victor. *The Politics of Reconciliation: Zimbabwe's First Decade*. Trenton, N.J.: Africa World Press, 1990.

De Waal, A. and R. Omaar. "The Genocide in Rwanda and the International Response." *Current History*, 4, 156-161.

DiPrizio, Robert C. *Armed Humanitarians: U.S. Interventions from Northern Iraq to Kosovo*. Baltimore, Md.: John Hopkins University Press, 2002.

Drew, Paul and Anthony Wooton. *Erving Goffman: Exploring the Interaction Order*. Boston: Northeastern University Press, 1988.

Drozdiak, William. "Retribution for Nazi Suffering: Germany Creates Special Fund to Compensate Forced Laborers and Slaves." *Gazette* (Montreal), July 18, 2000.

Eaglestone, Robert. *Ethical Criticism: Reading After Levinas*. Edinburgh: Edinburgh University Press, 1997.

Economist. "Waiting for May: Anti-Japan Protests in China," April 30, 2005.

Edmiston W. Allan III. "Showdown in the South China Sea: An International Incident Analysis of the So-Called Spy Plane Crisis." *Emory International Law Review* 16, no. 2 (Fall 2002): 639-688.

Edwards, Steven. "60 Tears, and Still No Shame: Failure to Atone for Wartime Atrocities Diminishes Japan." *National Post*, April 13, 2005.

Eltringham, Nigel. *Accounting for Horror: Post-Genocide Debates in Rwanda*. London: Pluto Press, 2004.

Erhard, Ludwig. "Address to the Council of Foreign Relations in New York, June 11, 1964," in *Common Values, Common Cause: German Statesmen in the United States, American Statesmen in Germany 1953-1983*, 60-70. Statements and Speeches. New York: German Information Center, 1983.

Esbenshade, Richard S. "Remembering to Forget: Memory, History, National Identity in Postwar East-Central Europe." *Representations 0*, no. 49, Special Issue: Identifying Histories: Eastern Europe Before and After 1989 (Winter 1995): 72-96.

Farmer, James. *Lay Bare the Heart: An Autobiography of the Civil Rights Movement*. New York: Plume/Penguin, 1985.

Feldman, Gerald D. "Holocaust Assets and German Business History: Beginning or End?" *German Studies Review* 25, no.1 (2002): 23-34.

Feldman, Lily Gardner. *The Special Relationship between West Germany and Israel.* Boston: George Allen & Unwin, 1984.

Felman, Shoshana. "In an Era of Testimony: Claude Lanzmann's Shoah." *Yale French Studies* 0, 97, 50 Years of Yale French Studies: A Commemorative Anthology. Part 2: 1980-1998 (2000): 103-150.

Financial Times. "China Says Apology for Anti-Japan Protests Not An Issue." June 16, 2005.

____. "South Korean President Demands Actions 'Suitable' to Past Japan's Apologies." May 6, 2005.

____. "Genocide Victims Body's Official for Investigation of 'Big Powers'." April 6, 2005.

Fisher, Marc. *After the Wall: Germany, the Germans and the Burdens of History.* New York: Simon & Schuster, 1995.

Fleishman, Jeffrey. "Permanent Memory of Holocaust Opens in Berlin." *Los Angeles Times,* May 12, 2005.

Fujitani, Takashi and Geoffrey M. White, and Lisa Yoneyama eds. *Perilous Memories: The Asia-Pacific War(s).* Durham, N.C.: Duke University Press, 2001.

Ganley, Elaine. "Chirac Acknowledges French Role in World War II Deportations." *Associated Press,* June 17, 1995.

Gao, Mobo C. F. "Sino-U.S. Love and Hate Relations," *Journal of Contemporary Asia,* 30, issue 4 (October 2000), 547-561.

Gazette (Montreal), "Belgium Apologizes for Inaction during Genocide," April 8, 2000.

Gerow, Aaron. "Consuming Asia, Consuming Japan: The New Neonationalistic Revisionism in Japan," in Laura Hein and Mark Selden (eds), *Censoring History: Citizenship and Memory in Japan, Germany and the United States,* 74-95. Armonk, N.Y.: M. E. Sharpe, 2000.

Getler, Michael. "Holocaust: A Shock to West Germans." *Washington Post,* January 24, 1979.

Gibney, Frank. ed. *The Nanjing Massacre: A Japanese Journalist Confronts Japan's National Shame.* Armonk, N.Y.: M.E. Sharpe, 1999.

Gibney, Mark and Erik Roxstrom. "The Status of State Apologies," *Human Rights Quarterly,* 23 (2001) 911-939.

Giddens, Anthony. *Central Problems in Social Theory: Action, Structure and Contradiction in Social Analysis.* Berkeley: University of California Press, 1979.

Gittings, John. "Pol Pot Men Say Sorry for Killing Fields." *Guardian* (London), December 30, 1998.

Global Newswire, "Rwanda Inaugurates National Genocide Memorial," April 7, 2004.

Goffman, Erving. *Relations in Public: Microstudies of the Public Order.* New York: Basic Books, 1971.

Goldberg, G. and Steven Green and Eric Sadler. "Saying You're Sorry," in *Negotiation Theory and Practice,* edited by Jeffe Z. Rubin and J. William Breslin, 141-146. Cambridge: Program on Negotiation Books, 1991.

Goldhagen, Daniel J. *Hitler's Willing Executioners: Ordinary Germans and the Holocaust.* New York: Alfred A. Knopf. 1996.

Goldstone, Richard J. *For Humanity: Reflections of a War Crimes Investigator.* New Haven, Conn.: Yale University Press, 2000.

Gong, Gerrit W. "The Beginning of History: Remembering and Forgetting as Strategic Issues." *Washington Quarterly* 24, 12 (Spring 2001): 45-57.

Gourevitch, Philip. *We Wish to Inform You that Tomorrow We Will Be Killed With Our Families: Stories from Rwanda.* New York: Farrar Straus and Giroux, 1998.

Govier, Trudy and Wilhelm Verwoed. "The Promise and Pitfalls of Apology." *Journal of Social Philosophy* 33, no. 1 (Spring 2002), 67-82.

Graybill, Lyn S. "South Africa's Truth and Reconciliation Commission: Ethical And Theological Perspectives." *Ethics and International Affairs* 12 (1998): 44-62.

Gries, Peter Hayes. *China's New Nationalism: Pride, Politics, and Diplomacy.* Berkeley: University of California Press, 2004.

____, "A 'China Threat'? Power and Passion in Chinese 'Face Nationalism'." *World Affairs*, 162, i2 (Fall 1999): 63-75.

Grunenberg, Antonia. "Totalitarian Lies and Post-Totalitarian Guilt: The Question of Ethics in Democratic Politics." *Social Research*, 69, no.2 (Summer 2002): 359-379.

Guardian (London) "American Reckoning; Clinton Finally Says Sorry," March 13, 1999.

Gudykunst, William B. "Diplomacy: A Special Case of Intergroup Communication," in *Communicating for Peace: Diplomacy and Neotiation*, eds. Felipe Korzenny and Stella Ting-Toomey, 9-39. Newbury Park, Ca: Sage Publications, 1990.

Guelph Mercury (Ontario). "Rwanda demands apology from UN." December 18, 1999, C8.

Haas, Mark L. "Reinhold Niebuhr's 'Christian Pragmatism': A Principled Alternative to Consequentialism." *The Review of Politics*, 61, no. 4, Christianity and Politics: Millennial Issue I 9Autumn, 1999), 605-636.

Habermas, Jurgen. *Between Facts and Norms: Contributions to a Discourse Theory of Law and Democracy.* Cambridge, Mass.: MIT Press, 1996.

____, 'Discourse Ethic," in *Moral Consciousness and Communicative Action.* Cambridge, Mass.: MIT Press, 1990, 43-115.

Hampshire, Stuart. "Public and Private Morality," in *Public and Private Morality* edited by Stuart Hampshire, 23-53. Cambridge: Cambridge University Press, 1978.

Haq, Farhan. "Annan's Qualified Apology for Inaction in Rwanda." *Inter Press Service*, May 2, 1998. <http://www.oneworld.org>

Hawthorne, Nathaniel. *The Scarlet Letter.* Bantam Classics, 1981.

Hein, Laura. "War Compensation: Claims against the Japanese Government and Japanese Corporations for War Crimes," in *Politics and the Past: On Repairing Historical Injustices*, edited by John Torpey, 127-148. Lanham: Roman and Littlefield, 2003.

Hein, Laura and Mark Selden, eds. *Censoring History: Citizenship and Memory in Japan, Germany and the United States.* Armond, N.Y.: M.E. Sharpe, 2000.

Henson, Maria Rosa. *Comfort Woman: A Filipina's Story of Prostitution and Slavery under the Japanese Military.* Lanham, Md: Rowman & Littlefield, 1999.

Herf, Jeffrey. *Divided Memory: The Nazi Past in the Two Germanys.* Cambridge, Mass.: Harvard University Press, 1997.

Hicks, George. "The Comfort Women Redress Movement." in *When Sorry Isn't Enough*, edited by Roy L. Brooks, 113-125, New York: New York University Press, 1999.

Hills, Ben. "Japan Expresses Remorse but Ducks Apology for War." *Sydney Morning Herald*, June 8, 1995.

Hodge, Carl Cavanagh. "Konrad Adenauer, Arms, and the Redemption of Germany," in *Ethics and Statescraft: The Moral Dimension of International Affairs*, edited by Cathal J. Nolan, 153-169. Westport, Conn.: Praeger, 1995.

Hu, Hsien Chin. "The Chinese Concepts of 'Face'." *American Anthropology*, 46 (1944): 45-64.

Human Rights Watch Report. "Leave None to Tell the Story," March 1999, 171-1, http://www.hrw.org/reports/1999/rwanda/ (accessed January 1, 2004).

Independent (London), "France Atones for 'Dark Spot' of the Dreyfus Case," January 9, 1998.

Independent (London), "Gay Activists Press for German Apology," November 1, 1997.

Independent (London), "Western Leaders Absent as Rwanda Mourns, 10 Years After the Genocide," April 8, 2004.

Janzen, John M., and Reinhild K. Janzen, *Do I Still Have a Life? Voices from The Aftermath of War in Rwanda and Burundi.* Publications in Anthropology. Lawrence, Kan.: University of Kansas, 2000.

Japan Economic Newswire. "Ex-comfort Women Sue Japan in U.S. Over Sex Slavery,"18 September 2000.

____, "Malaysian Lawmakers Demand Apology from Japan Over War Crimes," April 25, 2005.

____, "Ex-Comfort Women Sue Japan in U.S. Over Slavery,"   September 18, 2000.

Japan Times. "Comfort Women Exhibit Visits U.S." 28 December 2000.

____, "Court Rejects Chinese War Victims' Damages Case." September 22, 1999.

____, "Family Wins 20 Million Yen for Laborer's Time on Run." July 13, 2001.

____, "Former Sex Slaves Seek Justice in U.S.," September 17, 2000.

____, Second Wave if War Orphans Hits Government with Lawsuits." September 25, 2003.

____, "Koizumi Issues Rare War Apology." April 23, 2005.

____, "War Victims Unite Efforts to Win Redress from Japan." February 12, 1999.

____, "Unambiguous Apology Needed," November 5, 2003.

Jaspers, Karl. *The Question of German Guilt.* New York: Capricon Books, 1961.

Jensen, Soren Buus. *Trauma and Healing under Terrorism."* London: Zed Books, 1996.

Johnson, Peter. *Politics, Innocence, and the Limits of Goodness.* London: Routledge, 1988.

Jones, Bruce D. *Peacemaking in Rwanda: The Dynamics of Failure.* Boulder: Lynne Rienner Publishers, 2001.

Jubilee 2000: News. "Rwanda says debt hampers reconstruction." <http://www.jubilee2000uk.org/jubilee2000/news/rwand0909.html>

Kamukama, Dixon. *Rwanda Conflict: Its Roots and Regional Implications.* Kampala, Uganda: Fountain Publishers, 1997.

Karon, Tony. "Wanted: Some Diplomatic Choreography to End China Standoff." *Time,* April 4, 2001.

Katsuichi, Honda. *The Nanjing Massacre: A Japanese Journalist Confronts Japan's National Shame.* New York: M.E. Sharpe, 1999.

Keane, Fergal. *Season of Blood: A Rwandan Journey.* New York: Viking, 1995.

Kearney, Richard, and Mark Dooley, eds. *Questioning Ethics: Contemporary Debates in Philosophy.* New York: Routledge, 1999.

Kemp, Graham, and Douglas P. Fry, eds. *Keeping the Peace: Conflict Resolution and Peaceful Societies around the World.* New York: Routledge, 2004.

Khan, Shaharyan M. *The Shallow Graves of Rwanda.* New York: I. B. Tauris Publishers, 2000.

Kissinger, Henry. "Face to Face with China." *Newsweek* 137 no.16. 36-37, April 16, 2001.

Klinghoffer, Arthur Jay. *The International Dimension of Genocide in Rwanda*. Washington Square, N.Y.: New York University Press, 1998.

Knight, Christopher. "A Gray Grid Forms An Intangible Holocaust Memorial in Berlin." *Los Angeles Times*, June25, 2005.

Korea Times. "Hearts and Minds: Three Questions from Japan," June 28, 2000.

____, "Ethnic Korean Leads Publication of Book on Comfort Women in Japan," April 8, 2002.

____, "Comfort Women Seek Justice Apart from 1965 Korea-Japan Agreement," August 14, 2003.

Korey, William. The United States and the Genocide Convention. *Ethics and International Affairs*, (1997) 11: 272-290.

Korzenny, Felipe, Stella Ting-Toomey and Susan Douglas Ryan, eds. *Communicating for Peace: Diplomacy and Negotiation*. Newbury Park, Cal.: Sage Publications, 1990.

Krog, Antjie. *Country of My Skull: Guilt, Sorrow, and the Limits of Forgiveness in the New South Africa*. New York: Random House, 1999.

Krondorfer, Björn. *Remembrance and Reconciliation: Encounters between Young Jews and Germans*. New Haven, Conn.: Yale University Press, 1995.

Kwan, Weng Kin. "Revising History: Japan Wages War of Words." *Straits Times* (Singapore), May 6, 2001.

LaCapra, Dominick. "Lanzmann's 'Shoah': here there is no why." *Critical Inquiry* 23, no.2 (Winter 1997): 231-239.

____. *Writing History, Writing Trauma*. Baltimore: John Hopkins University Press, 2001.

____. *Representing the Holocaust: History, Theory, Trauma*. Ithaca, New York: Cornell University Press, 1994.

Lam, Willy. "Analysis: Behind the Scenes in Bejing's Corridors of Power." *CNN.com*, April 11, 2001. <http://www.cnn.com/2001/WORLD/asiapcf/east/04/11/china.plane.wlam> (June 8, 2004)

Lamko, Koulsy. *La Phalène des Collines*. Paris: Le Serpent à Plumes, 2002.

____. « Rwanda, mémoire d'un génocide, la parole des fantômes. » *L'Interdit*, Lille, <novembre 2000. www.interdits.net/2000nov/rwanda6.htm> (September 22, 2003).

Langfitt, Frank. "China Launches Battle for Public Opinion." *Baltimore Sun*. April 13, 2001.

Lapsley Michael. "Confronting the Past and Creating the Future: The Redemptive Value of Truth Telling." *Social Research* 65, i4 (Winter 1998): 741 (1).

Lauren, Paul G. *The Evolution of International Human Rights: Visions Seen*. Philadelphia: University of Pennsylvania Press, 1998.

Lavy, George. *Germany and Israel: Moral Debt and National Interest*. London and Portland: Frank Cass, 1966.

Lazare, Aaron. *On Apology*. Oxford; New York: Oxford University Press, 2004.

LeBaron, Michelle. *Bridging Cultural Conflicts: A New Approach for a Changing World*. San Francisco, Cal.: Jossey-Bass, 2003.

Lehmann, Jean-Pierre. "Japan in the Global Era: How to Avert the Risk of War with China." *Japan Times*, June 17, 2002.

Levinas, Emmanuel. *Ethics and Infinity: Conversations with Philippe Nemo*, translated by Richard A. Cohen. Pittsburgh, Penn.: Duquesne University Press. 1985.

Levy, Daniel. "The Future of the Past: Historiographical Disputes and Competing Memories in Germany and Israel." *History and Theory, Studies in the Philosophy of History* 38, no.1 (Fall 1999): 51-66.

Lindsey, Daryle, Alice Montgomery and Jake Tapper. "Ways of Words." *salon.com*. April 4, 2001.

Lister, David. "IRA issues Apology for Civilian Pain." *Times* (London), July 17, 2002.

Lumsden, Malvern. "Breaking the Cycle of Violence." *Journal of Peace Research* 34, no. 4 (November 1997), 377-383.

Lüth, Eric. *Akton Fried Mit Israel. We Ask Israel for Peace*. August 31, 1951.

Machiavelli, Niccolò. *The Prince and Discourses*. New York: Random House. 1950.

Mahmood, Mamdani. *When Victims Become Killers: Colonialism, Nativism, and the Genocide in Rwanda*. Princeton, New Jersey: Princeton University Press, 2001.

Marley, Tony. "Frontline: The Triumph of Evil." *PBS*, January 26, 1999.

Marrus, Michael R. "The Nuremberg Trial: Fifty Years After." *American Scholar* 66, no. 4 (Fall 1997): 563-570.

Marsh, Christopher and June Teufel. *U.S.-China Relations in the 21st Century: Policies, Prospects and Possibilities*. Lanham: Lexington Books, 2003.

Marzynski, Marian. "Good Guilt in Germany," *The Washington Post*, May 28, 2005.

Mathäs, Alexander. "The Presence of the Past: Martin Walser on Memoirs and Memorials." *German Studies Review* 25/1 (2002): 1-22.

McCool, Grant. "At Rwanda Memorial Panel, Annan Admits UN Blame." *Reuters*, March 26, 2004.

Medeiros, Evan S. and M. Taylor Fravel, "China's New Diplomacy." *Foreign Affairs* 82, no.6 (2003): 22-35.

Millet, Michael. "Japan's Take on History Upsets Neighbours." *Sydney Morning Herald*, March 3, 2001.

Mills, Nicolaus. "The New Culture of Apology." *Dissent*, 48, no.4 (Fall 2001): 113-116.

Mineur, Larry, and Philippe Guillot. *Soldiers to the Rescue: Humanitarian Lessons from Rwanda*. Development Centre of the Organization for Economic Co-operation and Development, 1996.

Ministry of Foreign Affairs of Japan. Comment by Minister of Foreign Affairs Makiko Tanaka on the Official Stance Conveyed by the Government of the Republic of Korea on the Decision to Authorize Japanese History Textbooks. May 8, 2001. <http://www.mofa.go.jp/announce/announce/2001/5/0508.html> (February 9, 2004).

____. Comments by the Chief Cabinet Secretary, Yasuo Fukuda on the history textbooks to be used in junior high schools from 2002. April 3, 2001. <http://www.mofa.go.jp/announce/announce/2001/4/0403.html> (February 9, 2004).

____. Affairs of Japan. Japan Republic of Korea Joint Declaration. "A New Japan-Republic of Korea Partnership toward the Twenty-First Century." October 8, 1998. <http://www.mofa.go.jp/region/asia-paci/korea/joint9810.html> (February 9, 2004).

____. Prime Minister's Address to the Diet. June 9, 1995. <http://www.mofa.go.jp/announce/press/pm/murayama/address9506.html> (February 18, 2004).

____. Address by Prime Minister Junichiro Koizumi at the 58th Memorial Ceremony for the War Dead. August 15, 2003. <http://www.kantei.go.jp/foreign/koizumispeech/2003/08/15sikiji_e.html> (October 13, 2005).

____. Observation by Prime Minister Junichiro Koizumi on the Visit to Yasukuni Shrine. April 21, 2002. <http://www.mofa.go.jp/announce/pm/koizumi/observe0204.html> (March 7, 2006).

____. Ministry of Foreign Affairs of Japan. On the Completion of the Atonement Project of the Asian Women's Fund (AWF) in the Netherlands. July 13, 2001. http://<www.mofa.go.jp/policy/women/fund/project0107-1.html > (February9, 2004).

_____. On the Issue of Wartime "Comfort Women." August 4, 1993. <http://www.mofa.go.jp/policy/postwar/issue9308.html> (February 9, 2004).

_____. Recent Policy of the Government of Japan on the issue known as "Wartime Comfort Women." June 2001. <http://www.mofa.go.jp/policy/women/fund/policy0011.html> (February 9, 2004).

_____. Ministry of Foreign Affairs of Japan. Remarks by Prime Minister Tomiichi Murayama During His May 1995 Visit to China. May 4, 1995. <http://www.mofa.go.jp/announce/press/pm/murayama/china.html> (March 7, 2006).

_____. Ministry of Foreign Affairs of Japan. Press Statement by Chief Cabinet Secretary Hidenao Nakagawa on the Asian Women's Fund. September 1, 2000. < http://www.mofa.go.jp/policy/postwar/state0009.html > (February 9, 2004).

_____. Ministry of Foreign Affairs of Japan. Statement by Chief Cabinet Secretary Kiichi Miyazawa on History Textbooks. August 26, 1982. <http://www.mofa.go.jp/policy/postwar/state8208.html> (February 9, 2004).

_____. Statement by Prime Minister Tomiichi Murayama on the "Peace, Friendship, and Exchange Initiative." August 31, 1994. <http://www.mofa.go.jp/announce/press/pm/murayama/state9408.html> (February 9, 2004).

_____. Statement by Prime Minister Tomiichi Murayama on the Occasion of the Establishment of the "Asian Women's Fund." July 1995. <http://www.mofa.go.jp/policy/women/fund/state9507.html> (February 9, 2004).

_____. Statement of Prime Minister Tomiichi Murayama "On the Occasion of the 50th Anniversary of the War's End." August 15, 1995. <http://www.mofa.go.jp/announce/press/pm/murayama/9508.html> (February 18, 2004).

_____. Statement by the Chief Cabinet Secretary Yohei Kono on the result of the study of the issue of "comfort women." August 4, 1993.   <http://www.mofa.go.jp/policy/women/fund/state9308.html > (February 9, 2004).

_____. Statement by Chief Cabinet Secretary Masaharu Gotoda on Official Visits to Yasukuni Shrine by the Prime Minister and Other State Ministers on August 15 of this year. August 14, 1986. <http://www.mofa.go.jp/policy/postwar/state8608.html> (February 9, 2004).

Ministry of Foreign Affairs of the P.R.C. "Chinese and U.S. Presidents Held Phone Conference." May 14, 1999. <http://www.fmprc.gov.cn/eng/wjdt/2649/t15797.htm> (March 7, 2006)

Minow, Martha. *Between Vengeance and Forgiveness: Facing History after Genocide and Mass Violence.* Boston: Beacon Press, 1998.

Mukarwego, Marie Césarie. "The Church and the Rwandan Tragedy of 1994." Chapter 9. In *Genocide in Rwanda: Complicity of the Churches*, edited by Carol Rittner, John K. Roth, Wendy Whitworth. Saint Paul, Minn.: Aegis ; Paragon House, 2004.

Myers, Steven Lee. "Chinese Military to Resume Contacts With Pentagon." *New York Times,* January 6, 2000.

_____. "C.I.A. Fires Officer blamed in Bombing of China Embassy." *New York Times,* April 9, 2000.

_____. "Chinese Embassy Bombing: A Wide Net of Blame." *New York Times.* 17 April 2000.

Nagel, Stuart ed. *Policymaking and Peace: A Multinational Anthology.* Lanham, Md.: Lexington Books, 2003.

Naradin, Terry, and R. Mapel., ed. *Traditions of International Ethics.* Cambridge: Cambridge University Press, 1992.

National Catholic Reporter. "Faith Group Broadcasts Apology for Abu Ghraib Abuse." July 7, 2004.

National Security Archive. ed. William Ferroggiaro. August 20, 2001. <www.nsarchive.org>

Nathan, Andrew. "Should States Apologize." Roundtable Discussion. Carnegie Council on Ethics and International Relations. April 2001. <http://www.cceia.org/lib_pov_apology.html> (May 21, 2001)

Negash, Girma. *"Apologia Politica*: An Examination of the Politics and Ethics of Public Remorse in International Affairs." *International Journal of Politics and Ethics* 2, 2 (2002): 119-143.

Neuffer, Elizabeth. *The Key to My Neighbor's House: Seeking Justice in Bosnia and Rwanda.* New York: Picador, 2001.

Neustadt, Amnon. "The Main Pillars Towards Understanding," in *Thirty Years of Diplomatic Relations between the Federal Republic of Germany and Israel,* edited by Otto R. Romberg and Heiner Lichtenstein, 115-123. Frankfurt: Tribüne-Books, 1995.

Newsweek, "Judgement of Bitburg," April 29, 1985.

New Times, "The Role of Re-Integration and Reconciliation and Reconciliation of Ex-prisoners." August 12, 2005.

New York Times, "A Payment to China for U.S. Bomb Error, "January 21, 2001.

____, "Blame in the Chinese Embassy Bombing," April 11, 2000.

Niebuhr, Rienhold. *Moral Man and Immoral Society: A Study in Ethics and Politics.* New York: Scribner, 1944.

Noddings, Ned. "Thinking, Feeling, and Moral Imagination." Pp.135-145 in *Philosophy of Emotions,* edited by Peter A. French and Howard K. Wettstein. *Midwest Studies in Philosophy* (Notre Dame, Ind.: University of Notre Dame Press, 1998).

Nolan, Cathal J. ed. *Ethics and Statecraft: The Moral Dimension of International Affairs.* Westport, Conn.: Praeger, 1995.

Nyankanzi, Edward L. *Genocide: Rwanda and Burundi.* Rochester, Vt.: Schenkman Books: 1998.

Ogawa, Shuko. "The Difficulty of Apology: Japan's Struggle with Memory and Guilt." *Harvard International Review* 22, i3 (Fall 2000): 42-47.

Okazaki, Tomiko. "Comment by Upper House Lawmaker from Minshuto." *Asahi Shimbun,* August 9, 2002.

Olick, Jeffrey K. and Brenda Coughlin. "The Politics of Regret: Analytical Frames." Pp. 37-62 in *Politics and the Past: On Repairing Historical Injustices,* edited by John Torpey. Lanham, Md.: Rowman and Littlefield, 2003.

Parker, Karen and Jennifer F. Chew, "Reparations: A Legal Analysis" Pp. 141-145 in *When Sorry Isn't Enough,* edited by Roy Brooks. New York: New York University Press, 1999.

Paterson, Tony. "Germany Unveils Monument to Its National Shame." *The Independent* (UK) May 11, 2005.

Pavon, Beatriz. "Rwanda Ten Years Later: Genocide Survivors Still Face an Uncertain Future." *UNChronicle,* (2004), issue 4.

Peace Treaty between Japan and the Allied Powers. East Asian Studies Documents. UCLA Center for East Asian Studies. <http://www.isop.ucla.edu/eas/documents/peace1951.htm> (January 3, 2005).

Perlez, J. "With Relations Warming Albright Presses China on Taiwan." *New York Times.* June 23, 2000.

Peterson, Scott. Me Against My Brother: At War in Somalia, Sudan, and Rwanda. New York: Routledge, 2000.

Pogatchnik, Shawn. "Widow Rejects IRA Men's Apology for Killing Irish Detective." The Associated Press, March 14, 2005.

Pope, Stephen J. "The Politics of Apology and Slaughter in Rwanda." America 180, i7 (March 6, 1999): 8(1)

Pottier, Johan. Re-imagining Rwanda: Conflict, Survival and Disinformation in the Late Twentieth Century. Cambridge, UK: Cambridge University Press, 2002.

Power, Samantha. A Problem from Hell: America and the Age of Genocide. New York: Basic Books, 2002.

____. "Bystanders to Genocide: Why the United States Let the Rwandan Tragedy Happen." The Atlantic, September 2001.

President Clinton. "Excerpts from Remarks at White House Strategy Meeting on Children, Violence, and Responsibility," State Department briefing, May 10, 1999.

Prince-Gibson, Eetta. "Europe's Jews Remembered at Berlin Memorial." Jerusalem Post, May 11, 2005.

Pross, Christian. Paying for the Past: The Struggle over Reparations for Surviving Victims of the Nazi Terror. Baltimore: John Hopkins University Press, 1998.

Public Broadcasting Service. "Frontline: The Triumph of Evil," January 26, 1999. Tony Marley interview. Transcript. <http://www.pbs.org/wgbh/pages/frontline/shows/evil/etc/script.html> (November 2001).

Raboteau, A.J. Slave Religion: The "Invisible Institution" in the Antebellum South. Oxford University Press, 1978.

Rafferty, Kevin. "Japan's 'Feeble' War Apology Angers Neighbours." Guardian. June 10, 1995.

Rennie, David. "Pilot is Forgotten in Anger at Crime Against State." Daily Telegraph. April 9, 2001.

Rigby, Andrew. Justice and Reconciliation. Boulder: Lynne Rienner, 2001.

____. "Three Contrasting Approaches for 'Dealing with the Past': Collective Amnesia, Retributive Justice and Prioritising Truth." Committee for Conflict Transformation Support. Newsletter 18. <http://www.c-r.org/ccts18/3apprch_htm>.

Rittner, Carol, John K. Roth and Wendy Whitworth, eds. Genocide in Rwanda: Complicity of the Churches? Saint Paul, Minn.: Aegis/Pargon House, 2004.

Robbennolt, Jennifer K. "Apologies and Legal Settlement: An Empirical Examination." Michigan Law Review. 102, i3 (December 2003): 460 (57).

Roeschlau, Frauke, and Ralf E. Kruegger. "German Minister in Emotional Apology to Namibia Herero." German Press Agency. August 15, 2004.

Rosenbaum, Arthur L. ed. U.S. China Relations and the Bush Administration: A New Paradigm or Continuing Modalities. Claremont, CA.: The Keek Center for International and Strategic Studies, Monograph Series, no. 15. 2002.

Rosenthal, Elizabeth. "Knotty Task of Beijing Talks on Plane: Reconciling Reality with Posturing." New York Times, April 18, 2001.

____, "U.S. Agrees to Pay China $28 Million for Bombing." New York Tim, December 16, 1999.

Rosenthal, Gabriele, ed. The Holocaust in Three Generations: Families of Victims and Perpetrators of the Nazi Regime. London U.K.: Cassell, 1998.

Rosenthal, Joel H. "Forward: Biography, Ethics, and Statescraft," in Ethics and Statescraft of International Affairs, edited by Cathal J. Nolan, xi-xvii, Westport, Conn.: Praeger, 1995.

Roth, Kenneth and Alison DesForges. "Crime and Punishment in Rwanda: An Exchange on Helena Cobban's 'The Legacies of Collective Violence.'" *Boston Review*, (Summer 2002)): 51-52.

Roth, Stanley O. "The Effects on U.S.-China Relations of the Accidental Bombing of the Chinese Embassy in Belgrade." Testimony before the Senate Committee on Foreign Relations Subcommittee on East-Asian and Pacific Affairs. Washington, D.C.: May 27, 1999.

Russel, Bertrand. *German Social Democracy*. London: George Allen and Unwin, 1965.

Sagi, Nana. *German Reparations: A History of Negotiations*. New York: St. Martin's Press, 1986.

Salpeter, Eliahu. "What will German Jewry Look Like in the Next Century?" *Financial Times* (Israel), August 17, 1999.

Schaap, Andrew. "Guilty Subjects and Political Responsibility: Arendt, Jaspers and the Resonance of the 'German Question' in Politics of Reconciliation." *Political Studies* 49, (2001): 749-766.

Schefer-Hughes, Nancy. "Undoing: Social Suffering and the Politics of Remorse in the New South Africa." *Social Justice* 254:74 (1998): 114-142.

Seattletimes.com. "Rwandans take Annan, U.N. to task for genocide," May 8, 1998. <http://seattletimes.com/news/nation-world/html/altrwan_050898.html>   (February 5, 2000).

Schellstede, Sangmie Choi. ed. *Comfort Women Speak: Testimony by Sex Slaves of the Japanese Military*. New York: Holmes and Meier, 2000.

Sefton, Dru. "Chinese Concept of 'Saving Face' Contributes to Spy Plane Stalemate." New House News Services. <http://www.newhousenews.com/archive/story1c040501.html>

Sehene, Benjamin. "Rwanda's Collective Amnsesia." *UNESCO Courrier*. December 1999, 33.

Semujanga, Josias. *Origins of Rwandan Genocide*. New York: Humanity Book, 2003.

Sereny, Gitta. *The Healing Wound: Experiences and Reflections on Germany, 1938-2001*. New York: W.W. Lorton & Co. 2001.

Shafir, Shlomo. *Ambiguous Relations: The American Jewish Community and Germany Since 1945*. Detroit, Mich.: Wayne State University Press, 1999.

Shapiro, Michael J. *Violent Cartographies: Mapping the Cultures of War*. Minneapolis, Minn.: University of Minnesota Press, 1997.

Shin, Paul. "Japanese Textbook Offends Koreans." *Chicago Sunday Times*, April 10, 2001.

Shriver, Donald.W. *An Ethic for Enemies: Forgiveness in Politics*. Oxford: Oxford University Press. 1995.

_____, "Can Nations Apologize?" *Christian Century* 12, no. 23 (1995): 732-733.

Sibomana, Andre. *Hope For Rwanda: Conversations with Laure Guibert and Herve Deguine*. Postscript and translation by Carina Tertsakian. London: Pluto Press. 1997.

Slama, Allan-Gerard. "An Apology Too Far?" *Le Point,* July 22, 1995.

Smith, Helmut W. ed. *The Holocaust and Other Genocides: History, Representation, Ethics*. Nashville, Tenn.: Vanderbilt University Press. 2002.

Sontag, D. "Barak Makes State Visit to Berlin: History Comes Full Circle as Israeli Leader Visits Former Concentration Camp." *Montreal Gazette*. September 23, 1999.

Soyinka, Wole. *Burden of Memory, the Muse of Forgiveness*. New York: Oxford University Press, 1999.

Star Tribune (Minneapolis, Minn.), "China Demands Fuller NATO Apology," May 11, 1999.

Stedman, J. S., R., Rothchild, and Elizabeth M. Cousens eds. *Ending Civil Wars: The Implementation of Peace Agreements*. Boulder, Co.: Lynne Rienner Publishers Inc. 2002.

Steele, William M. *Alternative Narratives in Modern Japanese History*. London: Routledge Curzon. 2003.

Sterling, Harry. "Japan Refuses to Face Up to its History." *Toronto Star*. January 8, 2001.

_____. "Whitewashing History: Japan Refuses to Come to Grips with its Military Past." *Montreal Gazette*. May 28, 2001.

Tanaka, Yuki. *Hidden Horrors: Japanese War Crimes in World War II*. Boulder, Co. Westview Press. 1996.

Tatman, Lucy "Forgiveness and Reconciliation: A Feminist Theological Reflection." *Peace news for Nonviolent Revolution*, (March/May 2000): 23-25.

Tavuchis, Nicholas. *Mea Culpa: A Sociology of Apology and Reconciliation*. Stanford, CA: Stanford University Press. 1991.

Taylor, Christopher C. *Sacrifice as Terror: The Rwandan Genocide of 1994*. Oxford; New York; Berg: 1999.

Thea, Carolee. "The Void: Daniel Libeskind's Jewish Museum as a Counter Monument." *Sculpture* (Washington D.C.) 119, no.9 (2000): 38-45.

Thomas, Caroline and Peter Wilkin eds. *Globalization, Human Security and the African Experience*. Boulder, Co: Lynne Rienner Publishers, Inc. 1999.

Ting-Toomey, Stella and Mark Cole. "Intergroup Diplomatic Communication: A Face Negotiation Perspective," in *Communicating for Peace: Diplomacy and Negotiation*, edited by Felipe Korzenny, Stella Ting-Toomey and Susan Douglas Ryan, 77-95. Newbury Park, Cal: Sage Publications, 1990.

Tomforde, Anna. "Khol says Belsen is Never-ending Shame," *Guardian* (London), April 22, 1985

_____. "Right Wingers Oppose Holocaust Bill: Tension Builds up over Denials that Nazis Killed 6 Million Jews/West Germany." *Guardian* (London), March 14, 1985.

Tomkins, Richard. "Commentary: It's all about 'Face'." *United Press International*. April 5, 2001.

Torpey John. ed. *Politics and the Past: On Repairing Historical Injustices*. New York: Rowman and Littlefield, 2003.

Trouillot, Michel-Rolph. "Abortive Rituals: Historical Apologies in the Global Era " *Interventions* 2, no. 2 (2000): 171-186.

Troverso, Enzo. *Understanding the Nazi Genocide: Marxism after Auschwitz*. London: Pluto Press, 1999.

Unger Jonathan. ed. *Using the Past to Serve the Present: Historiography and Politics in Contemporary China*. New York: M.E. Sharpe, 1993.

U.N. Press Release. "Secretary-General pledges support of U.N. for Rwanda's search for peace and progress." Secretary-General, SG/SM/6552.AFR/SG, May 6, 1998. <http://www.reliefweb.int> (May 19, 2004).

U.N. Wire. "Annan Accepts Blame for Rwandan Genocide." March 29, 2004. <http://www.unwire.org/UNWire/20040329/449_22259.asp> (December 5, 2004)

United Nations. *Economics and Social Council, Committee on Economic, Social and Cultural Rights*. 29th Session. Summary Record of 43rd Meeting. E/c.12/2001/SR.43, August 27, 2001.

_____. "Secretary- General Pledges Support of UN for Rwanda's Search for Peace and

Progress." November 22, 2004. <http://www.reliefweb>

United Press International, "China Official Echoes Demand for Apology." April 7, 2001.

_____, "China Scoffs at U.S. Apology." July 20, 1999.

U.S. Congress. House. Committee on International Relations, *Joint Hearing on the Ongoing Crisis in the Great Lakes.* 105th Cong., 2nd sess., March 5, 1998.

_____. House. Committee on International Relations, *Joint Hearing on Refugees in Eastern Zaire and Rwanda.* 104th Cong., 2nd sess., December 4, 1996.

_____. House Concurrent Resolution 157, 106th Congress, 1st session, July 16, 1999.

_____. House Concurrent Resolution 195. 107th Congr, 1st session, July 24, 2001.

United States Department of State, "United States Leads Support for Rwandan Reconstruction and Reconciliation." *All Africa,* April 1, 2004.

United States Information Service. "Clinton Meets with Rwanda Genocide Survivors," 1998 <http://www.usia.gov/regional/af/prestrip/w980325a.htm>

_____. "Clinton Addresses the Rwandan Survivors," Transcript, Washington File, March 25, 1998. <http://www.usia.gov/regional/af/prestrip/w980325a.htm> (February 9, 2000).

Uvin, Peter. *Aiding Violence: The Development Enterprise in Rwanda.* West Hartford, CT: Kumarian Press, 1998.

Valji, Nahla. "South Africa: No Justice Without Reparation." *Open Democracy.* February 7, 2003. <http://www.opendemocracy.com> (July 7, 2003).

Vancouver Sun (British Columbia), "Christian Group Retracing Steps of Crusaders Offers Apology for Killings." July 16, 1999. *Journal of Church and State* 39, (Spring 1997): 237-252.

Vincent, R. J. *Human Rights and International Relations,* New York: Cambridge University Press, 1992.

Vogel, Rolf. Ed. *The German Path to Israel: A Documentation,* Chester Springs, Penn.: Dufour Editions, 1969.

Waberi, Abdourahman A. *Moissons de Crânes: Textes pour le Rwanda.* Paris: Le Serpent à Plumes, 2000.

Walzer Michael. *Thick and Thin: Moral Argument at Home and Abroad.* Notre Dame, Ind.: University of Notre Dame Press, 1994.

Warner, Marina. "Scene Four: Red Dust by Gillian Slovo." *Open Democracy,* March 11, 2002. <http://www.opendemocracy.net>

_____. "Scene Two: St. Augustine's Confessions." http://www.opendemocracy.net (July 7, 2003)

_____. Sorry: the Present State of Apology." http://www.opendemocracy.net (July 7, 2003)

Wasserstrom, Jeffrey N. "China: Beyond the Matrix," *Nation,* 272, il8 (May 7, 2001), 32.

Watts, Jonathan. "North Korea Apologises to Japan for Bizarre Tale of Kidnap and Intrigue." *Guardian* (London), September 18, 2002.

_____. "Japan reclaims 'war hero'." *Guardian* (London), December 23, 1998.

Wawrynek, Christine. "World War II Comfort Women: Japan's Sex Slaves or Hired Prostitutes?" *New York Law School Journal of Human Rights.* 19, no.3 (Summer 2003): 913-922.

Wax, Emily and Nancy Trejos. "ten years Later, Rwanda Mourns." *Washington Post.com* (Foreign Service), April 8, 2004.

_____, "Japan reclaims 'war hero'." *Guardian* (London), December 23, 1998.

Wegner, Gregory. "The Power of Selective Tradition: Buchenwald Concentration Camp and Holocaust Education for Youth in the New Germany." Pp. 226-257 in *Censor-*

ing History: Citizenship and Memory in Japan, Germany and the United States, edited by Laura Elizabeth Hein and Mark Selden. Armond, NY: M.E. Sharpe, 2000.

Welch, David A. "Can We Think Systematically About Ethics and Statecraft?" *Ethics and International Affairs* 8 (1994): 23-37.

Weisman, Steven R. "The Art and Artifice of Apologizing to China." *New York Times,* April 13, 2001.

Weyeneth Robert R. "The Power of Apology and the Process of Historical Reconciliation." *Public Historian* 23, no. 13 (Summer 2001): 9-38.

Whitman, Jim and David Pocock, *After Rwanda: The Coordinatioon of the United Nations Humanitarian Assistance.* London: MacMillan Press, 1996.

Wiesenthal, Simon. *The Sunflower.* New York: Schocken Books, 1976.

Wolffson, Michael. *Eternal Guilt?: Forty Years of German-Jewish-Israeli Relations.* New York: Columbia University Press, 1993.

WuDunn, Sheryl. "Premier of Japan Offers 'Apology' for Its War Acts." *New York Times,* August 15, 1995.

Wu Pei-Yi. "Self Examination and Confession of Sins in Traditional China." *Harvard Journal of Asian Studies* 39, 1 (June 1979), 5-38.

Xinhua News Agency (Nairobi), "Site for Belgian Soldiers Lost in Genocide," April 2, 2004.

Yee, Albert S. "Semantic Ambiguity and Joint Deflections in the Hainan Negotiations." *China: an International Journal* 2, no. 1 (2004): 53-82.

Yoshiaki, Yoshimi. *Comfort Women: Sexual Slavery in the Japanese Military during World War II.* Translated by Suzanne O'Brien. New York: Columbia University Press, 2000.

Yoshida, Reiji. "Prime Minister Pledges Yasukuni Return," *Japan Times,* April 8, 2004.

Young, James E. *At Memory's Edge: After-Images of the Holocaust in Contemporary Art and Architecture.* New Haven, CT.: Yale University Press, 2000.

Zheng, Yongnian. *Discovering Chinese Nationalism in China: Modernization, Identity, and International Relations.* Cambridge, U.K.: Cambridge University Press, 1999.

Zimmerman, Michael J. "Negligence and Moral Responsibility." *Noo&ucic;s* 20, no.2 (June 1986): 199-218.

Zorbas, Eugenia. "Reconciliation in Post-Genocide Rwanda. *African Journal of Legal Studies* 1, no. 1 (2004): 29-52.

Zweig, Ronald W. *German Reparations and the Jewish World: A History of the Claims Conference.* Boulder, Co.: Westview Press, 1987.

Index

About the Author

Girma Negash (Ph.D. University of Colorado) is professor of political science at the University of South Carolina Aiken. He previously taught at the University of Colorado and University of Calabar, Nigeria. His current research focus is on apology and forgiveness in international relations and on the nexus between politics and the arts in political theory. His publications in these areas have appeared in *International Political Science Review*; *Peace Review*; *International Journal of Politics and Ethics*; *Social Identities: Journal for the Study of Race, Nation and Culture*; *Journal of African Cultural Studies*; and the recently published book *Justice and Violence, Pacifism And Cultural Transformation*.